Intimacies

Intimacies

Essay | Photographs

Kunal Basu | Kushal Ray

Curated by Ina Puri

NIYOGI
BOOKS

Overseas Distribution

USA and Canada
ACC Distribution
email: sales@accdistribution.com
www.accdistribution.com

United Kingdom, Ireland, Europe, Australia, New Zealand, Middle East and Latin America
Kodansha Europe Ltd.
email: info@kodansha.eu
www.kodansha.eu

Cambodia, Burma, Laos and Thailand
Paragon Asia Co. Ltd
email: info@paragonasia.com
www.paragonasia.com

Published by

NIYOGI BOOKS
D-78, Okhla Industrial Area, Phase-I
New Delhi-110 020, India
Tel: 91-11-26816301, 49327000
Fax: 91-11-26810483, 26813830
email: niyogibooks@gmail.com
www.niyogibooks.com

Curated by: Ina Puri
Design: Abhijit Gupta & Ajoy Kumar Das/Niyogi Books

ISBN: 978-93-81523-11-7
Year of Publication: 2012

Printed at: Niyogi Offset Pvt. Ltd., New Delhi, India

for

Manju Chatterjee

L'amour de l'art fait perdre l'amour vrai

[Love of art brings loss of real love]

Jean Richepin

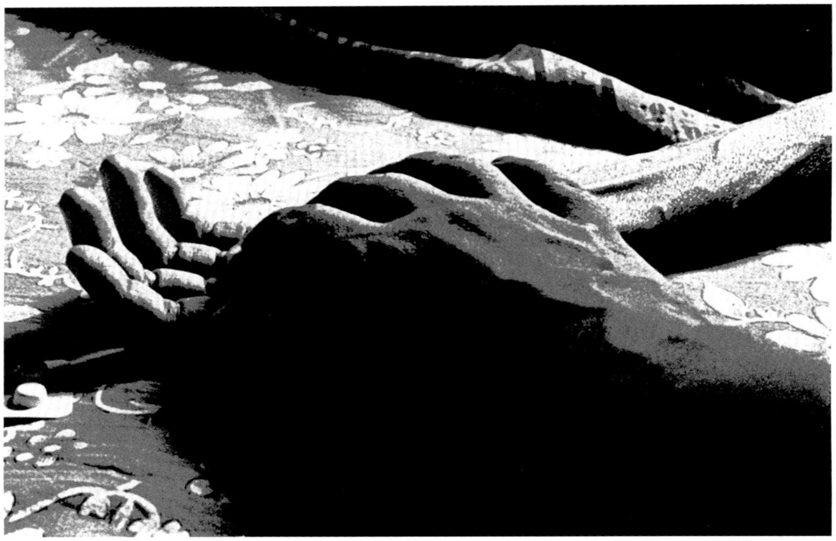

Intimacies

Kunal Basu

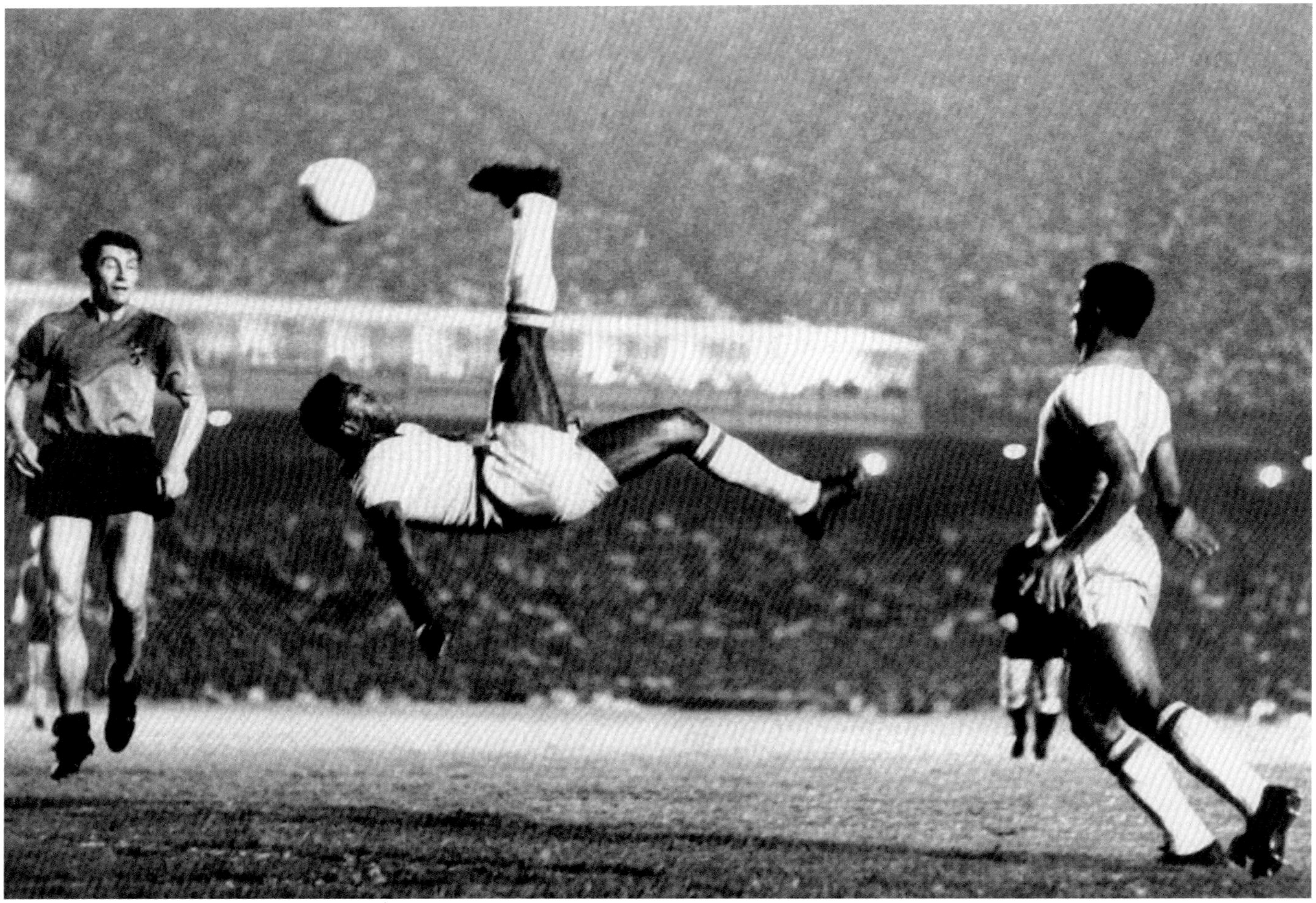

The Locked Knee

At eighteen he was a year older than Pelé when the master had made his World Cup debut. It had taken Kushal – Kajol at home – 7 years of daily practice with poor marks in school to qualify for the annual trials of Kidderpore SC, known as the dark horse of Kolkata's Football League and the nursery of India's brightest talents. The fabled coach, Coco-da, Achyut Banerjee, had his eye on the young prospect. The boy was known for his speed and a cool head. He could tackle opponents twice his size and just like Pelé, play the magical bicycle kick. There wouldn't be a better moment than this for him to show what he could do with a ball at his feet.

By May 1978, when he appeared for the trials, Kushal Ray's story had already fallen into a familiar pattern. Born into middle class Kolkata, he was the exception, the sole athlete among 3 boys – a studious elder and a happy-go-lucky younger brother. His parents Geeta and Ashim, the noted author/journalist, had given in to their son's single-minded devotion to football that came at the expense of his studies. At 11 he'd started to play for his school's under-height team, joined the senior team soon after and captained it by the time he was fifteen. He practised twice a day, smuggled in a football to school and showed off his dribbling skills to his friends during breaks; he skipped classes to watch his favourite stars at Kolkata's club grounds. Managing to scrape along with his studies, he fared badly in the science subjects. But by then, even his teachers had become his fans. Besides football, only reading caught his mind – reading about the game. He'd learned the bicycle kick by thumbing through the step-by-step guide *Play Football with Pelé*, having badgered his father to buy him a copy for 100 Rupees. But it was Pelé's autobiography, *My Life and the Beautiful* Game, that moved him the most. At first he needed a dictionary to read the 350 pages. Then he read them over and over again till he could recite them from memory: 'If it moves, kick it. If it doesn't move, kick it and make it move. If it's too big to kick, trade it in for something smaller and kick that.'

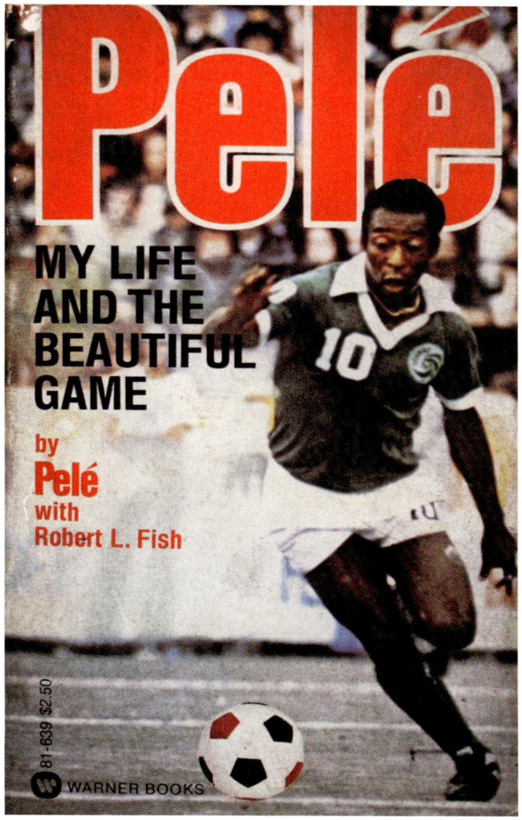

In 1976 he had his first taste of injury. Deshapriya Park, just minutes from their home, had dried out after the rains. The uneven surface was tricky even for the practice match he was playing. Surprisingly, it was his mentor Kailash who'd brought him down with a ferocious tackle. There were rumours that he envied his protégé, although it was he who had shaped Kushal's game, suggested that he move from the position of a 'speedy forward' to that of an 'attacking defender'. 'Only I can dribble past the "boy wonder",' Kailash would brag openly. From the moment he fell, Kushal knew it was serious. Pelé's father came instantly to mind, the unlucky Dondinho, who had torn a ligament early in his career and had to play through his injury just to support his family. He knew there'd be pressures now for him to quit football. Just when he had recovered with regular physiotherapy, he was injured again. This time, a rickshaw had to be pulled up to the centre of the grounds to carry him back home. The family doctor referred him to Kolkata's best orthopaedic surgeon, and on 5 February 1977 he was operated upon at St Mary's Hospital to fix the torn cartilage of his left knee.

Displaying a resolute streak that was to become his trademark, Kushal went straight from hospital to rehab, helped on by his mother who had to practically carry her son from his bed to the only bathroom in the house with a western style commode. He was back in practice in less than 4 months, having built his own device with pulley and weights to save money on physiotherapy. Word of his recurring injury though had spread by then, and opponents who in the past had fought shy of him, now took him aggressively on. He felt he had lost speed, and had to depend on his friend Apurba, a skilful midfielder, for support on the flanks. At the end of 1977 he decided to make a fully-fledged comeback, subjecting himself to gruelling workouts, outdoing his fellow trainees and fitter opponents. It was around this time that word came from Kidderpore SC to appear at their yearly trials in May.

A good two decades and more later, Kushal hesitates talking about the trials. When probed, he starts from the day before, when he'd gone over to the Dakhineshwar temple in the city's suburbs to meet his elderly friend Alok Mukherjee, a Ramakrishna devotee. A bachelor with a magnetic personality, Alok had expanded Kushal's horizon about football. It was more than a game, Alok had explained to him. It was a way to bring joy to people. Footballers belonged in the same camp as artists, filmmakers, dramatists, ascetics and poets – Pelé and Satyajit Ray, Badal Sircar and Ramakrishna were soul brothers – possessed of a nobler calling than all those who simply ingratiated themselves in pursuit of routine careers. It calmed Kushal to spend time with Alok, distracted him from the fierce rivalries of fellow footballers and the uncertainties attached to his own ambition. As before, he had spent the afternoon chatting with his friend about the virtues of plain living and high thinking.

He remembers that afternoon for another reason. Not far from the garden where they sat, a tantric occultist had snared a tourist, a western woman, and was about to hypnotise her when Alok rushed to her aid and shooed the scoundrel away. Kushal had returned home late that night, woken up later than usual next morning and missed his warm up session with the 'iron shoe' designed specially to keep his knee in shape.

Reaching the grounds, he didn't have time to feel nervous as Coco-da mixed the new recruits with seniors and assigned them into two teams to start the trial match. As the attacking right back, Kushal knew his job was to stop Tapan Dutta, the breezy left-winger of the rival team, from scoring a goal, from repeating the performance that had made him such a rising star of the Kolkata League. The equation was simple enough: Tapan scores and he loses his chance to play with a Kidderpore jersey on his back; he'd fulfil his dreams if the left-winger went goalless.

Midway through the first half, his plan seemed to be working. He was doing well against Tapan with his well-honed 'man marking' skills, denying the left-winger any possession of the ball and the chance to dribble and dazzle his opponents. He was outrunning Tapan by his sheer speed, frustrating him, making him swear. He could almost see Coco-da's admiring looks from the sidelines. Everything he'd learnt so far, every hour of practice, every class he'd skipped to play football, every exam he'd failed, every moment of pain before and after his surgery seemed to be paying off. With minutes to go before half time, Tapan fell back and collected a pass, then rushed down the flanks dodging past Kushal and closed in on the goal. Turning around Kushal gave chase to the left-winger and caught up with him. Ready for the final tackle, he knew it was his last chance to clear the ball. As he reached out with his right foot, his left knee twisted and locked, sending him crashing down on the ground. Lying on his back, he watched Tapan swerve by him easily and kick the ball into the net.

At that very moment Kushal knew he had lost everything – he'd never play football again. The locked knee had broken his heart.

Fellow players picked him up and brought him over to the sidelines. Numbness followed ten minutes of intense pain. He couldn't bear to watch the game anymore and hobbled into the tent. Someone offered him tiffin – boiled egg, bread, banana and juice. He couldn't eat. Coco-da came over at half time, examined his swollen leg. 'Old injury?' he asked, passed his hand over the scalpel scars then shook his head. The game was well near over when he left Kidderpore SC and dragged himself over to the nearest stop and took the Number 24 tram to go home. About to leave the grounds, he grabbed his boots and hurled them over to the greens.

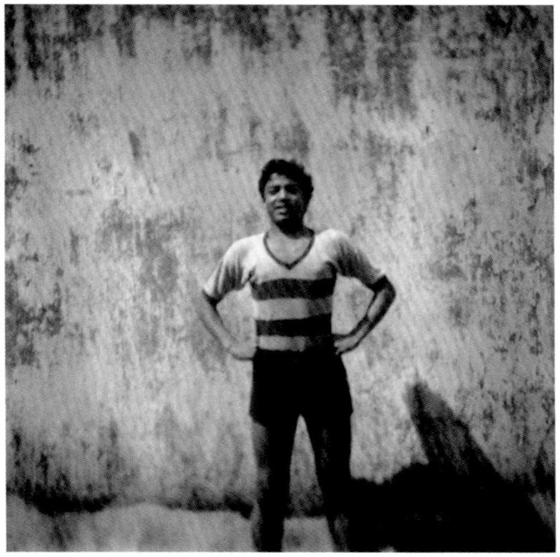

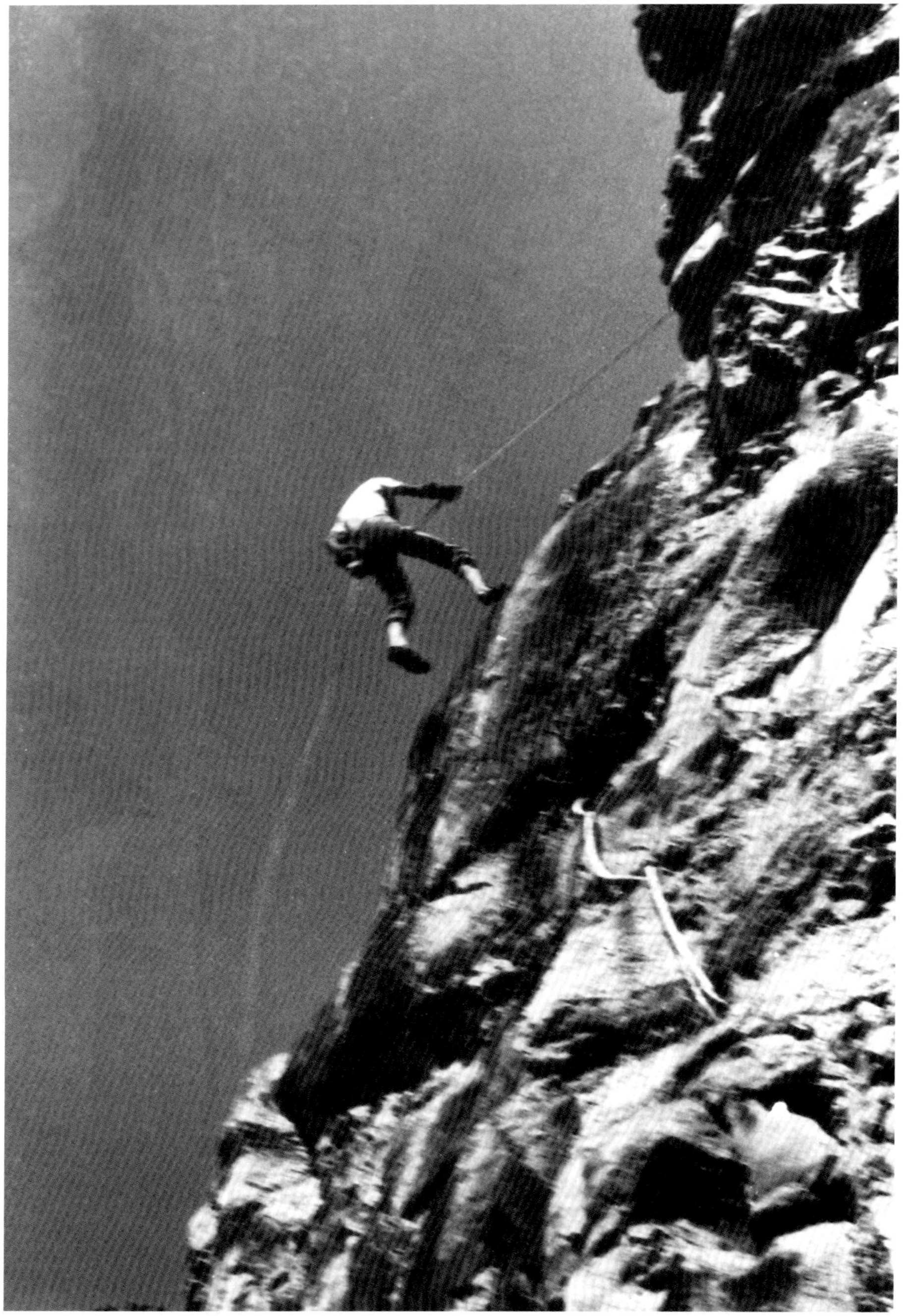

Unheard Melodies

As with most artists, the stories of Kushal Ray's life provide clues to his photographs. They prompt us to see what he sees, what he considers worthy of capturing on film, what he rejects, what he considers to be central and peripheral, and more fundamentally, what sense he makes of his art as a viewer. The circumstances that made him pick up a camera and do more with it than the average shutterbug, are just as curious as his images of the Kalighat house and unravel the plot that has led him to photograph the few hundred square feet of space with such manic intensity. Back in 1978 while he was yet to recover from the devastation of the Kidderpore trials, Susan Sontag had written about photographs as being 'perhaps the most mysterious of all the objects that make up and thicken the environment'. The 'thickening' one finds in Kushal's Kalighat photographs derives necessary pigments from the trajectory that had its beginning on the football field in the single-mindedness of an 'attacking defender'.

What purpose does he serve by locking us up inside the 12 rooms of this house with its 10 residents? I asked myself as I viewed the album. Why this unrelenting gaze at the ordinary, the unglamorous, the ugly, the uneventful? Why no digression, no elaborations on the theme? What 'theme' does he espouse anyway, and why? That these aren't impersonal records is obvious, not the state-of-the-art of a declining joint family in lower middle class Kolkata, or a commentary on the somewhat antiquated usage of domestic space. The knowledge that drives the photographer isn't simply that of functional family matters, but an ethical and political knowledge. And the feeling they generate goes beyond sentimentalism into a complex terrain populated by cross currents of intimacies.

The intimacies in Kushal's Kalighat photographs had struck me when I'd seen them first. They seemed to belie the common view of the photographer as the intruder, the trespasser, the distorter, the expropriator and the exploiter. These weren't acts of aggression, a passive aggression conducted from a safe distance with professional detachment, but the result of some deep engagement that had turned the photographer into a friend, a care giver, even a protector. In photograph after photograph, he seemed to be embracing the world he'd photographed, giving us a glimpse of who he is.

The locked knee had, of course, meant more than the end of his footballing career, but an outright demotion as well from the status of a star athlete to that of an average student. He was shocked to discover how far he had fallen behind others at his college, how much more they knew about almost anything than him. A fellow student could recite the *Mahabharata* by heart; heads no longer turned when he entered the classroom and took his seat. The shift from studying science to the arts though, had served him well. Even before his fateful injury, he'd started attending the lectures regularly. Whereas in school he'd cut classes for football, he hurried through practice to rush back to college just for literature and history: *The Merchant of Venice*; English Romantic poets ('Heard melodies are sweet, but those unheard are sweeter,' recited eloquently by his favourite teacher); Lamb's essays, alongside the poetry and fiction of Buddhadev Basu, Amiyo Chakraborty and

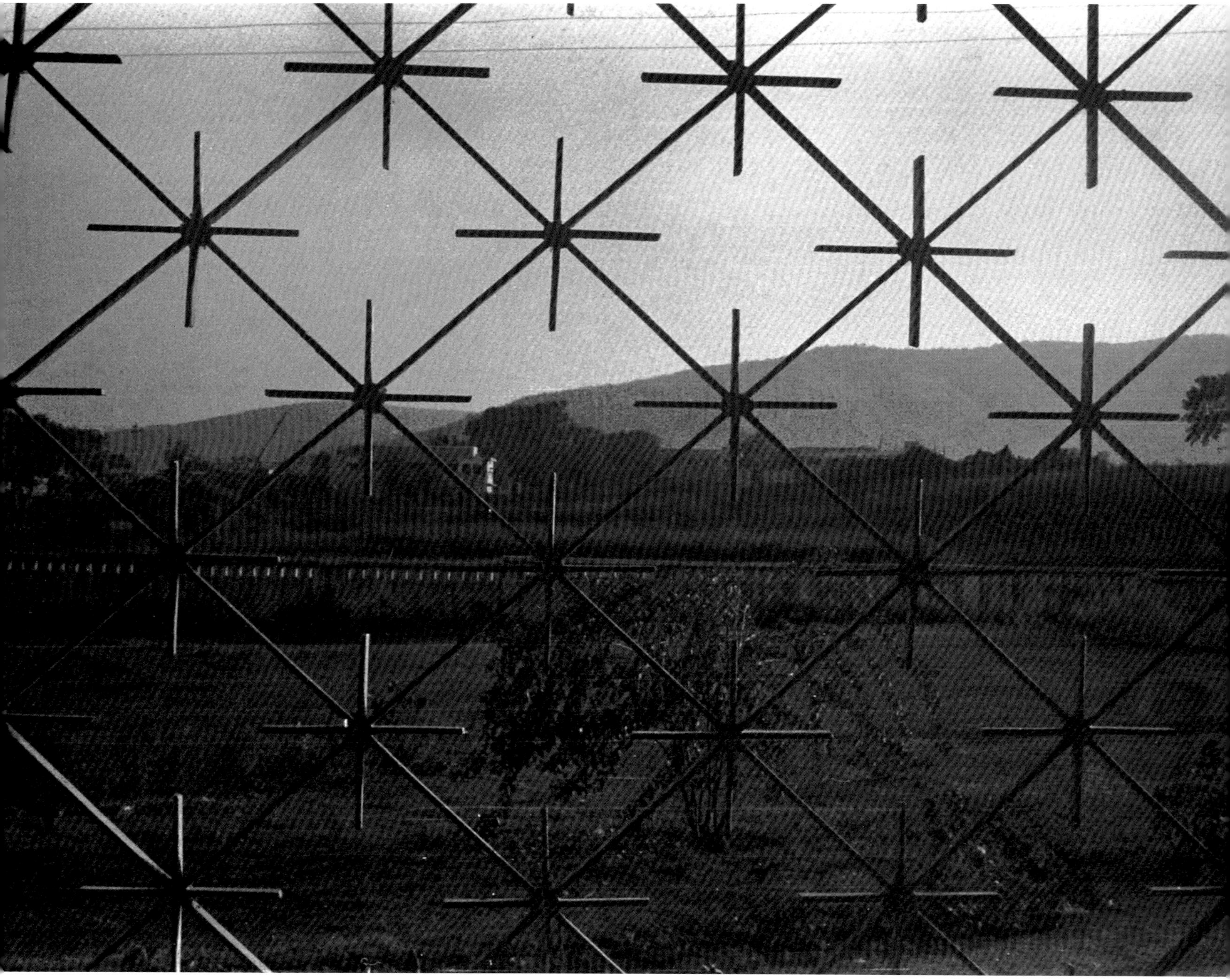

Kushal Ray's first photo taken in Rajgir

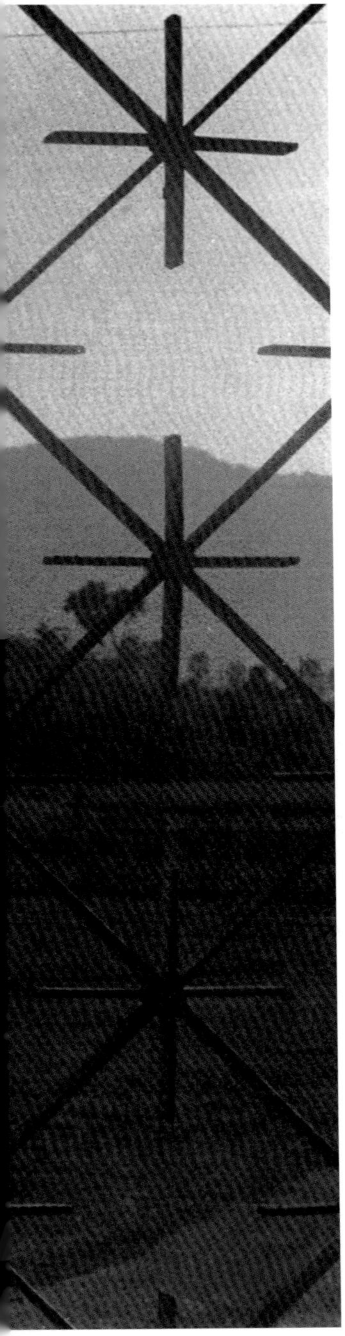

others. His father nudged him towards E.H. Carr's *What is History?* The family that had supported his football stood steadfast behind him during his rehab, to help him stage yet another comeback to a new game with its own rules and practice regime.

The gift of Bengali intelligentsia – a library full of books and the company of famous visitors to the Ray household – helped Kushal rediscover his love for painting and reading that had lain dormant under the heavy veneer of football. Artists like Nirod Majumdar, Paritosh Sen and Prakash Karmakar, poets Bishnu Dey and Subhash Mukhopadhyay helped to fire up a different sort of imagination. If he was good enough for football, then he'd be good enough for the arts – his parents believed, and he proved them right by turning into a bookworm and graduating from college with high marks in English. Football, though, wasn't fully out of his head, and he refused office jobs to seek apprenticeship as a sports reporter.

How could 14-hour shifts at the sub-editor's desk keep his love for the arts or of sports alive? I asked him to tell me more about the dozen years or so that he'd spent at a variety of newspapers, ending up at *The Telegraph*. Not surprisingly, he hadn't found journalism to be his calling. After the early challenge – proving his mettle among colleagues who exuded the garrulous confidence of English medium grooming – had waned, he took refuge in mountaineering. For a while it served as the perfect diversion, harking back to his former suite of preparation, perseverance, and trials. He devoured Chris Bonington's *Annapurna and Everest, the Hard Way*, Herman Buhl's *Nanga Parbat* and many more; he idolised Mallory, Herzog, Messner and Hillary like Pelé, Garrincha, Zito and Vavá. Then, in 1983, he bought his first camera, a Zenith TTL, for 1,000 Rupees from Muslim, a well known dealer in the grey market adjacent to Metro cinema house that sold everything foreign from Ronson gas lighters to Taiwanese condoms and cameras.

As Kushal admits freely today, a deep-seated sense of deprivation made him buy his first camera. At their joint family home, his grandmother and uncle openly favoured his older brother Ujjal when it came to gifts and the best portions of a meal. In addition to gifting Ujjal a Click 3 viewfinder camera, his uncle had lent him his prized Voigtländer 35 mm on the eve of a family vacation to Rajgir renowned for its hot springs. Ujjal guarded the two cameras zealously, kept them beyond bounds of his younger siblings. One day when the family left their holiday home for a dip in the hot springs, Kushal stayed back under some pretext or other. He knew where Ujjal had hidden the Voigtländer. Digging it out of a suitcase, he found all but 2 of the 36 frames exposed. He decided to take just one shot, so as not to arouse too much suspicion. Even now his eyes gleam when he describes that photograph – of the distant hills taken from behind a grilled up window. He, of course, knew nothing about photography, had never before held a camera in his hands. But the exposure had turned out to be miraculously right in a wellcomposed frame, and stunned his older brother into admiration when the mischief was later discovered on print.

The eighties were bullish years for the newly launched *The Telegraph*, and its iconoclastic editor, M.J. Akbar, was hungry for stories, stories that came with pictures. Bored by now with his rounds, Kushal started to take his camera along, incurring frowns from staff photographers. But he shot more than football, returning from the national games in Goa with photos of fishermen, and ignored athletes altogether for classical dancers during a winter jamboree in the city. One of his holiday albums was commissioned for a centrespread. The headiness of it all turned his mind to the challenge of becoming a 'real' photographer. At 40 Rupees a copy, subscription to *Practical Photography* taxed his junior reporter's wallet, but he was willing to stretch his budget. In a bold move from outdoors to indoors, he started to take his camera to work, used high speed film and set the timer to

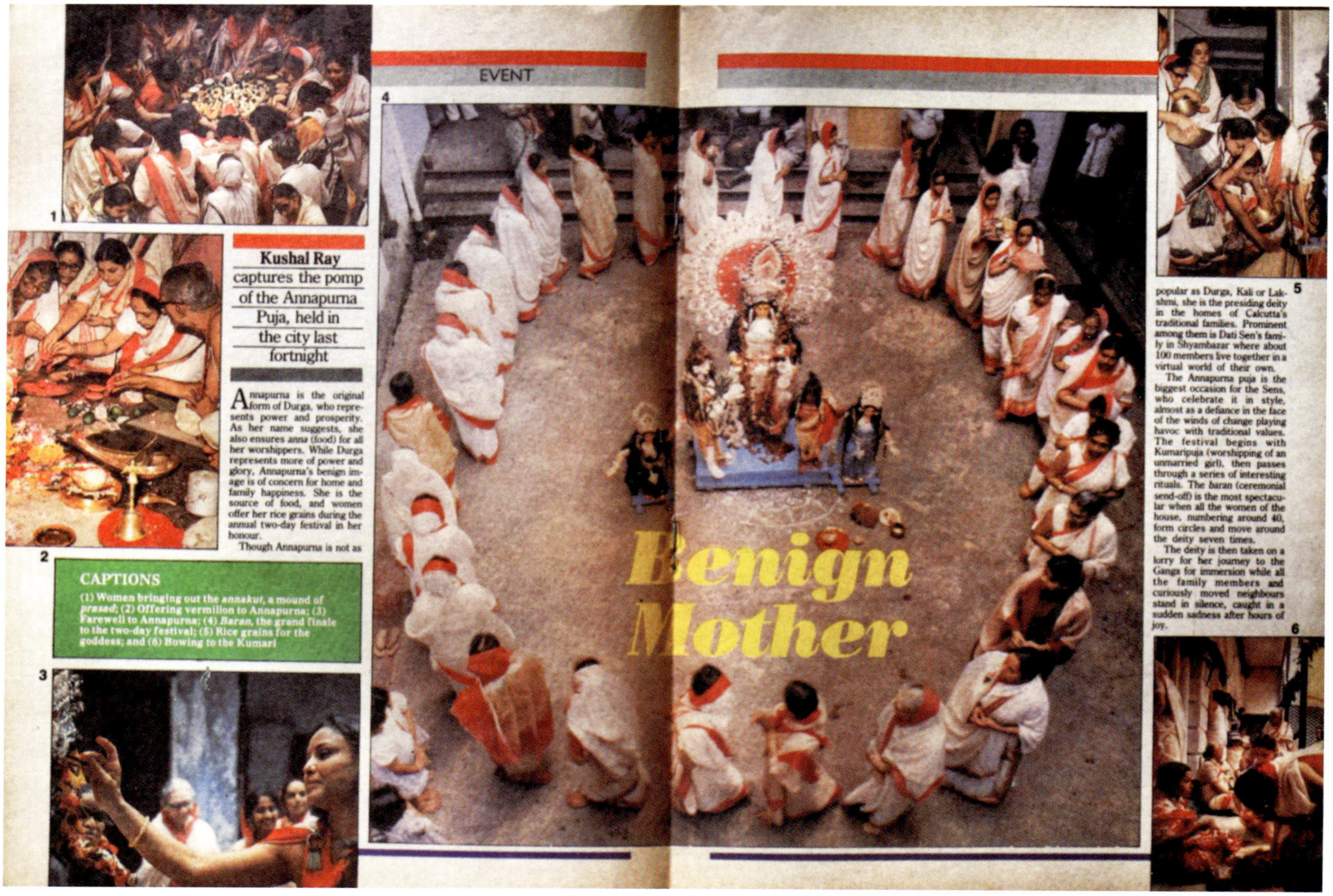

EVENT

Benign Mother

Kushal Ray captures the pomp of the Annapurna Puja, held in the city last fortnight

Annapurna is the original form of Durga, who represents power and prosperity. As her name suggests, she also ensures *anna* (food) for all her worshippers. While Durga represents more of power and glory, Annapurna's benign image is of concern for home and family happiness. She is the source of food, and women offer her rice grains during the annual two-day festival in her honour.

Though Annapurna is not as popular as Durga, Kali or Lakshmi, she is the presiding deity in the homes of Calcutta's traditional families. Prominent among them is Dati Sen's family in Shyambazar where about 100 members live together in a virtual world of their own.

The Annapurna puja is the biggest occasion for the Sens, who celebrate it in style, almost as a defiance in the face of the winds of change playing havoc with traditional values. The festival begins with Kumaripuja (worshipping of an unmarried girl), then passes through a series of interesting rituals. The *baran* (ceremonial send-off) is the most spectacular when all the women of the house, numbering around 40, form circles and move around the deity seven times.

The deity is then taken on a lorry for her journey to the Ganga for immersion while all the family members and curiously moved neighbours stand in silence, caught in a sudden sadness after hours of joy.

CAPTIONS

(1) Women bringing out the *annakut*, a mound of *prasad*; (2) Offering vermilion to Annapurna; (3) Farewell to Annapurna; (4) *Baran*, the grand finale to the two-day festival; (5) Rice grains for the goddess; and (6) Bowing to the Kumari

take candid shots of his colleagues: girls smoking cigarettes; the drama of nightshifts, and the play that goes with work. Then, he returned to Muslim to splurge on a Nikomat with a 50 mm, 1.4 lens that has remained his favourite over all these years.

Ladakh in many ways was the watershed. Inspired by Vikram Seth's *From Heaven Lake*, he spotted the perfect intersection: between his love for the mountains and the camera. *The Telegraph* paid 150 Rupees for each published photograph, and this time the staff photographers didn't take matters lightly. Kushal too was conscious that his passion had outpaced his technique, that experiential learning alone couldn't elevate him to artistic heights, dooming him to hack photography. Going abroad to study was unthinkable; like everything else in his life, photography too would have to be self-taught, laboriously acquired through reading, by trial and error, and most of all by patience. Recently promoted as senior sub-editor, he asked his boss for a month's leave. It was an unreasonable request. After much toing and froing, he offered his employers a deal they couldn't refuse: a month's night duty in exchange, when the norm was a mere week.

That month was meant for a return visit to the Himalayas to retrace the footsteps of Raghubir Singh, to emulate his favourite photographer's Ganga series. Did Raghubir come here? – he asked around at every village, temple, teashop and hotel that he visited, from Hardwar to Rishikesh and on to Devprayag, Gangotri, Gomukh and Tapoban. Like Raghubir, he met sadhus, lived rough at their threadbare ashrams, listened to their sermons, contracted stomach diseases, and composed frames in his mind's eye sleeping around bonfires late into the night.

Back in Kolkata, he published his first series of serious photography. *The Telegraph*'s colour magazine carried his homage to Annapurna, the goddess of domestic bliss, worshipped at an old Kolkata home. No less than Raghubir! – this time the praises rang sweet in his ears.

By 1990, he had lost both parents prematurely, but was already knee deep into his favourite diversion. He had read Susan Sontag. Photography had become the new football.

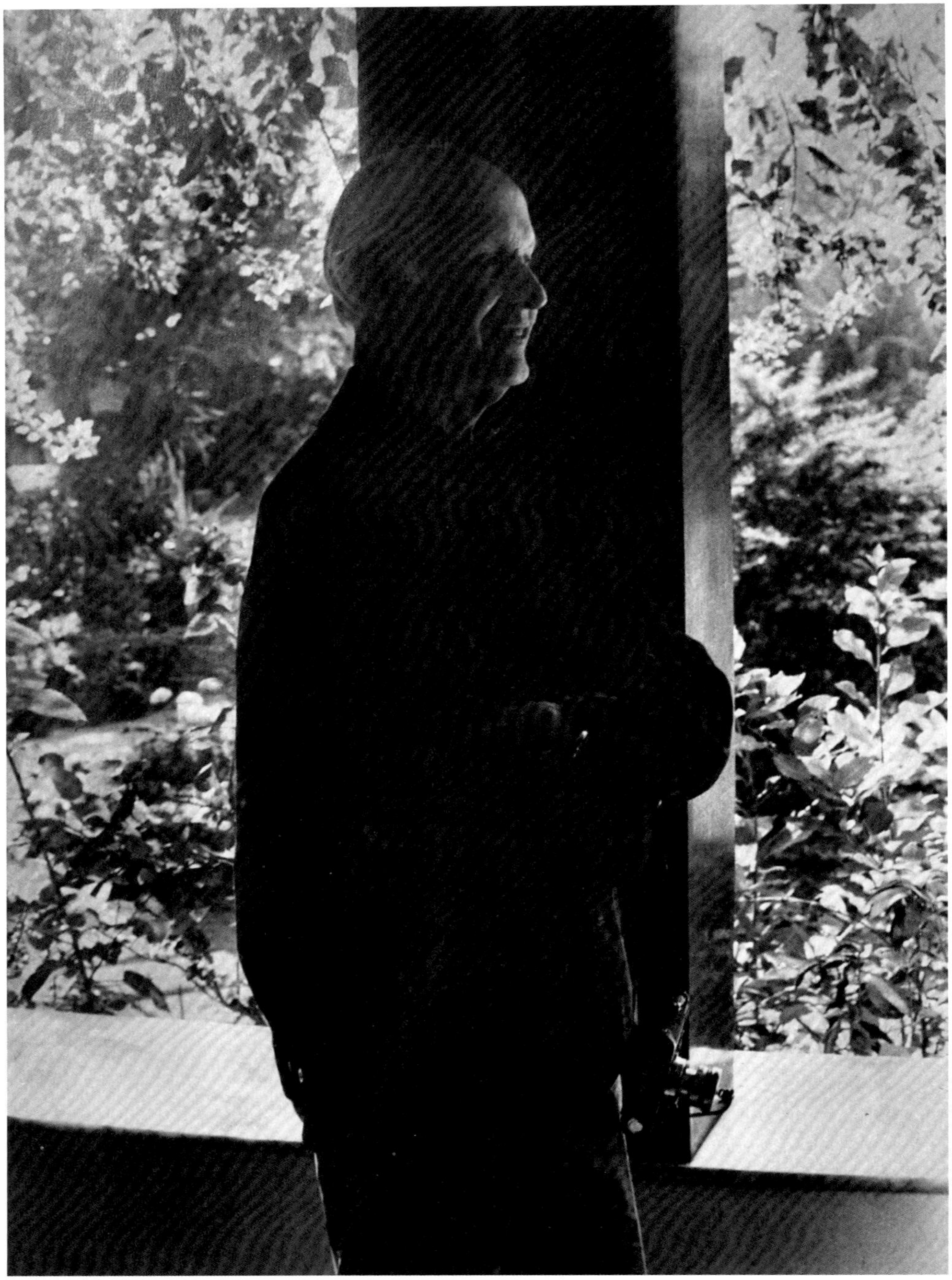

A Friend of Cartier-Bresson

The camera arrived in Kolkata in 1840, and by the nineties had captured the hearts and minds of the masses. Among dead ancestors and living legends or simply those that were curious to have their portraits taken, photography had encountered lesser resistance and fewer adverse commentaries compared to other foreign imports such as the gas light, the steam engine, the bicycle, the gramophone, the railways or the motor car. Unlike imperial photographers who were keen to capture the natives on daguerreotype or film as ethnographic record, the Bengali intelligentsia took to the camera as the novel child of science and art, giving rise to photography societies, training classes, richly illustrated learning manuals and a slew of commercial studios. In his monumental work *Chobi Tola: Bangali-r Photography Chorcha* (*Taking Photos: The Pursuit of Photography among Bengalis, 1988*), Siddharta Ghosh provides an amazing list of thirty-six shops selling photographic equipment in Kolkata as early as in 1915 and twenty-four studios for picture taking, not counting the innumerable establishments at the China Bazaar. Luckily, the debate over photography's claim to artistic status hadn't taken root in Indian soil, and its roster in the early decades of the twentieth century was graced by luminaries such as Upendrakishore Ray, Sukumar Ray and Aryakumar Chowdhury, spreading an aura of gentlemanly affectation over the novel machine.

Established in 1961, Image Photographers owned by Jyotish Chakrabarty in Bhowanipore was a chip off the old block of photography studios. Feared for his martial temperament and nicknamed 'Military Man', he was admired equally for being the 'know all' of film processing. The only lab in Kolkata to use Kodak's original chemicals imported from abroad, Image

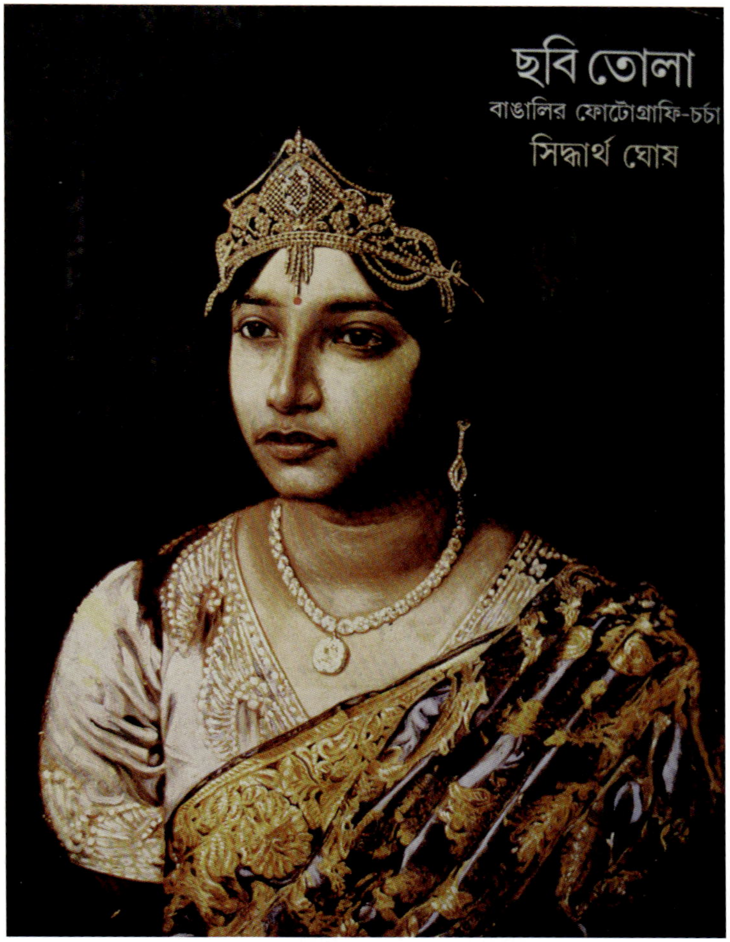

Cover of Siddharta Ghosh's Bangali-r Photography Chorcha

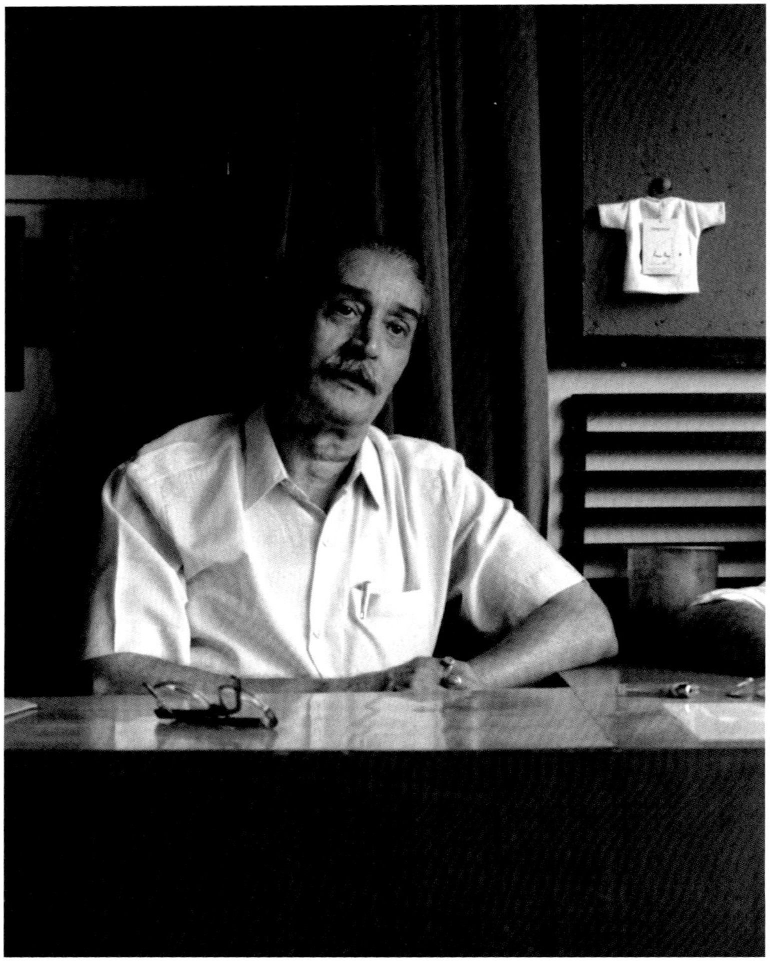
Jyotish Chakrabarty at his studio

Photographers counted many celebrities among its clientele, including Satyajit Ray. A commercial photographer and portraitist of some repute, Jyotish was more a buff than a businessman and would turn customers away if he didn't like their looks or doubted their intent for serious work. Only those he considered worthy earned the right to sit on the couch across his desk and receive his sermon on the prints hot off his laboratory's press. Myths flew about Military Man, how for instance he had thrown out Uttam Kumar, the matinée idol of Bengali cinema when he'd shown up drunk at his shop, but didn't bat an eyelid at the debauchery of his pet photographers. Among his more famous friends was Henri Cartier-Bresson.

The actor Vasant Chowdhury took Jyotish to the house of a wealthy industrialist who was host to Cartier-Bresson during his visit to Kolkata in 1986. He had come to photograph the solar eclipse, the spectacle of the masses not of the sun. After the two had been introduced, Cartier-Bresson handed Jyotish his Leica and said, 'Bless my camera'. It took a while for the two to start talking, for the Frenchman to finish a whole pot of tea, before Jyotish asked to take a photo of him. The visitor recoiled instantly. He had never allowed anyone the honour, but after the flush of initial reluctance had paled he agreed with an expansive sweep of his arm: 'Because I consider you a friend, I'll let you take one. Just one, mind you. But you can never publish it while I am alive.'

Favoured customers at Image Photographers had heard the story countless times: How a wily Cartier-Bresson had tried to trick Jyotish by posing at a spot marked by extreme contrast in lighting. Military Man though had risen to the challenge and produced, in the celebrated photographer's opinion, the best portrait ever taken of Cartier-Bresson. A real friendship had started between them, which helped considerably to elevate Jyotish Chakrabarty's esteem in the eyes of his many admirers.

In 1989 Kushal was looking for a reliable lab for his Himalayan photographs when a friend brought him to the Bhowanipore studio. Besides suggesting a filter to reduce the blue cast on his photographs, Jyotish offered him no further advice. As he started to frequent Image Photographers, Kushal longed to sit on the couch and receive the wisdom of Cartier-Bresson's friend. A hand stretched out to receive his prints, he'd wait for the nod to stay back and join the photographers of the inner circle. With each visit, his impatience grew. Jyotish preferred black and white over colour, and Kushal considered making a switch. These were hard times: day duty at *The Telegraph* wasn't conducive to following his photographer's muse. He'd arrive at work to receive his boss's missive: *need a scoopish and anchorish story today*, and the pressure to produce one waylaid him for most of the day. Night duty worked better. He'd work from 8 at night to 3 in the morning; slept for a few hours, setting the alarm to rise at 6:30 and left home with his camera. He'd come back for a second bout of sleeping at 10, only to leave again at 3 to catch the afternoon light before reporting for night duty. The routine worked well the first two days of the week. Then he'd doze at work. His boss gave him suspicious looks: 'You're taking photos again, aren't you?' Colleagues covered for him whenever he was late. Crisscrossing the city several times a day and night, he must've resembled a somnambulist on a motorbike.

Strangely enough, what drew him into Jyotish's inner circle was a series on classical dancers rather than the street life that he shot compulsively, following in the footsteps of Cartier-Bresson. Casting his frown on the photos, Jyotish had taken out his own folio of dancers, before offering Kushal what was till then his most substantial piece of advice: 'Wait for the dancer's body to become still. Wait for that fraction of time then shoot. A dancer's face is most expressive when she slows down to change posture. Follow her. Learn as much as you can about dance. Then she'll dance in your photographs.'

The switch from colour to black and white at Jyotish's behest was followed by yet another piece of advice – from Lee Friedlander, the American photographer whose urban landscapes held much appeal at the time for Kushal. Friedlander had spoken about 'mastering a single lens' to master one's eye – a logic he found compelling enough to sell off his wide angle and zoom lenses and embark on a yearlong experiment shooting 268 rolls in total with only a normal lens. The almost devotional tenor of his regime worried Jyotish, who failed to dissuade him despite offering him his precious 24mm wide, in what must've been the ultimate sign of trust. Recalling that year, Kushal goes back to his favourite quote from Cartier-Bresson from his early days as a street photographer: 'I went to Marseille. A small allowance enabled me to get along, and I worked with enjoyment. I had just discovered the Leica. It became the extension of my eye…I prowled the streets all day, feeling very strung up and ready to pounce, determined to "trap" life – to preserve life in the act of living.... '

Like others of his generation, Kushal too had been shaped by Cartier-Bresson's notion of the 'defining moment' and the power of form – the visual configuration that captures everything, connects the dots of time, combines several conversations – that appeared at 'the instant when chaos coalesces into order before dissolving into chaos again,' as Michael Brenson has written. That very moment held the potential to 'thicken' this world by exposing the density and magic of everyday life and flag off several journeys within both viewer and photographer. Following Cartier-Bresson's street work in Paris, Cordoba, Trieste and Mexico City, Kushal became aware of the dialogue between the photographer's eye and his heart. The master had cast his unblinking gaze at mean poverty, pitching it right at the centre of his photographs, his early albums in particular palpating with the thrust of both pictorial and narrative climax centred on the hard life lived by many in most parts of the world.

Yet Cartier-Bresson wasn't his sole inspiration. Raghubir Singh's controversial article, 'Illustration, Accidents and Ignorance', had alerted Kushal to a broader learning agenda: 'If one is to be a photographer or comment on photography, it is essential that the practitioner have an excellent grounding in the history of photography.' Raghubir convinced him that a sophisticated sensibility must compliment sight otherwise he'd remain a 'primitive', condemned forever to reinventing the wheel. Like Picasso who'd stood on the shoulders of Courbet and Cezanne, he must find the right shoulders to stand on and decide which ones to avoid. Browsing at Foreign Publishers Agency on Esplanade, he discovered the masters, and badgered the shop owner to keep importing their albums against the grain of market demand.

Quizzed about his early influences, Kushal digs out a slim black volume devoted to American photographers of the Depression as part of the Pantheon Photo Library series. Set up by President Roosevelt in 1930 at the height of the Great Depression, Farm Security Administration or FSA had employed a handful of photographers to document the lives of poor sharecroppers and tenant farmers who had lost their land and were scouring the country in search of a livelihood. The works of Dorothea Lange, Russell Lee, Walker Evans and others not only evoke the full ravages of those years, but also represent one of the most ambitious projects to capture a society's defining images in a given period. As we turned the pages, Kushal paused over wrought faces of men and women, a child's grave, men in dungarees looking lost as they held relief checks in their hands.

Yet another photographer of the 1930s, W. Eugene Smith, had startled him with the photograph of a mother cradling her daughter emaciated by mercury poisoning. A staffer of *Life* magazine who later joined the prestigious Magnum photo agency, Smith believed that it simply wasn't enough to take exciting pictures and moved away from celebrity coverage to depict the struggles of ordinary people. Two photo essays by Smith had left their mark on Kushal: the first documented a doctor's daily practice in a rural Colorado clinic, with the photographer 'fading into the wallpaper' to record the densely interlocking networks of that community. Here was the unmannered rawness that Kushal was looking for, not the accident of the decisive moment, not a voyeuristic search for oddities, not the endless street prowling that he'd grown accustomed to, but a photographer's deliberate grip on his subject matter, a sympathetic but unsentimental gaze that made no excuses, striding brazenly from fact to fiction.

The second, started barely a few years after the Colorado essay, had Smith perching himself in a grimy studio loft in the flower district in lower Manhattan. Sitting at his windowsill for years, he photographed the varied characters and activities outside – street musicians, hobos, cops, conmen and whores – an extraordinary mélange that seemed to fit quite naturally into the same family tree.

Atget, Arbus, Stieglitz, Sander, Frank, Friedlander, Winogrand – encircled by stacks of books that he had devoured early on goaded by Raghubir, Kushal spoke about the argument that had started to brew in him between the 'primitive' and the fast maturing artist. It was an argument that had started with Cartier-Bresson. 'If you take care of form, the content will take care of itself,' Cartier-Bresson had advised photographers; every decent photographer has a fair idea of the substance matter of a photograph, and avoiding content heaviness was vital if one were to aspire to develop one's own unique form. It was the same argument wielded by Raghubir Singh in his wake-up call to Indian photographers: 'our photographers have consistently put the cart before the horse, subject matter before form.' But the world was full of subjects. As sub-editor at *The Telegraph*, Kushal had had his full quota of matters that were considered newsworthy, worthy of being recorded. Given his footballing background, he could keep shooting sports or important personalities that he routinely met on his rounds. It'd take slight lateral movement to land into the world of high fashion and the catwalk, and if he managed to strike a truce with the staff photographers he could keep on shooting mountains and rivers, street scenes and dancers forever, trespass even into nine to five photojournalism, bite off a few juicy pieces from political rallies, corpses and natural disasters. In a subject rich world it was the photographer's luxury to choose his subject, a choice that was no less revealing of his genius than the idiosyncrasy of his craft. The masters that Kushal admired were just as noteworthy for what they had chosen to train their camera on as that special form they'd developed for the purpose: the selectivity of Atget's empty streets made poignant by the way he'd filled them with life in the absence of humans; Robert Frank's America serving up just a slice of that nation for Jack Kerouac to pen a poem:

Robert Frank, Swiss, unobtrusive
nice, with that little camera that he raises
and snaps with one hand he sucked a sad poem
right out of America onto film, taking rank
among the tragic poets of the world.

Although Cartier-Bresson himself was no aesthete and had never gone looking for the picturesque image, Kushal recognised the danger of a slide towards formulaic perfection armed with a Bressonian grammar. He felt impatient as well at the parsimony of solitary images, mere glimpses into unfamiliar worlds: who were the prostitutes captured in Cartier-Bresson's decisive moment as they peeked through their windows in Mexico City's Calle Cuauhtemocztin? Whose mothers were they, whose daughter, whose friend? What did they do after they'd wiped the paint off their faces? He longed to see them at their kitchens, at the market stalls, in their baths, with their pimps and in bed. The 'subject' hadn't fully been explored, he felt, despite the superior form of its presentation. As the argument gathered steam within him, unexpected support arrived from yet another source.

Writing in *Success and Failure of Picasso*, John Berger argued that 'the painter's choice of a subject is a far more complicated question that it would at first seem. A subject begins when the artist selects something *for special mention*...In truth, the subject is literally the beginning and end of a painting.' Berger had then proceeded to trace one of the major ways in which a painter decided what to paint – painters like Van Gogh, or Gauguin in the South Seas – by identifying themselves with the people they painted. These were lonely artists, Berger had written, and 'because they wanted to belong, they became socially conscious'. That's me!! – Kushal had scribbled on the margins of the page. Here was the missing piece of the puzzle that he'd been searching for all along to fit into his photographer's arsenal of sophisticated sensibility coupled with sound technique and an eye that was alert to magical moments. Here was the mind of the photographer, his take on history and contemporary events, his allegiances to people, his relationship to power – his ideology.

Luckily, he had encountered Bruce Davidson before the puzzle could drive him into a conceptual dead end. The grandson of immigrant Polish Jews, Davidson was raised in poverty by his single mother and had a varied career in photography. After his stint as an army photographer, he'd been a Magnum man in Paris then returned to America to photograph Brooklyn gangs and worked with Michelangelo Antonioni in Hollywood during filming of *Zabriskie Point*. Then he started a novel project: 'At the end of 1966 I met Emily, my future wife, in New York. I was beginning to photograph what people called the worst block in the city: East 100th Street. I took pictures of everything, the people, their homes, the ruined buildings, vacant lots, rooftops. We began to be accepted by the community. ...People asked me into their homes to make records for the citizen's committee of leaks, cracks and unheated buildings. Later at night I developed the negatives and made prints for the next day. After nearly two years I felt my work there had come to an end. Two thousand pictures... In the fall of 1970, *East 100th Street* was published and given an exhibition at the Museum of Modern Art. People from 100th Street came to see themselves.'

Like Davidson, Kushal had an abiding interest in the commonplace, not the self conscious architecture of an imagined or pretended and ultimately stylised world, but one where the photographed were stakeholders themselves. Marc Asnin's folios too held their draw with intimate stories of clustered communities with whom the gonzo photographer had more than rubbed shoulders, be they gravediggers or skinheads. He found Asnin's work disturbing, gratuitous even in its depiction of violence and tragedy, but compelling still given the proximity of the subject and the clear view of the why and the what in the photographs. The family photographs of Dayanita Singh, ultimately, hinted at an opening that he grasped with both hands.

Unlike some others of his generation who exclusively followed the works of western photographers and saw themselves as diligent contributors to Eurocentric paradigms of artistic/cultural thought, Kushal had a curious eye out for native shoulders providing sanctuary to his early thinking on photography. These were days preceding the internet. It was hard to get a hold of unpublished photographs, and books were expensive. *The Telegraph*'s library had thrown him a lifeline, and the outdoor works of the two Rs had inspired him considerably: Raghu Rai by infecting him with the sheer joy of taking pictures, and Raghubir impressing with his strong form, presenting his subjects without sensationalism and with dignity. His mentor Jyotish spoke highly of Pablo Bartholomew, the bohemian, the enfant terrible who formed the third of the illustrious troika, and the little that Kushal saw of his work struck him with its unusual spontaneity and furtive glimpses of urban subcultures. Dayanita's series of posed portraits of families in middle and upper middle class Indian homes held out the promise of doing a Davidson with close focus on a single family, but rather than follow in her precise footsteps, he could do a Eugene Smith and become the 'wallpaper at the Colorado clinic' to arrest life as it happens. The family too would have to be different. Not only would an upper class home be beyond his social reach, it wouldn't appeal to him as a subject. He must find a family he could recognise as his own, and members who could double as his kin.

Kushal's much thumbed copy of *East 100th Street* opens naturally at the last page of the introduction penned by the photographer himself. 'So I have done what I wanted to do,' Davidson had written. 'I have seen everything, misery, celebrity, the beautiful people, the wicked ones, generosity and hatred. But I think I have gone beyond my vision...in the heart of my life, in the heart of other people's lives. Perhaps that is the most important thing I have done.' By year end in 1990, Kushal had resigned his post at *The Telegraph* and was ready to do the most important thing he'd done so far in his life.

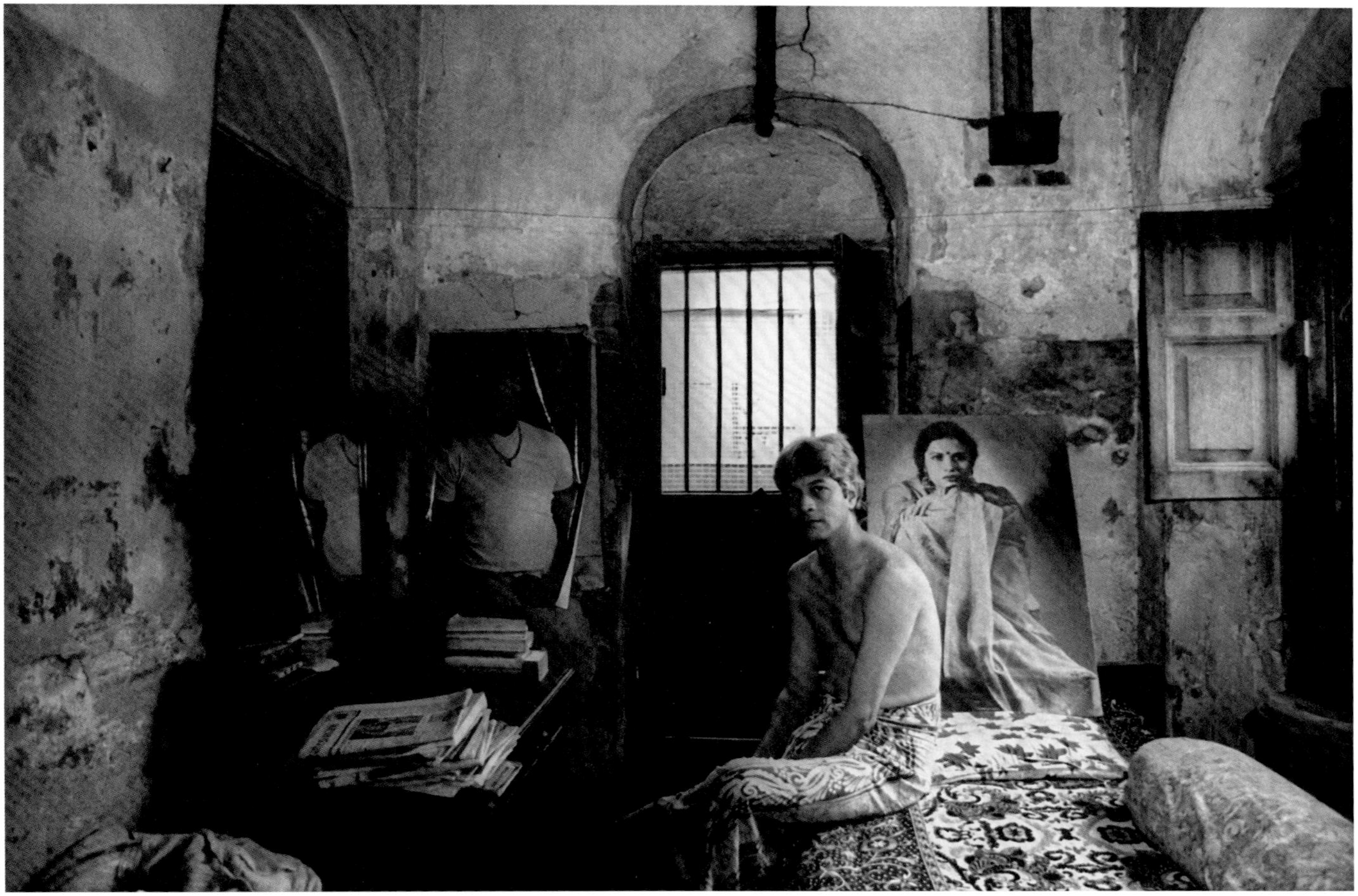

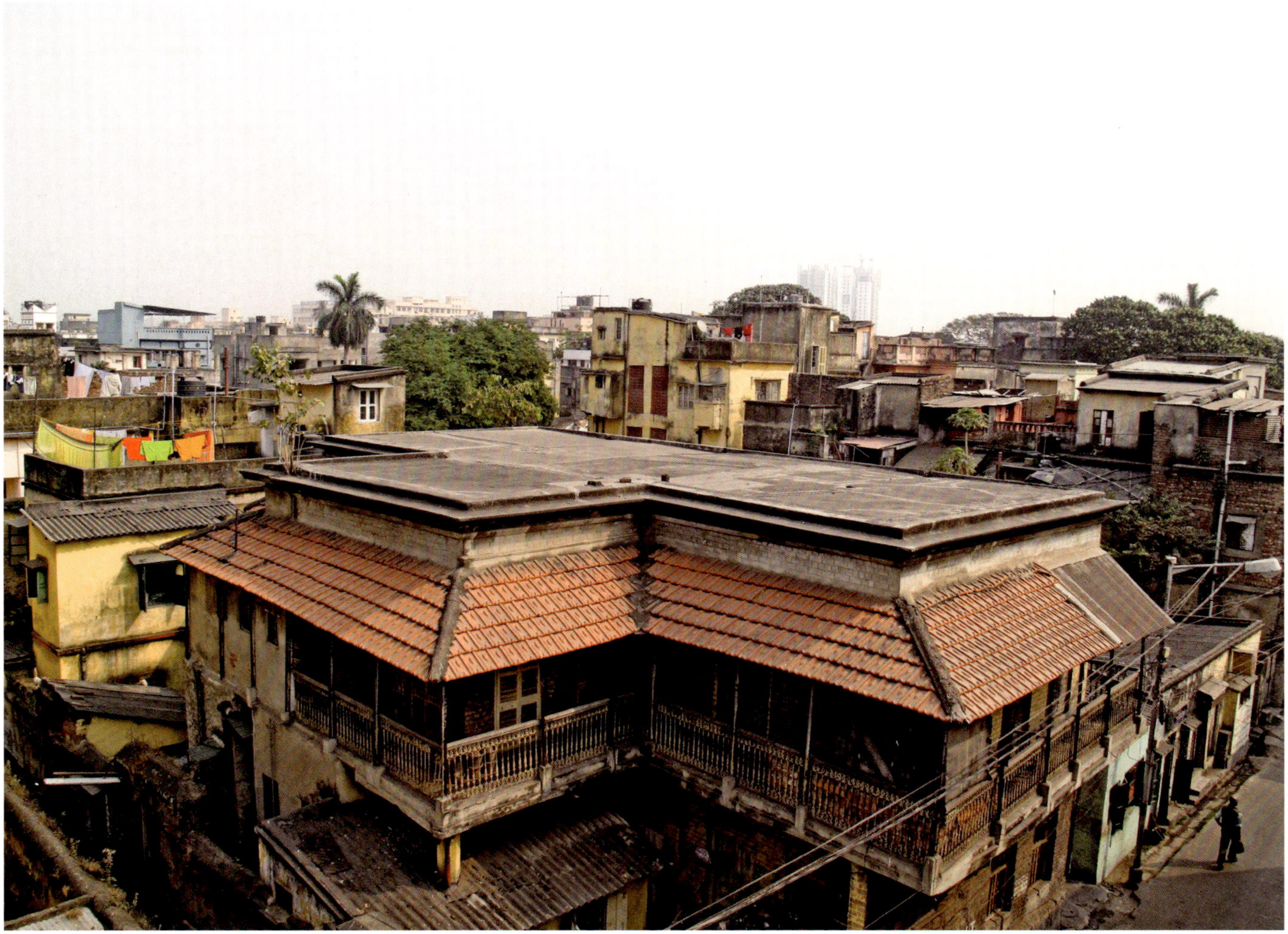

The Kalighat House

Kushal's copy of *Henri Cartier-Bresson–The Early Work* bears the inscription: *presented to Kushal by Manju Chatterjee in the hope of better days*. Much had transpired between his first visit to Image Photographers and the time when he'd received the gift from his friend MC. His job was the key obstacle to his ambition, he had concluded, as he went about building his own library of books and cruising the streets with his gear. He was reminded often of his father who had to straddle journalism and fiction all his life against his wishes. 'I am not really a journalist, although I work for a paper,' Ashim had written to Geeta when he was courting her. His father rose early and did his 'essential work' – writing his novels and short stories – before he left to do office work purely for pay. 'Don't give in to the demand of others,' Ashim had written in his memoirs – perhaps as a warning to his middle son who resembled him most – 'but your own. That way you can preserve your zest for life.' Kushal knew he'd end up being just a Sunday photographer if he didn't take his chances soon. Worse, his passion would burn him down to a cinder leaving behind the ashes of a successful subeditor, well liked by his colleagues and considered a hot marriage prospect by family and friends.

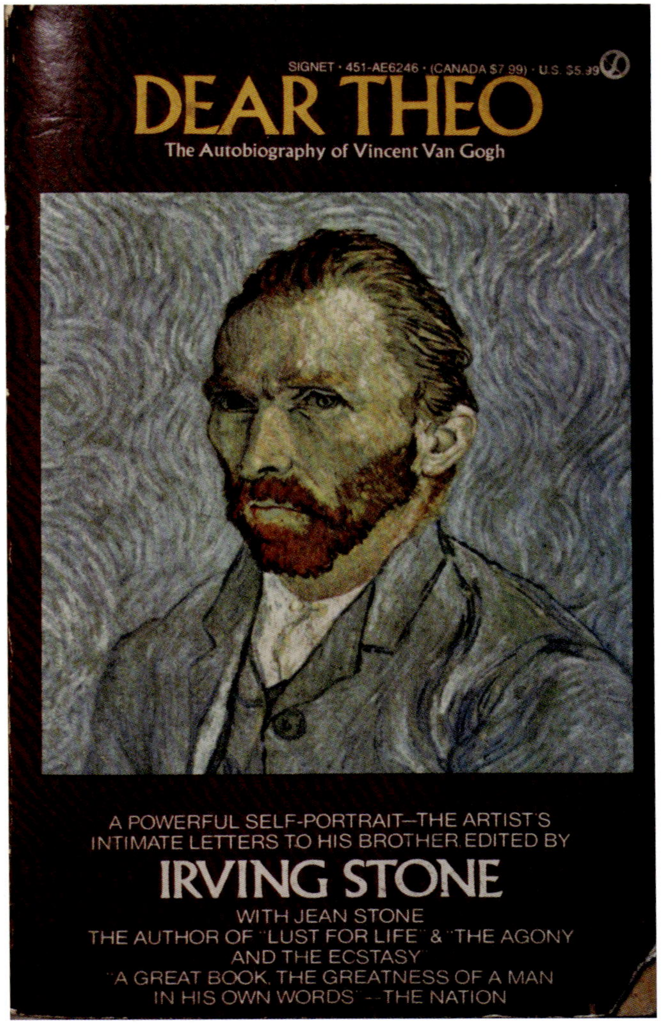

An avid reader from his college days, he found Irving Stone's Lust for Life to be more than a biography but a life manual of sorts. Stone's dramatic rendition of the exchange between a struggling Van Gogh and Johan Weissenbruch, a painter of the Hague School, assumed great significance given his state of mind. At a party thrown by Van Gogh's cousin Mauve, Weissenbruch 'got Vincent off into the corner by the fire, spat into the flames at frequent intervals to hear the pleasant sound of the hiss, and fondled a plaster foot.

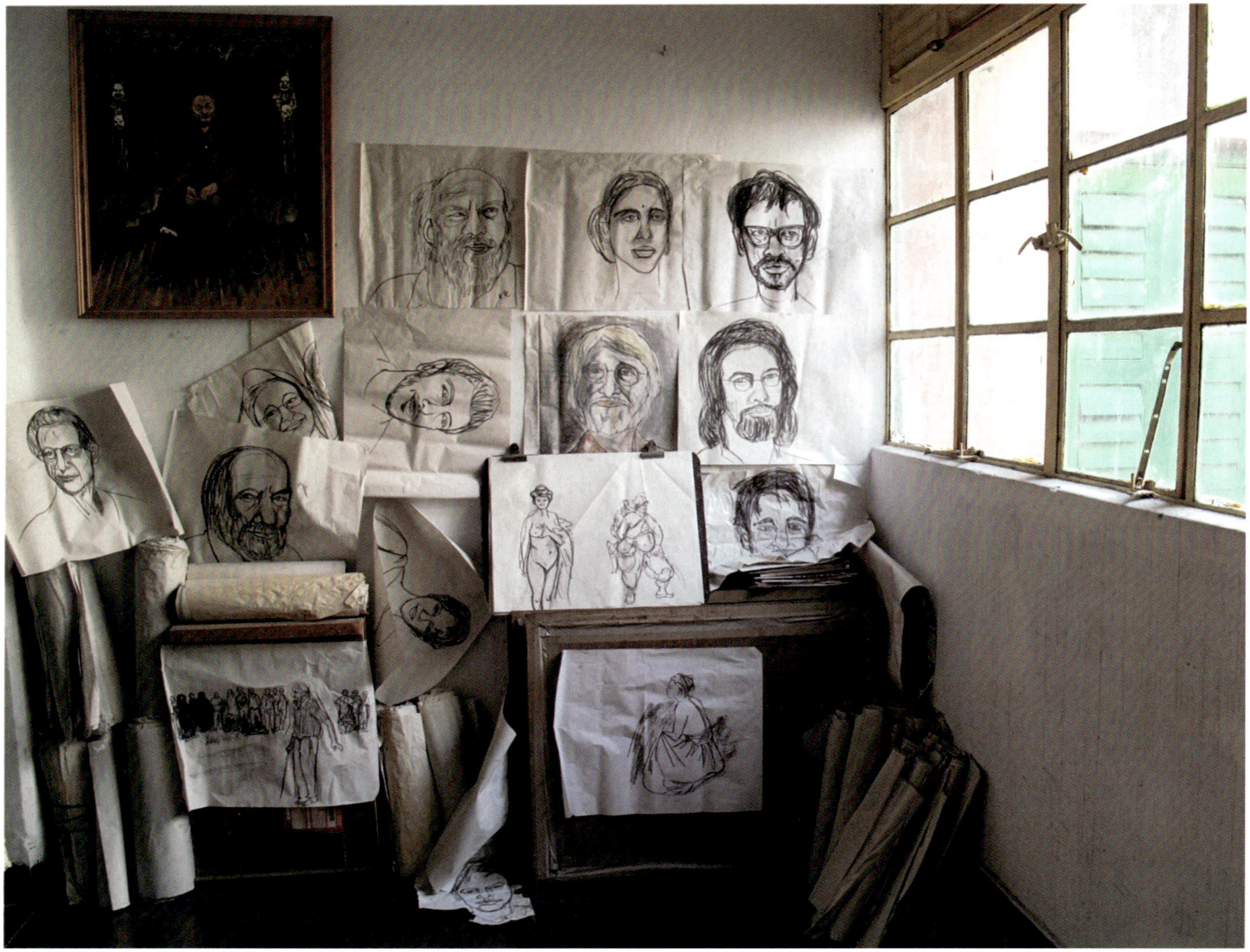

'I hear you're a Van Gogh,' he said. 'Do you paint as successfully as your uncles sell pictures?'

'No, I don't do anything successfully.'

'And a damn good thing for you. Every artist ought to starve until he's sixty. Then perhaps he would turn out a few good pieces of canvas.'

'Why are you so interested in seeing me suffer?'

'Because it'll make a real artist out of you. The more you suffer the more grateful you ought to be. That's the stuff out of which first-rate painters are made. An empty stomach is better than a full one, Van Gogh, and a broken heart is better than happiness. Never forget that!'

'That's a lot of rot, Weissenbruch, and you know it. Poverty destroys.'

'Yes, it destroys the weak. But not the strong!'

So here was the life philosophy that could serve his art, a philosophy that he didn't find life threatening. While he had never found money to be an inspiring subject, the fall in income from a princely 5,000 Rupees a month to the paltry interest that he received on his meagre savings didn't stop him from taking a momentous decision about his future. Invited to a friend's home, he was introduced to the family and a young woman of marriageable age. The two of them were left alone to chat among themselves in what turned out to be an enjoyable evening. He was invited back, and this time the father of the lady broached the matter of an arranged marriage. He was under some difficulty, Kushal lied. There was trouble at *The Telegraph*. The paper wasn't doing as well as expected, and there was talk of redundancies. Emboldened by his lies, he went ahead and declared that he had in fact already received the notice of dismissal and was unemployed for all practical purposes. The bride's father paled at the unexpected news and withdrew his offer.

His resignation from *The Telegraph* prompted surprise and sympathy. Well-wishers, including Jyotish Chakrabarty, were taken aback by this act of old fashioned romanticism and self-sacrifice. He was too young to know what a lifetime of photography meant, and at least a dozen photographers tried to dissuade him with well honed arguments. Free of day and night duty, he started immediately to put his plan into action, drawing and painting at a frenzied pace. Besides giving vent to his early passion for art, he wished to emulate Cartier-Bresson – the artist turned photographer – and refine his eye. Waking at 5, he'd start to copy the masters: Titian and Tintoretto, Degas, Lautrec, Picasso and Hockney, following in the footsteps of Van Gogh who had exerted himself similarly with Millet and Delacroix, and of Pissarro, his other idol, copying the works of Rubens and Veronese. M.F. Husain too had advised his son to copy no less than 100 paintings every day to gain mastery over his craft, and Kushal took his advice to heart, working dawn to dusk to reach the magic 100. He felt he needed to perfect the nude, and like Van Gogh was certain that he wouldn't be able to get anyone to pose for him. Fortunately, he was luckier than Vincent, helped by an ex-footballer friend who like him had been forced to switch careers after injury. Looking back at the early '90s, he recalls being hungry all the time, living alone and going for meals at his elder brother's home or to local eateries. It hadn't taken very long to replace the persona of the sub-editor with that of a Parisian bohemian, and by 1996 he'd managed to emulate the masters by contracting tuberculosis.

It wasn't painting but photography that was responsible for the swollen lymph node. Taking breaks from the masters he'd go out of Kolkata on shoots, to Benares and Rajasthan or Kutch, and back to Ladakh, his favourite. After one such trip to the mountains he returned with severe sunburn, which took a year to heal. But of greater damage was the infection he'd picked up living in a hotel that charged a mere 25 Rupees a night for a room that had only recently been occupied by a TB patient. As the gland enlarged, he ignored the symptoms – the evening fever, the staggering weakness – then dabbled in homeopathy as matters seemed to get out of hand. It took a whole year before he visited an allopath, to be operated upon within 48 hours.

Of Kushal's footballing friends, only Apurba Chatterjee had remained in his inner circle following his college days – the very same Apurba who was his training partner, the midfielder who covered for Kushal when he'd lost speed after his knee surgery. His family lived nearby in Kalighat, on the ground floor of an old two storied house that looked older than its eighty odd years and had two street addresses to its credit: 28/12 Library Road, and 28/12 Nakuleshwar Bhattacharya Lane. When still a rising footballer, Kushal had visited Apurba's home on his birthday in 1974. The house had reminded him of his maternal grandparents' home in North Kolkata. He was moved by the warmth of the Chatterjees that stood in stark contrast to the neglect he'd suffered within his own extended family. Apurba's father owned a catering business and the meal was sumptuous, although there was nothing to beat the *paes* prepared by Apurba's mother. The two friends had kept in touch despite little commonality between their careers, and the contact strengthened following the death of Kushal's parents in the late eighties. The family, headed by Apurba's grandparents, with their three sons and two daughters, a daughter in law, a granddaughter, a dog and many cats, provided the perfect getaway for the solitary Kushal whose links to his own family including his two brothers had waned over the years. At the Kalighat house, a special friendship developed between him and Manju Chatterjee, Apurba's unmarried aunt, a senior lecturer in philosophy at a women's college, then approaching fifty.

It didn't take long for Manju Chatterjee, dubbed MC by her students, to become an ardent supporter of Kushal's work. She was different to the rest of her brood, and soon they'd be meeting every day for wide ranging discussions on photography and art, plays and novels, including Kushal's father's books. A lonely Atget, pushing his handcart full of prints through the streets of Paris, appealed to them both, along with characters – real and fictional – that seemed just as lost in their respective trajectories. MC too had had tuberculosis, and suffered severely from asthma. Between the two it was a friendship of minds, of pain and solitariness. In time it came to glow with the shared dream around Kushal's work. She bought him valuable books he couldn't afford, paid for his film and film processing, kept press clippings of his articles, reviews of his two art exhibitions and those that followed his first solo show of the Ladakh series at the prestigious Piramal Gallery in Bombay. She sent over his dinner in hot boxes before he left for night shifts, came to his house to feed him breakfast when he had French classes to attend at Alliance Française. She sent her maid to clean up his studio and to do his laundry. Sub-editors die early for the lack of proper nourishment, Kushal's father used to joke. With MC as friend and protector, Kushal had escaped the risk inherent in his employment.

Far from slowing him down, recovery from tuberculosis marked a period of even greater intensity when he resumed copying the masters. It also marked a departure in his photography: from outdoors to indoors, down from the mountains back into the city; from assembling a portfolio of single shots to building up a detailed portrait of a familiar space. By now he was tired of travelling: living rough, skipping meals, living constantly in fear of theft of his expensive equipment, and picking up infections in cheap hotels with questionable hygiene. His regular visits to the Kalighat house to meet MC sparked an idea. In fact he was fast approaching the decisive moment of his life when early influences would blend with a decade of hope and preparation to create just the right feed for the next stage of his work. Was he thinking of Bruce Davidson and East 100 Street when he shot the Kalighat house for the very first time? Was he reminded of Dayanita Singh's close focus on families? Did he wish to become a fly on the walls of the twelve-room house? Was this deliberate strategy or the case of a well-honed instinct that had found its perch in part by chance?

Whatever the impulse, inspiration came from the painters he'd copied. 'It's necessary to draw, draw and draw,' he heard Pissarro in his ear, 'until one is no longer an outsider looking in but an integral part of the picture looking out'. He shot, shot and shot scenes of daily enactments at the Kalighat house, not bothering with novel angles or special moments. Each frame was special and held the potential to ripen with time and present something that was more complete and truer than anything he'd done before. Arriving early in the morning, he took pictures of Apurba's family lounging around and reading the papers, or rushing through breakfast and bath on their way to work. Apurba's father watched the chief minister deliver stern sermons on TV, as his granddaughter Teesta finished her last minute homework. Muni, Apurba's grandmother, the matriarch, gazed absentmindedly through the window; Apurba's brother Amal washed hurriedly in the courtyard; a line formed before the only toilet. A poster of Shahrukh Khan covered up the rich patina of water seepage on a wall, and drying laundry blew in the breeze. MC enticed him with lunch to stay back and take more pictures. Some afternoons were unlike others. Sheila, a young Muslim woman, came to offer her 'beauty treatment' to Manju and her unmarried sister Leena. As Sheila applied henna to MC's hair and did her facial, Muni watched from her bed. At Leena's turn, MC sat Sheila's daughter Pinky down and showed her a Van Gogh album. As Muni's health declined, a different visitor came – the family physician, with everyone crowding around her bed. She could no longer do her own things, and her two daughters took turns to help her. They combed her hair, lifted her up from bed; Teesta fed her grandmother; MC gave her a bath as she sat on a chair in the courtyard. She died in 2001.

'One must work as much and with as few pretensions as a peasant,' Van Gogh had written in a letter to his brother Theo. Between 1999, when he started his work, and 2003, Kushal had amassed a substantial portfolio on the Kalighat house and shared them with his close associates. The reaction was mixed. The celebrated Bangladeshi photographer Shahidul Alam, who had founded the prestigious photo agency Drik, commended him for creating such strong relationship-based images. It was impossible for a photographer to get this close to his subjects unless he himself was a part of the web of characters. Jyotish Chakrabarty though was guarded with his praise. He hadn't seen this sort of work before, didn't know how far Kushal could go with it, how it'd be received by viewers. A visiting Neil Burgess, ex-Magnum and hugely influential as a photo editor, voiced the same concern – over marketability. When Robert Pledge, the great champion of photographers, came to Kolkata on his way to Dhaka, Kushal showed him a selection of his photographs. Pledge advised him to protect his work against piracy, and identify websites that could end up selling his portfolio. The view of Suvendu Chatterjee, fellow photographer and friend, troubled him most: the Kalighat family was ordinary, too ordinary perhaps, not one that'd stir curiosity seekers or activists. It simply didn't have the same draw as sex workers, say, or HIV/AIDS patients.

He shared his frustration with MC. It was true he hadn't worked with an eye towards the market. But he disagreed with the complaint of 'ordinariness'. Wasn't it true that Bibhutibhusan Bandopadhyay's *Pather Panchali* was a story about an ordinary family? More ordinary than the Chatterjees of Kalighat? Did Satyajit Ray shy away from depicting the ordinary lives of common people? And it had 'sold' the world over, hadn't it? It depressed MC as well. By then she had become his co-conspirator, the 'resident informer' who helped to prepare his eye, advising him about the varied businesses of the Kalighat family that might offer him suitable photo opportunities. She too disagreed with the undue emphasis on the exotic. Together they dreamt of better times.

The chance to shoot the exotic came soon afterwards. UNICEF had launched a novel project in the brothels of Kolkata, and Suvendu broached Kushal with the offer of teaching photography to the children of sex workers. The monthly stipend of 5,000 Rupees for two years was attractive, as was the chance of contributing to a worthwhile cause – instilling pride among the underprivileged children, and equipping them with visual literacy to explore their world. Taking time off from his Kalighat work, he started visiting Titagarh twice a week. It was the most notorious of all the red light areas, catering to the poorest of clients. The pimps and local gangs didn't allow anyone but customers to enter the homes. His dedication and rapport with the children soon endeared Kushal to the community. He was treated like a prince, fed and hugged; some of the women tried to drag him over to their rooms when he arrived to teach. Surprisingly, he didn't take up the golden opportunity to make full use of his unusual surroundings and subject. Foreign photographers had already discovered Kolkata's brothels. In Sonagachi, Kushal met Zana Birski, an American photographer. She too taught photography to the children of sex workers and photographed their mothers in exchange. A film based on her experiences won Zana an Oscar for best documentary feature, but invited widespread criticism for racial stereotyping and unethical use of prostitutes for profit. He met the French-Cambodian Tian Doan Na Champassak, who was making his own rounds of Sonagachi, scandalising his Indian friends by his explicit – almost pornographic – shots of female and *hijra* sex workers. 'How are you able to take these shots?' Kushal asked him. 'The prostitutes are happy to let me shoot them as I'm a foreigner not a local like you,' boasted Tian.

The UNICEF period is revealing on account of what Kushal chose not to photograph. He knew he had entered a goldmine when he set foot in Titagarh. Here he could compose his essay on the forbidden and the exotic; he could stun foreign and domestic audiences with a kind of ethno-journalism that was fast gaining ground in a world bored with packaged universalisms. To start with, he didn't want to influence the children with his own work, holding it up as a standard before their unpolluted gaze. But more fundamentally, he saw his chief drawback as being the outsider who could never become part of the community through friendship, transaction or activism. However great his skill as a photographer, he'd be doomed to well-intentioned cultural voyeurism at best, lacking the most basic and nonnegotiable asset – intimacy.

Two years visiting the brothels alongside his painting and photography led to yet another health breakdown. He was copying the works of Dali when fever and weakness returned, and this time he was diagnosed with a quartet of conditions: tuberculosis, pleurisy, an enlarged thyroid, and hepatomegaly. His elder brother's family living next door was afraid of the infection spreading, and he had very little money. MC, once again, came to his rescue, and had him admitted to a nursing home. He lived on a strict regime of medicine and injections following his release, but developed an intense fear of death. MC responded to his call at midnight and came over; the next day she took him back with her to the Kalighat house. There he lived for 4 years at a stretch in a small antechamber next to MC's bedroom, becoming one of the Chatterjees, reading, painting and taking pictures after he recovered – 8,000 shots in total, four times more than Davidson in lower Manhattan.

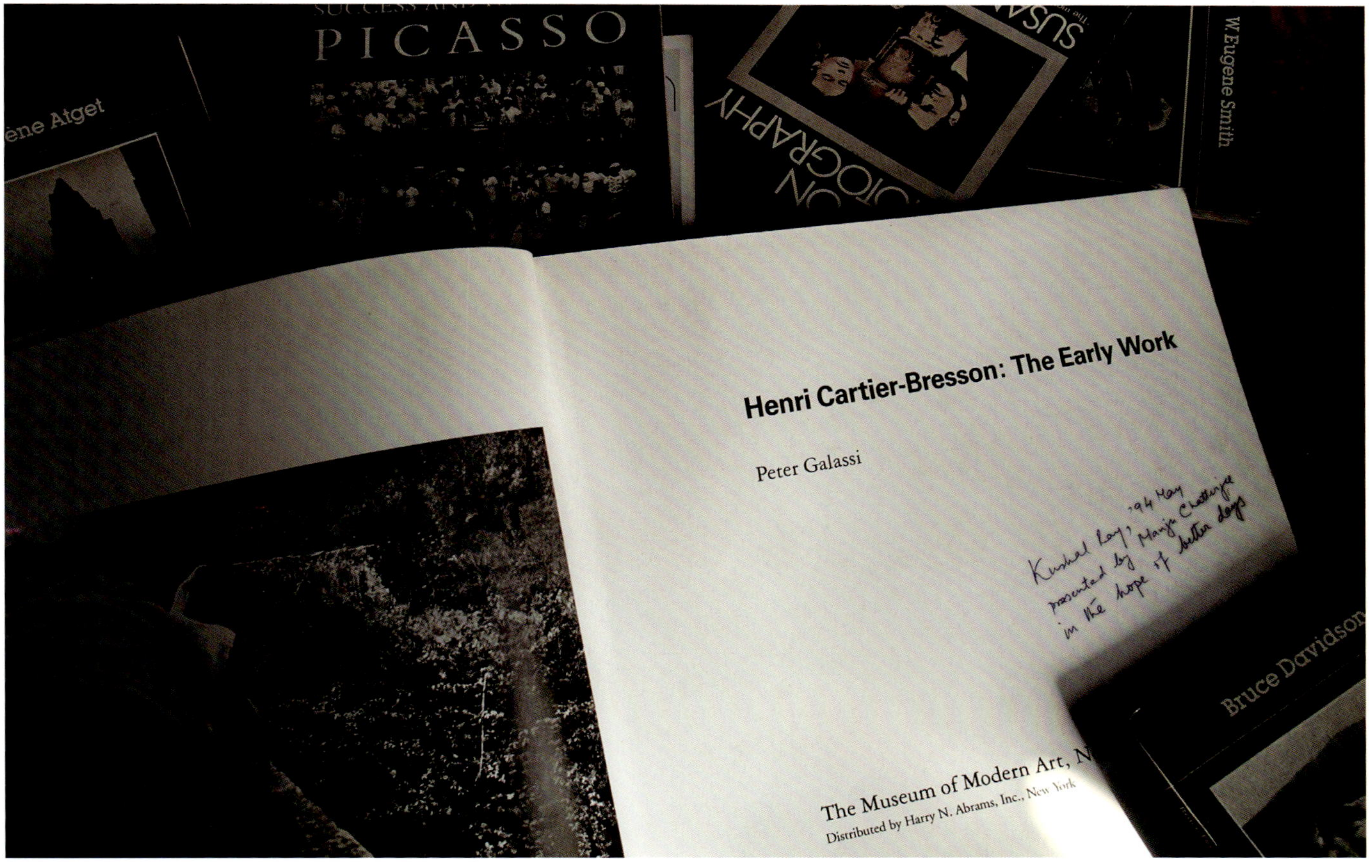

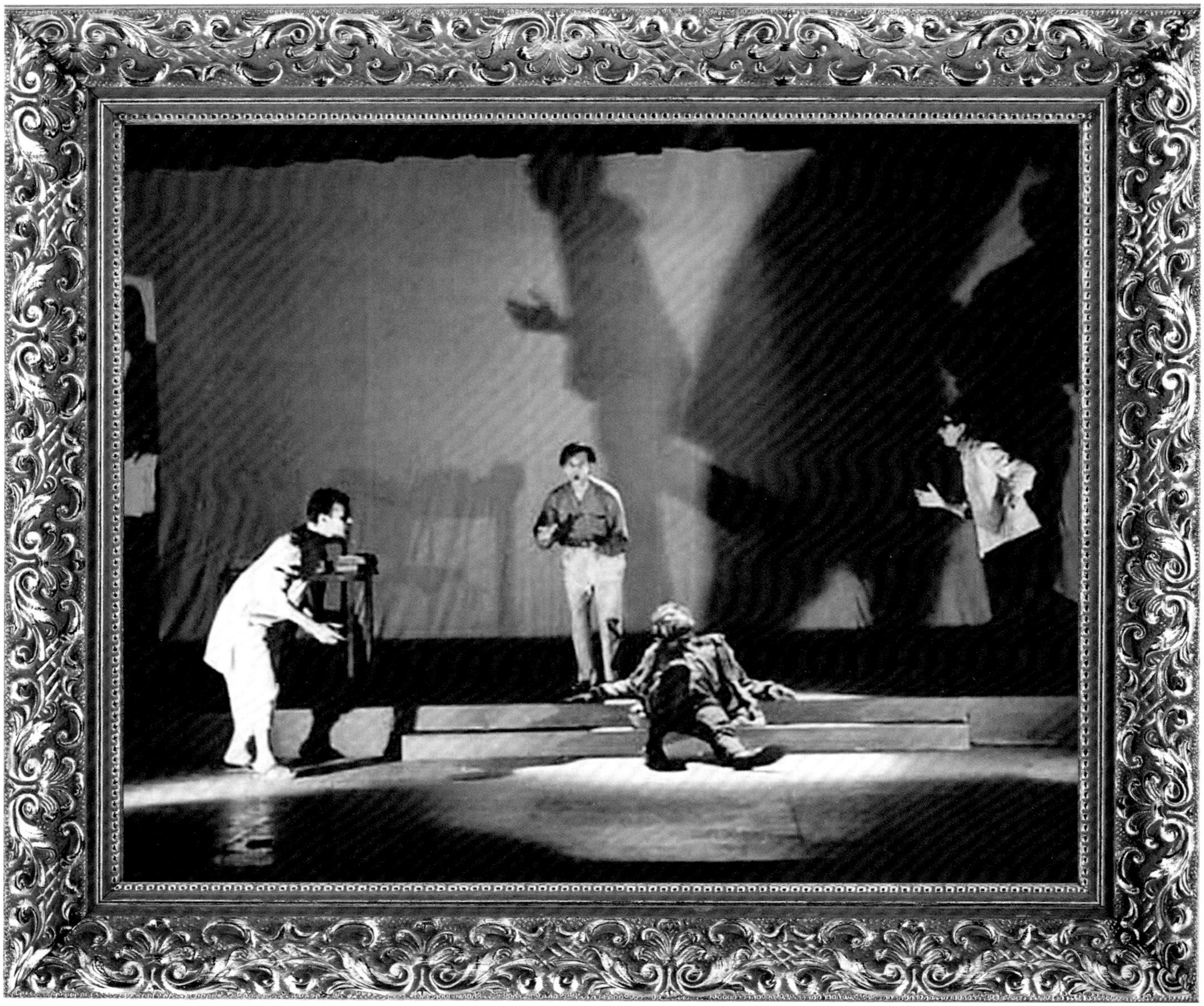

A scene from Badal Sircar's Ebong Indrajit

Photo courtesy: Bharati Chatterjee

Unsuccessful Men

'A novel is more than a plot; it's an author's contemplation of his life and his world,' Ashim Ray had written in his memoirs. 'It isn't just documentary evidence of our existence or mass media entertainment; it's the story of a mind.' Kushal's father had written candidly about a lover, who had challenged him once: 'I know you'll take refuge in history and in literature to claim that truth is a complex matter. I'll say no, you're wrong. Truth is but a simple thing.' As I flipped through the Kalighat album, the photographs did not appear to be complex statements about life so much as pieces of it. And their simplicity made me think about the world Kushal had grown up in.

The texture of the black and white interiors brought to mind Mrinal Sen's films of the '70s, especially his Kolkata trilogy. In *Interview* (1971), Ranjit, a young man, holds a low paying job as a typesetter in a printing press and shares a small home with his mother and unmarried sister. An affluent relative promises him a plum position in a foreign firm. All that's needed for Ranjit to bag the job is to appear for the interview smartly dressed in a suit. The film revolves around Ranjit's efforts to find a workable suit on the day of the interview. It's a simple enough task but fate wills otherwise. A strike called by workers means that he's unable to recover his own suit from the laundry. His father's suit doesn't fit him well and he manages to borrow his friend's only to lose it in a curious and funny incident. Ranjit has no option but to show up for the interview in native *dhuti-panjabi*, and fails to win his dream job. Obviously disappointed, he meets his fiancé at a museum and somehow the two manage to cheer each other up. At the end of the film the audience, speaking in the voice of the invisible director, quiz him on the day's events:

Audience: 'You were saying you aren't sad that you didn't get the job. Why did you waste your time running around town all day then?'

Ranjit: (angry) 'I told you I already have a job. It's a small job, but that's enough to support my family. Lots of people live that way.'

Audience: 'Yes, but you wanted a bigger job, didn't you? A job that'd pay you more salary, more commission. These are not my words, but yours...to your mother, remember? You wanted to climb up the stairs.'

Ranjit: (now erupts) 'I had everything, except a wardrobe.' (He becomes angrier and gives a fiery speech on the injustice of it all. But the phantom audience has left by the time he finishes. Roaming the empty streets he spots a smart clothing shop displaying a suited mannequin. Ranjit thinks for a moment or two then breaks into the showcase. He quietly disrobes the mannequin and leaves it standing comically naked).

Growing up in the '70s, Kushal had imbibed the most powerful drug of the decade: rebellion. Violent eruptions on the streets were matched by those on screen, on stage and in the pages of clandestine magazines. It was the hour of Che Guevara and Mao, Napalm and Uncle Sam, parallel cinema, street theatre, blank verse and graffiti. He couldn't have missed the drama of election frauds and general strikes, not to mention the horror of mass killings and jailbreaks that left their mark on all those that were lucky or unlucky to have lived through the '70s. Yet for Kushal the lure of doctrine was less powerful than the lives of men and women he met regularly in his father's study, at work and on the streets. Over time, they came to occupy the core of his consciousness. 'They go by different names,' as the dramatist Badal Sircar wrote in his cult classic *Ebong Indrajit* (And Indrajit; 1963), 'names like Amal, Bimal and Kamal – the middle class intellectuals, the educated, the genteel, whose lives are bereft of colour, texture and substance – un-dramatic.' As photographer and artist,

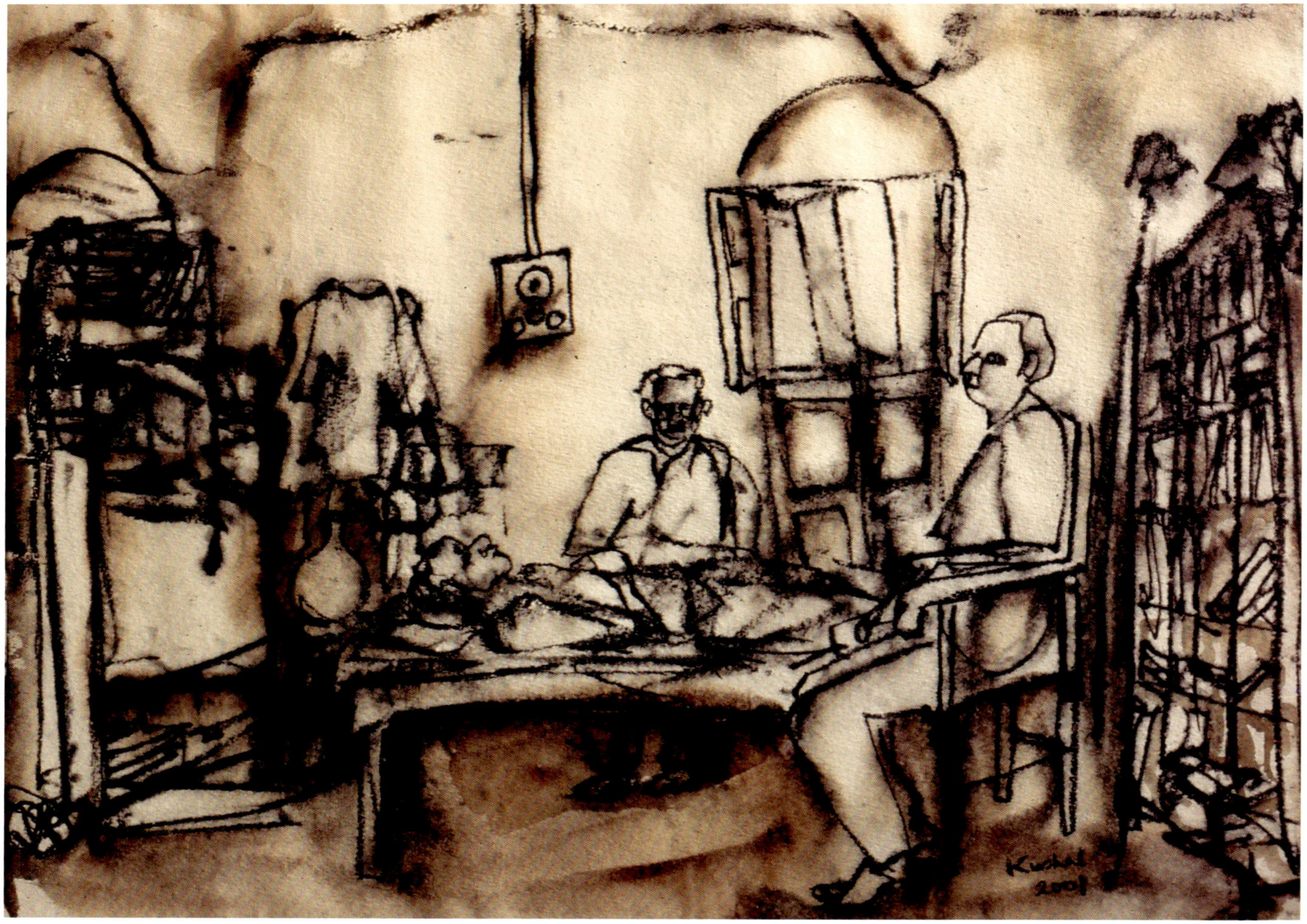

he must've seen the shadow of Amal, Bimal and Kamal hovering over his favourites – a lonely Atget, a tortured Van Gogh, his father Ashim dying unfulfilled, perhaps even hovering over himself, the failed footballer and self taught artist struggling to find his feet among aesthetes.

The flashback to the '70s helped me to see the residents of the Kalighat house as they must have appeared to Kushal when he met them first: not as subjects of photography but as actors on a familiar stage. I wondered if he'd heard Shakti Chattopadhyay, the poet of the decade, calling out as he passed those un-plastered walls:

Here they cry, come stand by them
Here they've set a trap for you, fly in like a bird
Here they're alone, come join them by their side

His first exhibition of paintings was titled *Unsuccessful Men*. Pre-dating the Kalighat photos, they depict similar domestic spaces inhabited mostly by middle- aged men going through their chores: undressing and bathing, chatting in a circle, smoking cigarettes and drinking tea as their much darned clothes hang limp from door nails under flapping wall calendars and framed images of deities. It's hard to miss the striking similarity between the paintings and the photographs. This, unmistakably, is his brood, those he feels closest to, spotting them with ease through windows of dimly lit rooms, in alleys that stink of rubbish, or ramshackle balconies with crisscrossing lines of drying laundry. This is the dead centre of his world, where his mind and his heart align with his sight. In drawing and photographing the office goers, the unemployed, the petty clerks, the retirees, the ageing and the unglamorous, he announces not just a sentimental bond born out of familiarity but also his loyalty towards those who've lost out in the race for success, for whom life must and does go on without unnecessary pathos. *This* then is his subversion – shifting one's gaze from odd anecdotes to the blindingly obvious texts of daily life. Unlike Diane Arbus's violent subversion, Kushal's is a quiet retelling of a parable that simply can't be suppressed notwithstanding the assault of contemporaneous fads and so called cultural universalisms. His parting of ways from a diffused Bressonian humanism has landed him closer to Sebastiao Salgado, the Brazilian master, in a shared solidarity with those who must somehow go on living for others to thrive, for whom the truth of life is simple enough – that of struggle borne with patience, humour and guts.

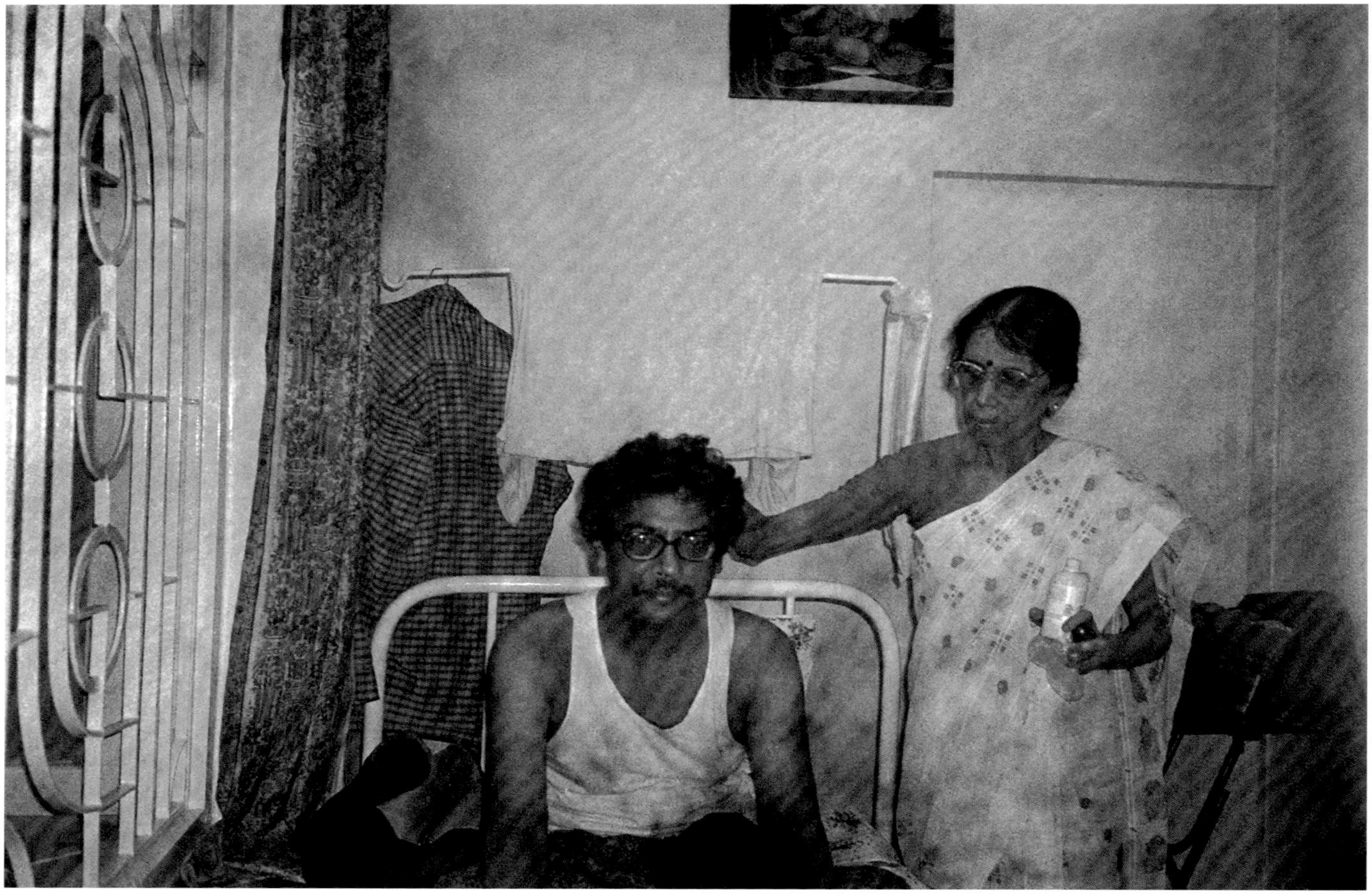

'My only wish is that I live long enough to see his success' – Manju Chatterjee

Intimacies

No less remarkable than Kushal's photographs is the reaction of his subjects to the incessant gaze of an outsider. 'The click of the shutter is like an insect sting,' Cartier- Bresson had written. 'You have to reach the subject in a moment of inner silence, as lightly as possible, so that he can scarcely feel it, so that the sting is as painless as possible.' Did the Chatterjees not feel the sting in ten long years? In the absence of posed portraits, the photographer couldn't possibly have gained admission into their private world by simply stroking their vanity. Yet they betray no reservations, not the 'anxiety of the primitive,' as Susan Sontag described, nor the 'fear of the camera's disapproval.' It is clichéd to call these photographs 'natural', given the unnatural disregard displayed by the subjects towards the photographer who'd hardly had to creep up to them on his belly like a combat soldier or approach on tiptoes like a pickpocket. Far from being surreptitious images, they are brazen acts, un-negotiated, conducted with full knowledge. It is as if the camera had turned into a mirror requiring no courtesy or apology; into the ceiling fan even, its unrelenting drone falling daily on deaf ears.

MC, of course, was Kushal's rock. She had rescued him from TB, fed him a wrestler's diet and presided over his recovery. She bought him art supplies and raw stock, paid for expensive processing and prints, chipped in a hefty share when he needed to buy a new camera and passed on a regular book allowance. Most importantly, she managed the micro politics at the Chatterjee household to pave the way for the outsider who in the eyes of some did nothing all day but play with his camera.

He struck special bonds with the others as well: Teesta, Apurba's young niece, benefited immensely from Kushal's skill as a graphic artist. 'She was doing poorly in homework, till I took over and copied illustrations from story books to her art teacher's delight.' He taught her to sing Rabindrasangeet, not in the traditional way but following the avant-garde George Biswas and Pijushkanti Sarkar. During long nights of power cuts, Kushal, Teesta, MC and her sister Leena would gather around the courtyard for musical soirees. He got Leena and Teesta's mother Padmini to pose for him. Amal, Apurba's younger brother, was a mountain lover, and Kushal took him along to Ladakh on a visit. It didn't take him long to fit right into the Chatterjees' mode of living, making frequent appearances in MC's daily diary, turning quickly into an insider with his own share of tantrums, heartaches and fisticuffs.

Not everyone took a benign view of his presence, especially after he'd recovered. 'Why's he still around?' MC's brother Anupam would complain. He was the successful product of the family, who lived apart with his wife Gopa and son Sounak. His visits to the Kalighat house made MC tense. Anupam and Kushal didn't get along well, although it was the very same Anupam who'd come to Kushal's aid when he was desperately sick, visiting him in the hospital and helping to boost his confidence on the eve of a MRI scan. 'He saw me as weak, as an unsuccessful man, and treated my views about everything with disdain. My photography failed to win him over.' Anupam had once asked Kushal to take a portrait of his son who was on the verge of becoming a successful singer. It wouldn't be a candid shot like his other work though, but a 'real portrait'. The Chatterjees worried for Kushal as he made his preparations. He too felt a bit unsure of the assignment and consulted with Jyotish Chakrabarty. Himself a commercial photographer, Jyotish had approved of the results, but Anupam trashed them. 'You call these photographs!' he scoffed at the prints and took his son over to a 'proper studio.' There were occasional tiffs with Bani, Apurba's mother. Kushal and MC, the 'intellectuals', were the targets of her barbs. Apurba too would rile him from time to time for 'wasting his money' on photography. 'But,' as Kushal insisted, 'there weren't any villains in this piece. None more sinister than what you'd expect in a Bengali middle class home.' There was no need to turn the coin over to find the coexistence of extreme generosity with daily pettiness, unbounded affection with domestic malice – the ordinary sharing the frame with the extraordinary.

The alley cat episode is perhaps illustrative of the state of the heart at the Kalighat house. *Shadababu* – Mr White – came to live among the Chatterjees and was adopted willingly by the residents. Despite her asthma and allergy towards anything furry, MC fed him regularly as did Leena and Padmini, herself a cat lover. Kushal bought him fish from the market and called him his son. Like Ditto the dog and several other cats it became one of the clan till it fell sick and died. Mr White's last days were anything but serene for the Chatterjees: invectives flew over who was to blame in inviting such a piece of nuisance into the house, and eventually, who'd be responsible for disposing off the corpse.

While there weren't any major takers yet for his photographs, the Kalighat album was at last beginning to impress Kushal's friends. Overcoming his initial doubts, Suvendu became an active champion and included photographs of MC and Leena caring for their mother Muni in *Indian Women: The Roles Revised*, a show curated by him in Bangalore, fetching Kushal the grand sum of 10,000 Rupees. Sunil Gupta, the iconoclastic artist, writer and cultural activist, and the author/curator Radhika Singh also took an active interest in the Kalighat photographs, featuring them in their exhibition *Relative Values: Some Current Trends in Indian Photography* at the University of Southampton. These were later published in the book *Click! Contemporary Photography in India* (2008). The 'better days' that MC and Kushal had hoped for in 1994 seemed closer than ever in 2007.

A chronic sufferer of asthma, MC had battled her condition with Kushal's help for years, but fell seriously sick at the end of 2007. Doctors diagnosed her with osteoarthritis, but couldn't cure her back pain and fever. By early 2008 the pain had spread to her left elbow and Dr Bhattacharya, the house physician, was forced to conduct an X-ray. Kushal accompanied MC and Anupam to the doctor's chamber and handed over the plate. 'I remember the scene vividly,' he told me, recounting the day's events. 'The doctor took a look at the X-ray, then quickly covered his face with it. He asked MC to be taken out of the room. I left with her, settled her down at the antechamber and rushed back. Dr Bhattacharya was explaining things to Anupam. He suspected cancer, a stage four malignancy in the lungs. Only a CT scan could confirm his suspicion, and he told us to admit the patient immediately to a nursing home for further tests.'

'Who broke the news to her?' I asked.

'It wasn't necessary. She knew.' MC had come home and complained bitterly about Dr Bhattacharya. 'Why did he have to cover his face like that? Why did he make me leave the room? I'm not a child!'

Kushal took her to a nursing home the next day, and a CT scan confirmed lung cancer.

There are two entries in Manju Chatterjee's diary on 18 April, the day she visited Dr Bhattacharya: a record of the doctor's fees and the taxi fare to and from his chamber. The pages are blank for the next few weeks. The first of seven sessions of Chemotherapy started soon thereafter, and on June 23 she had her next diary entry:

> *Birthday. 67th year. This is a new kind of birthday. Now I'm no longer a patient of asthma. Now I am a patient of osteoporosis and lung cancer. I've had 2 chemos already, and shall be admitted again to the nursing home on 6 July. These words may make me sound very pessimistic. My inner strength makes me an optimist. It's for Kushal that I didn't lose my will to live even when I found out about the cancer. It's for many years now that Kushal has cared for me. It's rare to find such intimacy. My only wish on my birthday is that I live long enough to see his success. If I could live for 4 or 5 years more, it might be possible I think.*

It wasn't MC but Kushal who suffered a breakdown. He googled Lung Cancer and found out that the typical longevity of patients was no more than 10 months. For nights on end he kept marching up and down the cramped quarters of the Kalighat house unable to sleep. Every vein of his body pulsed violently, and his face darkened like burnt log. Manju called Kushal over from her hospital bed and made him promise that he'd see a psychiatrist. 'Don't make her suffer any more by seeing you like this,' the psychiatrist counselled him and prescribed pills to get over his depression. What followed in the next few months took Kushal some time to tell me between bouts of silence.

'I had once taken her out for a ride on my motorbike. This was when she was well, while she was still a teacher in her college. We went to the deserted Eastern Metropolitan Bypass at night, and I revved up my bike to 100 kph. Most of my ex-colleagues at *The Telegraph* would've been frightened to death riding pillion with me at that speed. But not her. She kept holding me tight and whispering into my ear ...*concentrate, concentrate*...' As she declined, Kushal started to photograph her and the house with even greater concentration. As much as it pained him to see her suffer, seeing her turn into a helpless bedridden creature living from one bout of radiation and chemo to the next, he clung on to each precious moment seen through his viewfinder. 'Friends have asked me later, how I could do this. It wasn't as if I wanted to chronicle a dying patient and become famous for these difficult photographs. I simply wanted to keep a record of my own life, a large part of which was ending with MC. It was as if I was trying to keep her alive by taking her pictures.'

Manju's diaries were full of everyday details: lists of food and medicine that she paid for, record of visits by family and friends, fairly detailed accounts of her discomforts, complaints against nurses and doctors, and most significantly, proud reports of Kushal's successes.

July 29th

Today's special news is that Kushal's photographs have been selected for a show in Singapore. 800 entries were accepted from 6,000 submissions!

And again:

October 8th

A new college for photography will be founded in Kolkata, Suvendu has told Kushal. They'll ask him to be a teacher there. An Italian magazine has asked for his Ladakh photo

A deep sorrow entered Kushal's photographs from the time when MC fell sick. As her primary care giver, he lost track of everything except the demands of cancer. For a while he pinned his hopes on a wonder drug, an Ayurvedic remedy, fought with Anupam to have her take it regularly; consulted astrological charts and took over managing MC's investments to meet the rising expenditures. He lost his head over small matters. More than once, he tried to distract MC from her pain. 'What do you suffer from most?' He asked her one day. 'From the fact that I can't talk to you properly,' she managed to whisper.

She didn't mind him taking her pictures, even in the most embarrassing of situations when she was urinating in a bedpan, or gasping for breath with an oxygen mask on her face. 'To photograph people is to violate them,' Susan Sontag had pronounced. Even as she waited at the Thakurpukur Cancer Centre for her radiotherapy to start, MC egged Kushal on to take out his smallest camera disguised as a cell phone and take photographs. She seemed to dare him to shoot, just as her mother Muni had when she was 90, confessing to Kushal: 'now I live just for you to take my photo...'

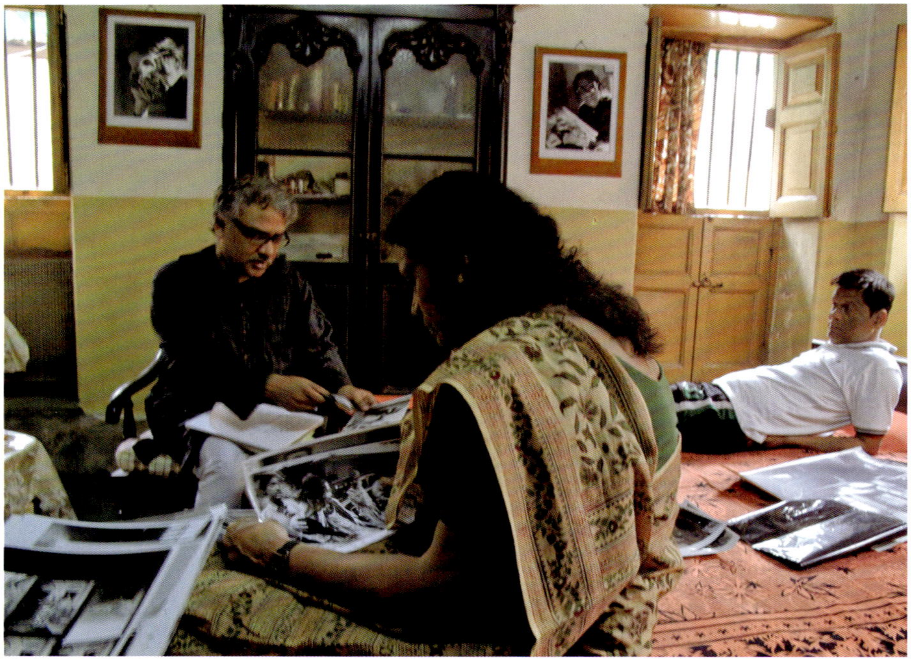

'Take one more picture,' MC had urged Kushal after she'd been brought home after her seventh chemo. She had described the frame that she wanted:

'Put your hand in mine and take a photo of our hands.'

Intimacy had turned to union with the click of the shutter.

It'd be unfair, I thought, to write about Kushal's photographs in a formalistic way, ignoring the real stories that give them character. It'd be unfair to him and to MC, indeed to all those who'd stepped before Kushal's lens if I simply were to treat the album as fodder for analysis. Just as critical as the aesthetics of the work is the journey, the will, the friendships, the loves and the loss that shaped Kushal's photographs. Writing about them made me see why he has spent almost a quarter of his life on this project, why he carries the Kalighat house inside his head even after he'd stopped living there following Manju Chatterjee's death. These aren't dispassionate images, and I couldn't be bloodless in my observations. Neither are they simply artistic statements, leaving me no room to hide behind the mask of a critic. Built piece by piece from shared moments, they filled me with a sense of belonging and an unexpected fear of loss. More than once, I was tempted to emulate John Berger and invent a fictional character, a photographer along with his muse, just as Berger had done with Janos Lavin, an émigré Hungarian artist in London and his wife Diana, for his first novel *A Painter of Our Time* (1958). At the end of that novel, the artist disappears never to be found again. Perhaps I could script a different ending to my own fiction, I thought, one that'd prolong MC's life by 4 to 5 years just as she'd wished, to see Kushal's success.

Armed with 150 or so photographs I visited the Kalighat house with Kushal. The Chatterjees were expecting me with tea and biscuits. I crossed the same courtyard where Kushal had shot Apurba bathing, and entered the house that was instantly recognisable from the photographs. We went into Manju Chatterjee's room and I sat on her favourite chair under a pair of her framed portraits. Apurba and Leena lounged on the neatly made up bed that filled more than half the space between the walls. The refrigerator hummed; street noise blew in through the curtains. I enquired about Teesta and was told that she had left with her mother Padmini and her new husband to settle in America. Bani came in after a while, as did Amal, Apurba's younger brother, and his wife Mithu. Sipping my tea, I answered Apurba's questions about this and that, waiting for the right moment to conduct my experiment. Everyone seemed fairly relaxed talking about Kushal and encouraged by the proceedings, I laid out the photographs on the bed, asking them to pick their favourites and those that they disliked for whatever reason. Pen poised on paper, I waited as they ran their eyes silently over them.

'Anyone who comes to this house gets photographed!' Apurba laughed and broke the ice. The others laughed too, but none answered my question, turning their gaze back at the bed and recalling a few things about the photos, simple things such as when they were taken, and what they were doing at that very moment. It was silly to ask them these questions, I realised after a while. They didn't see the photographs as photographs, but as pieces of their life that didn't warrant approval or disapproval. It was enough to locate them in time, which alone was the most significant marker of all.

Ready to leave, I looked around for Kushal. He'd disappeared, and I caught sight of him fleeting into the room with his camera. Then he disappeared again, busy taking photographs, as he always had at the Kalighat house, under the gaze of his MC.

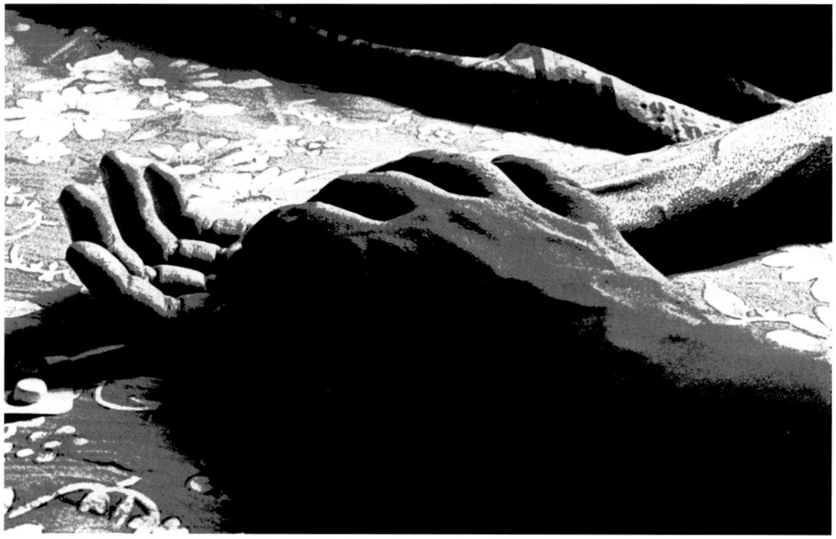

Intimacies

Kushal Ray

Muni and her late husband

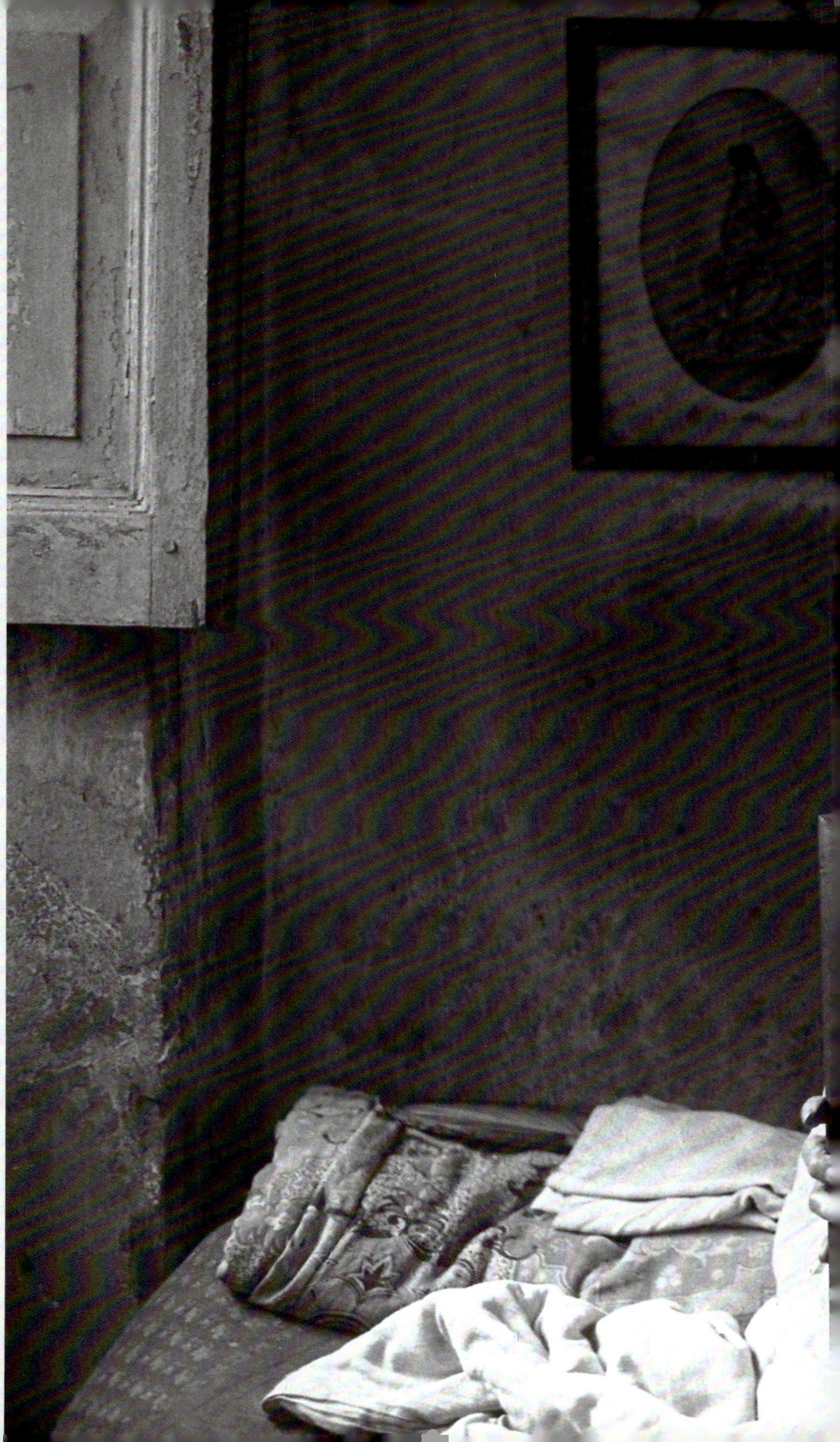

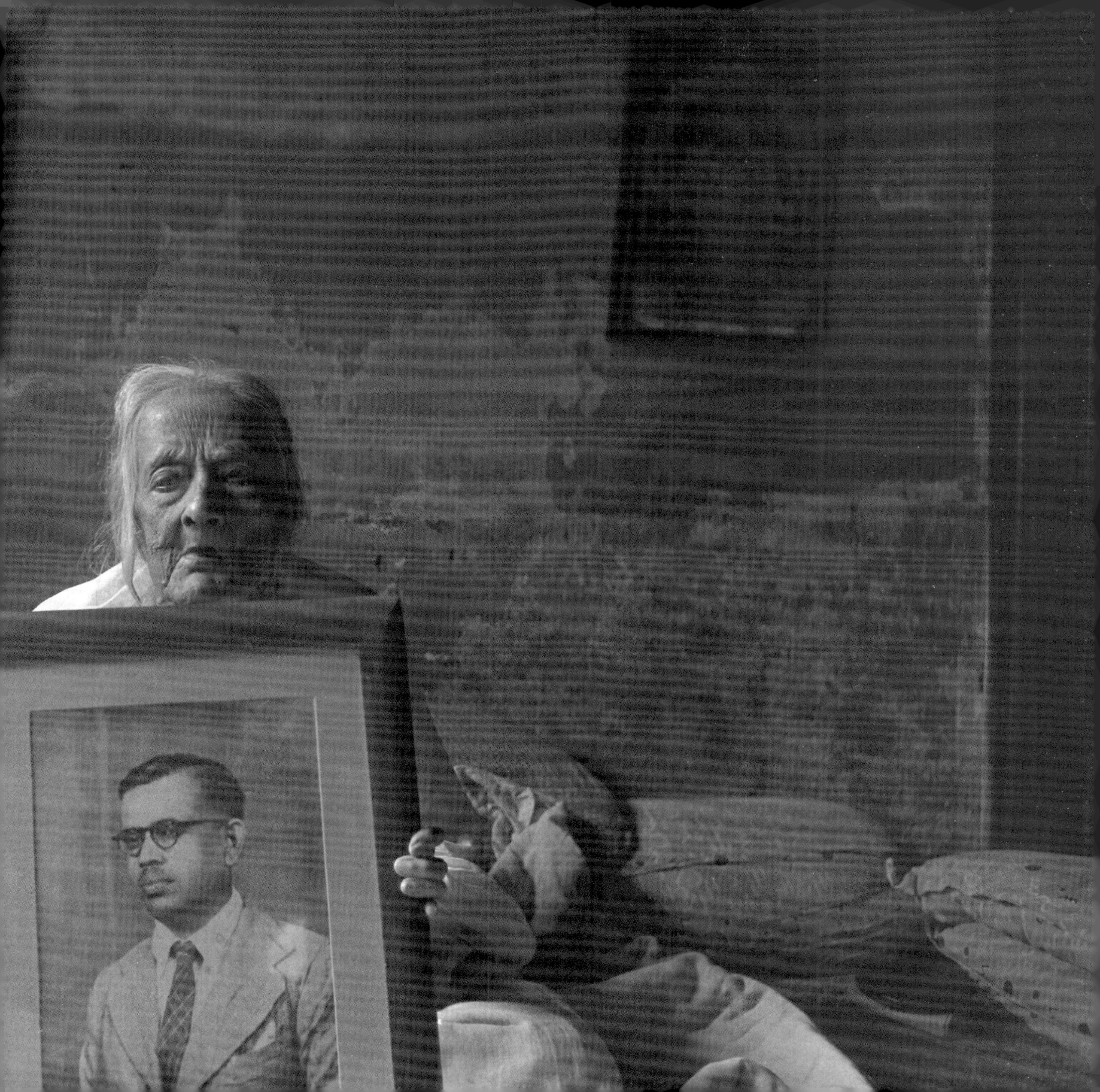

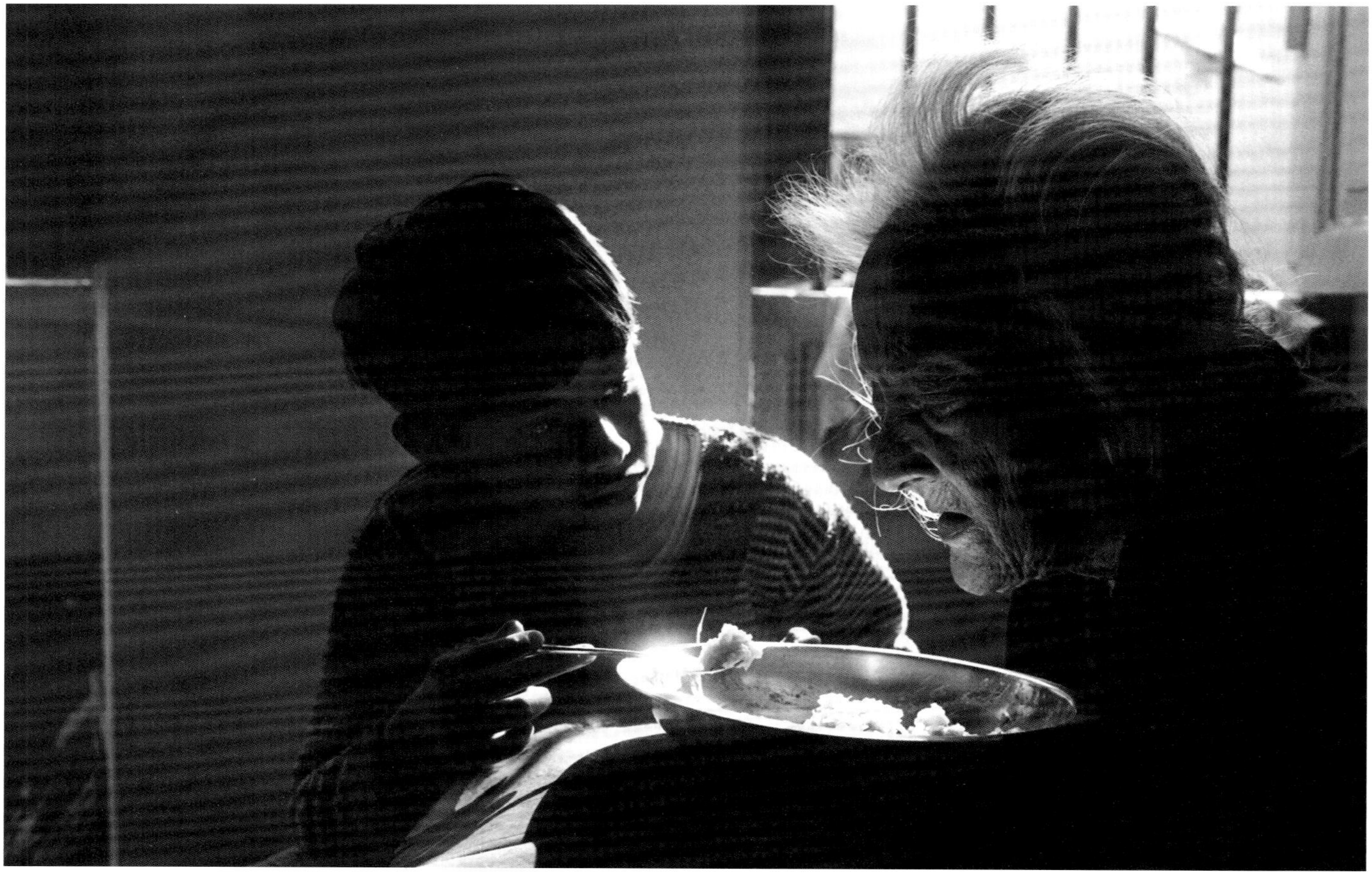

Muni and her great granddaughter Teesta

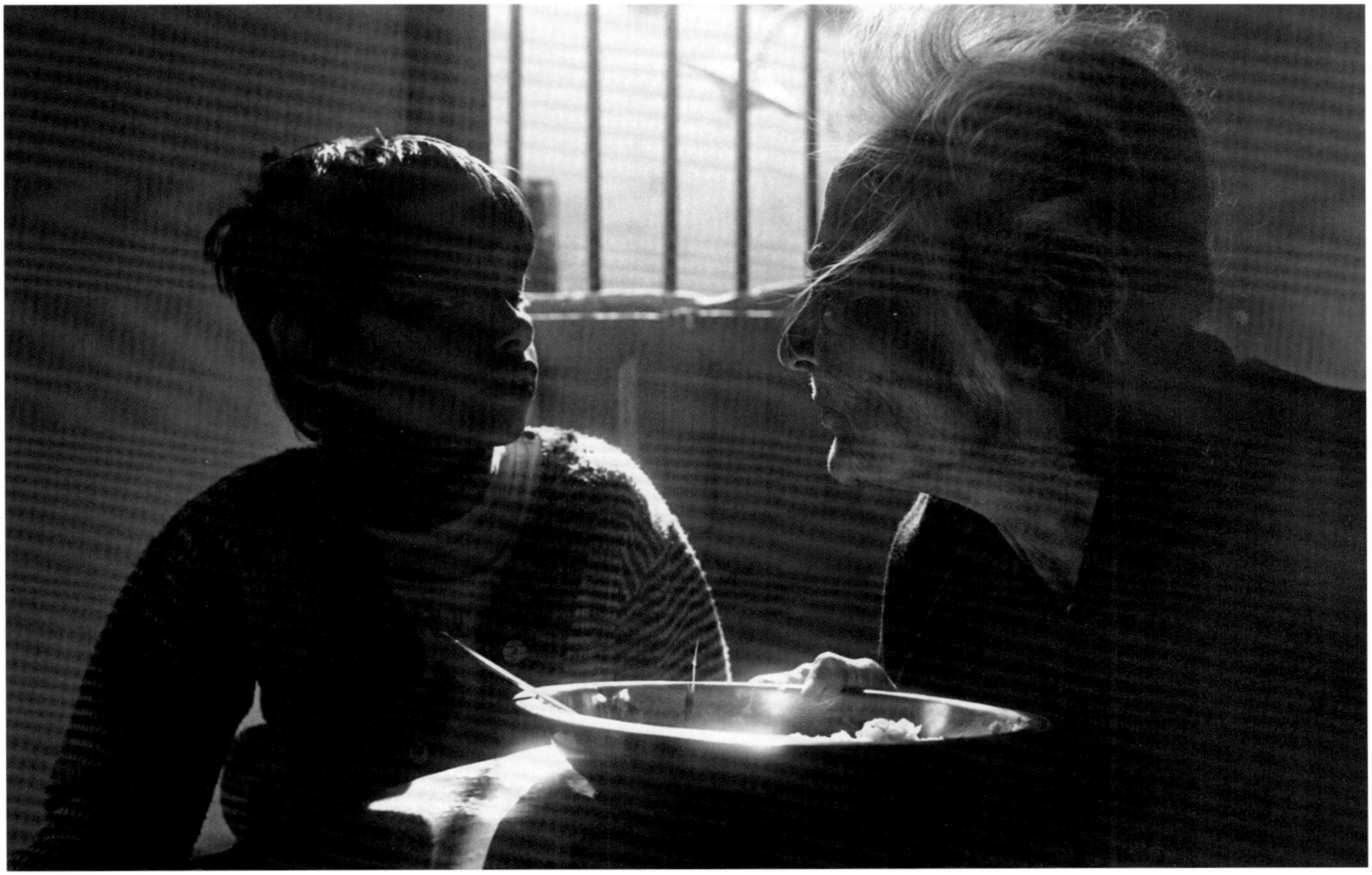

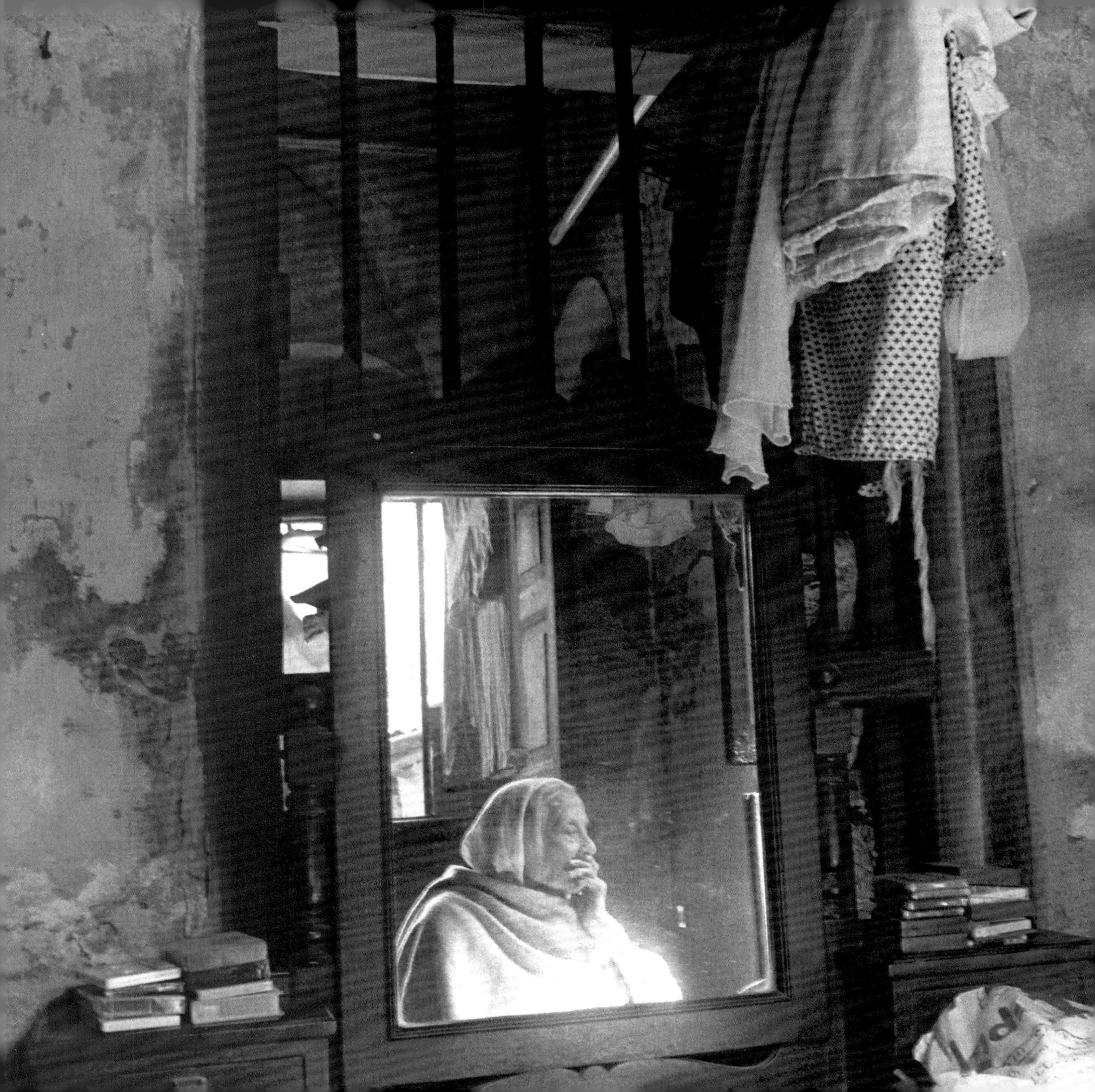

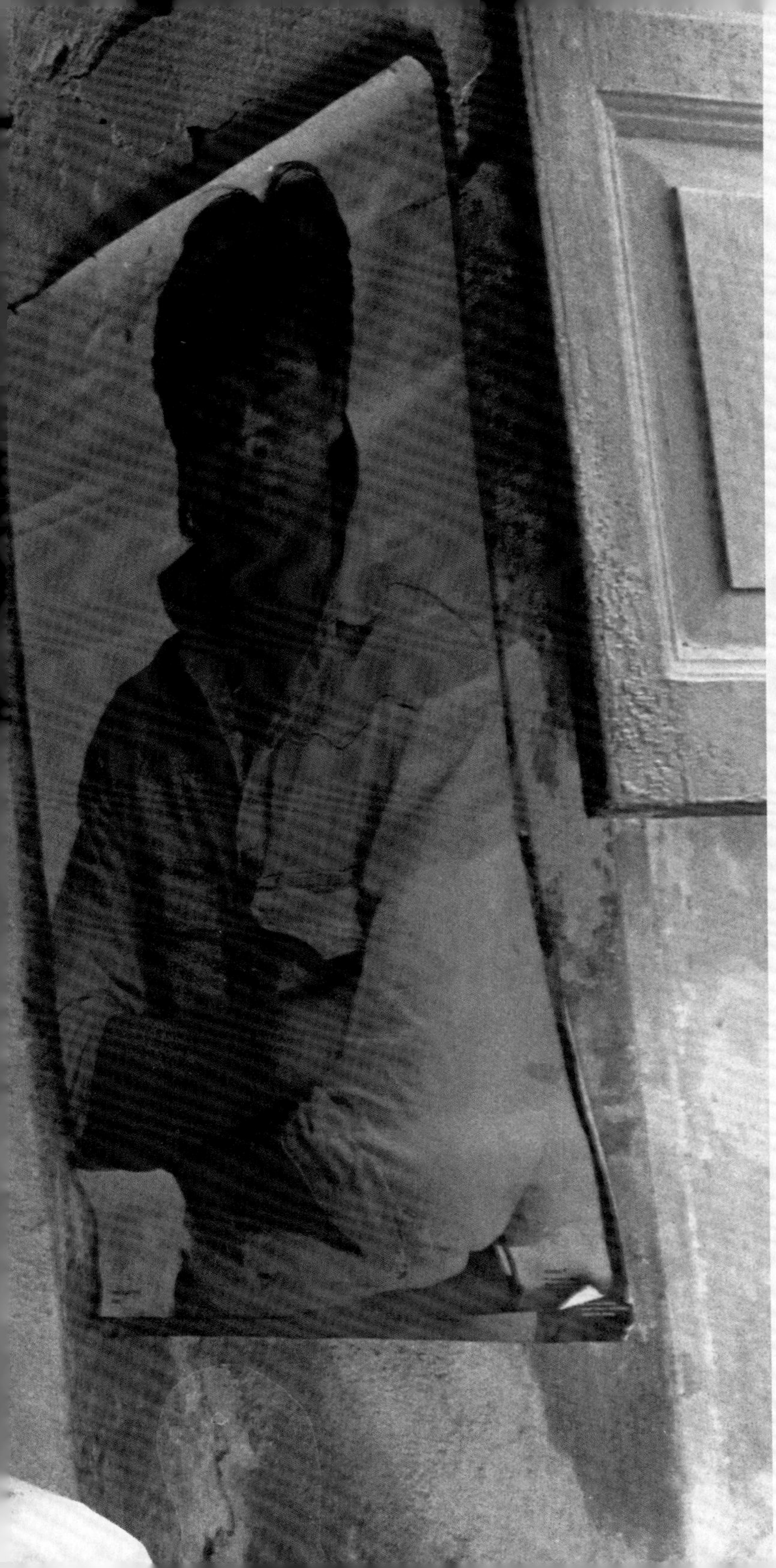

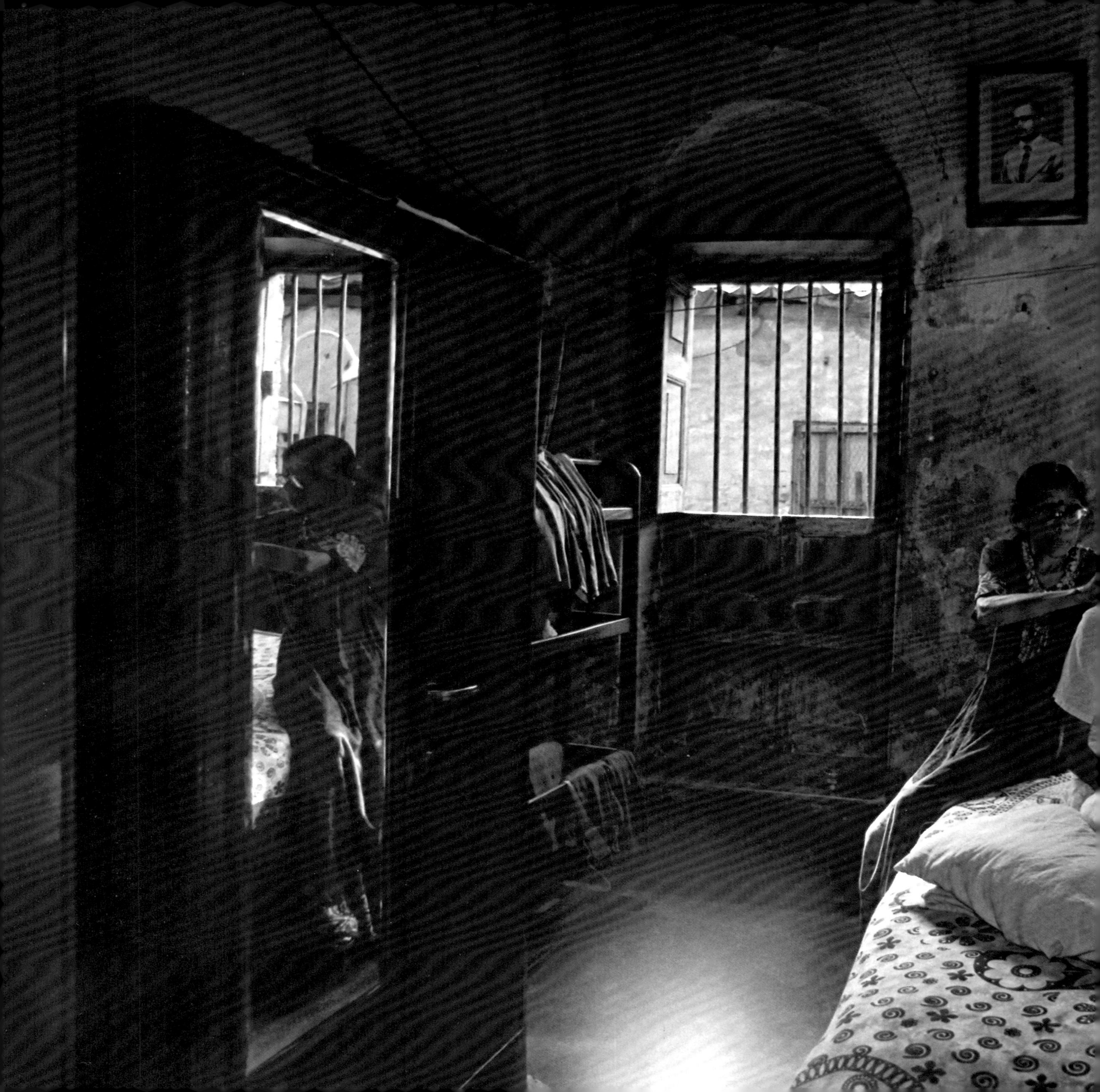

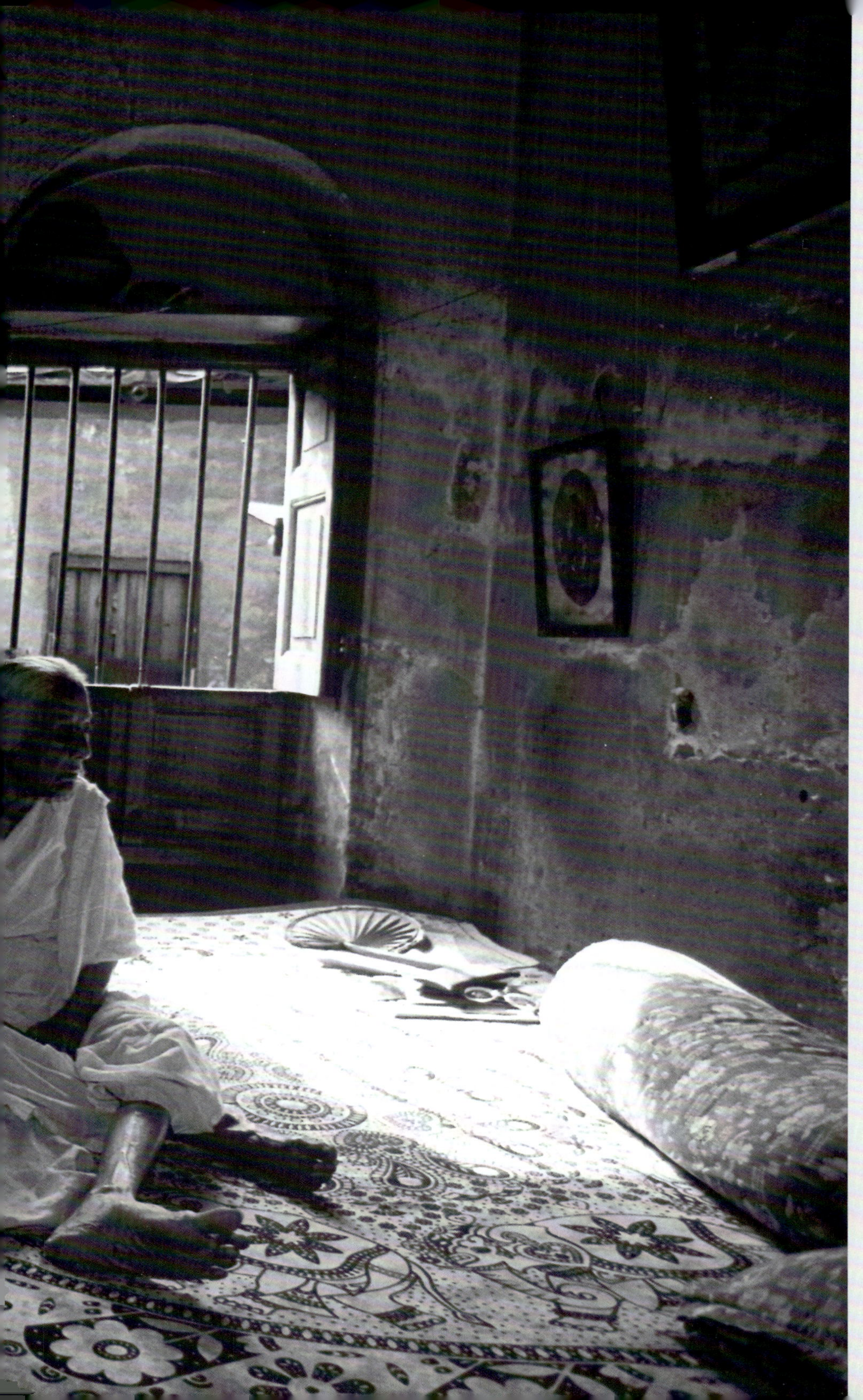

...whose lives are bereft of colour,
texture and substance...un-dramatic

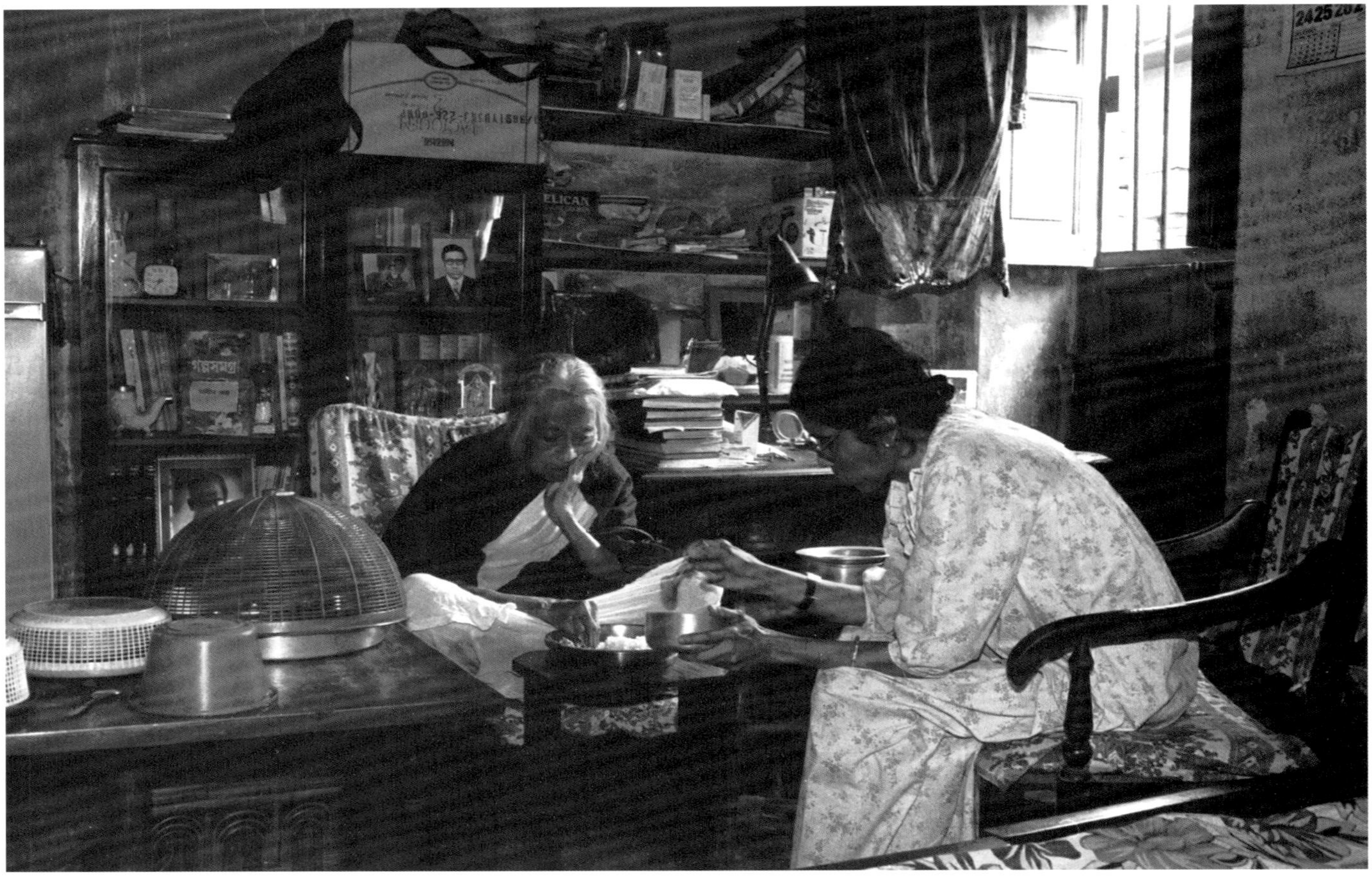

Muni and her daughter Manju

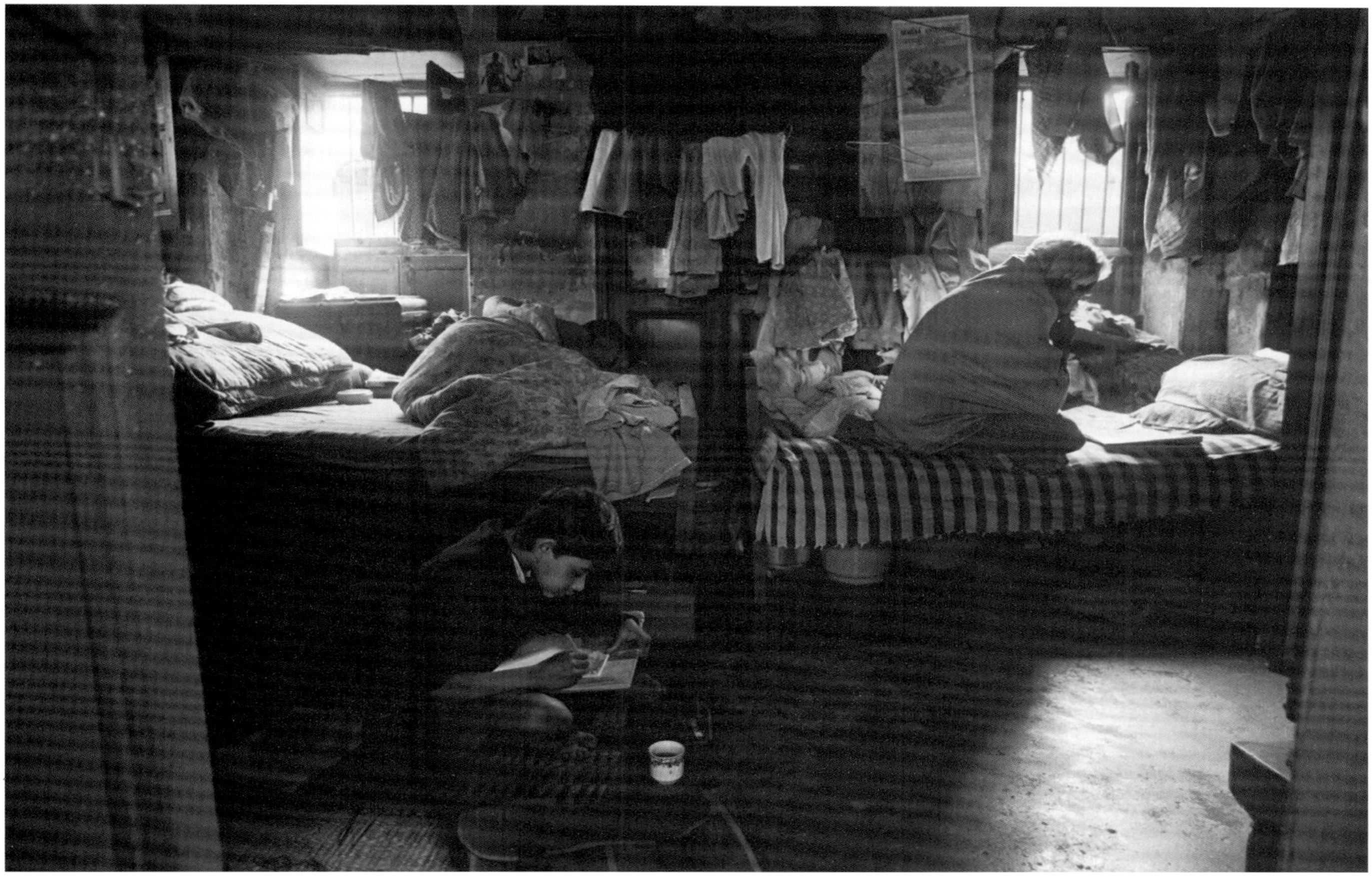

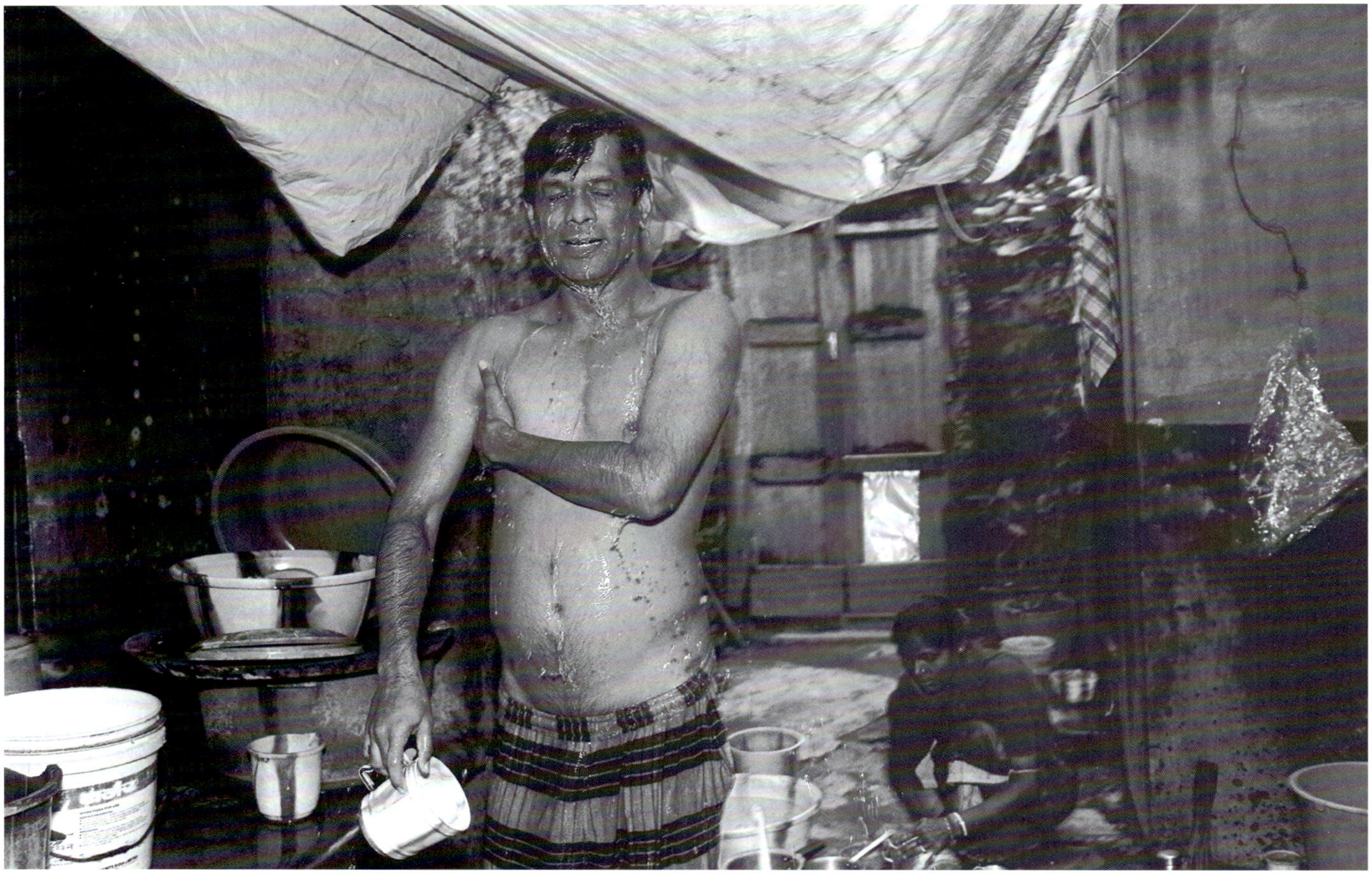

'Anyone who comes to this house gets photographed!'- Kushal's friend Apurba

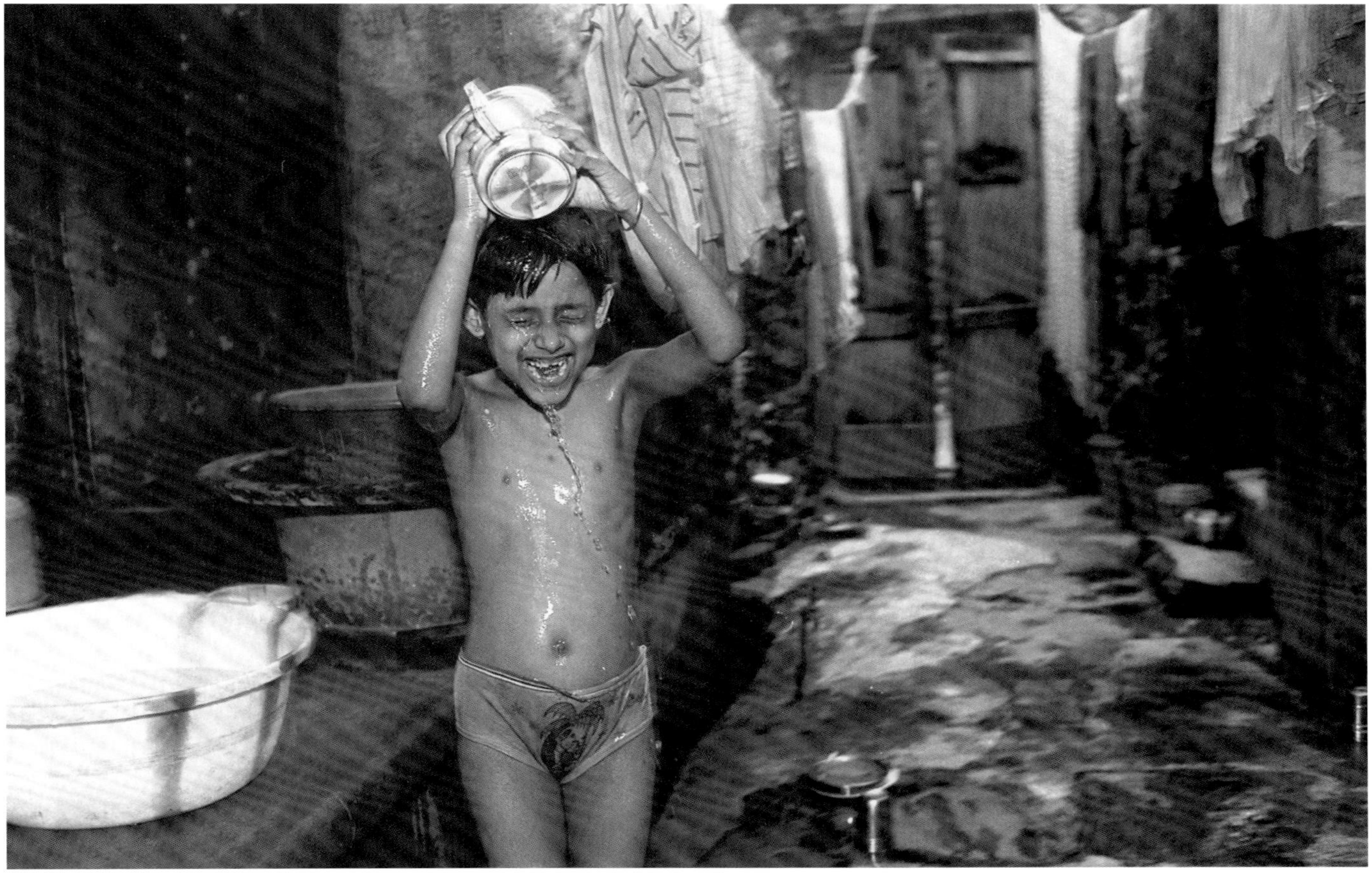

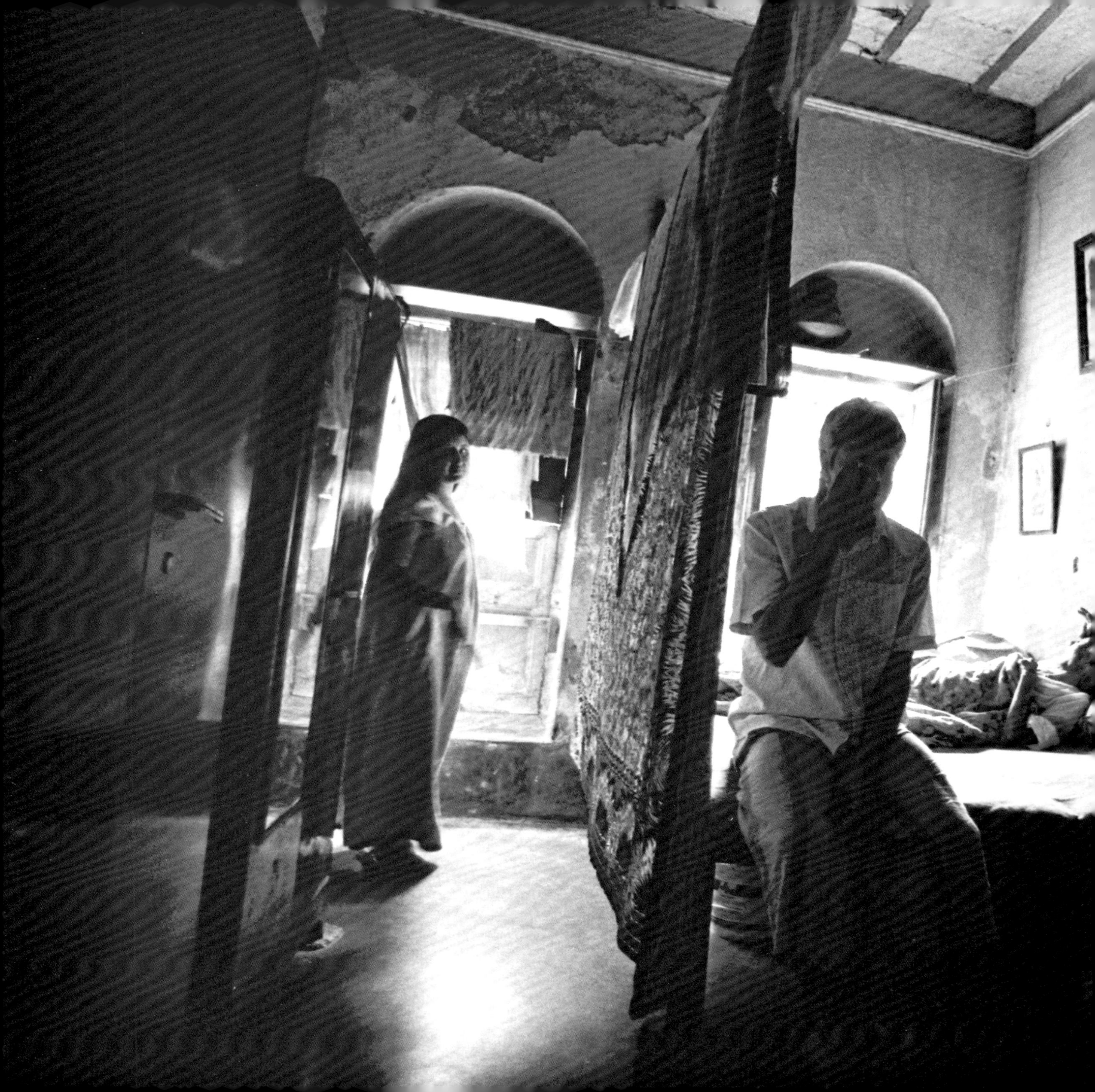

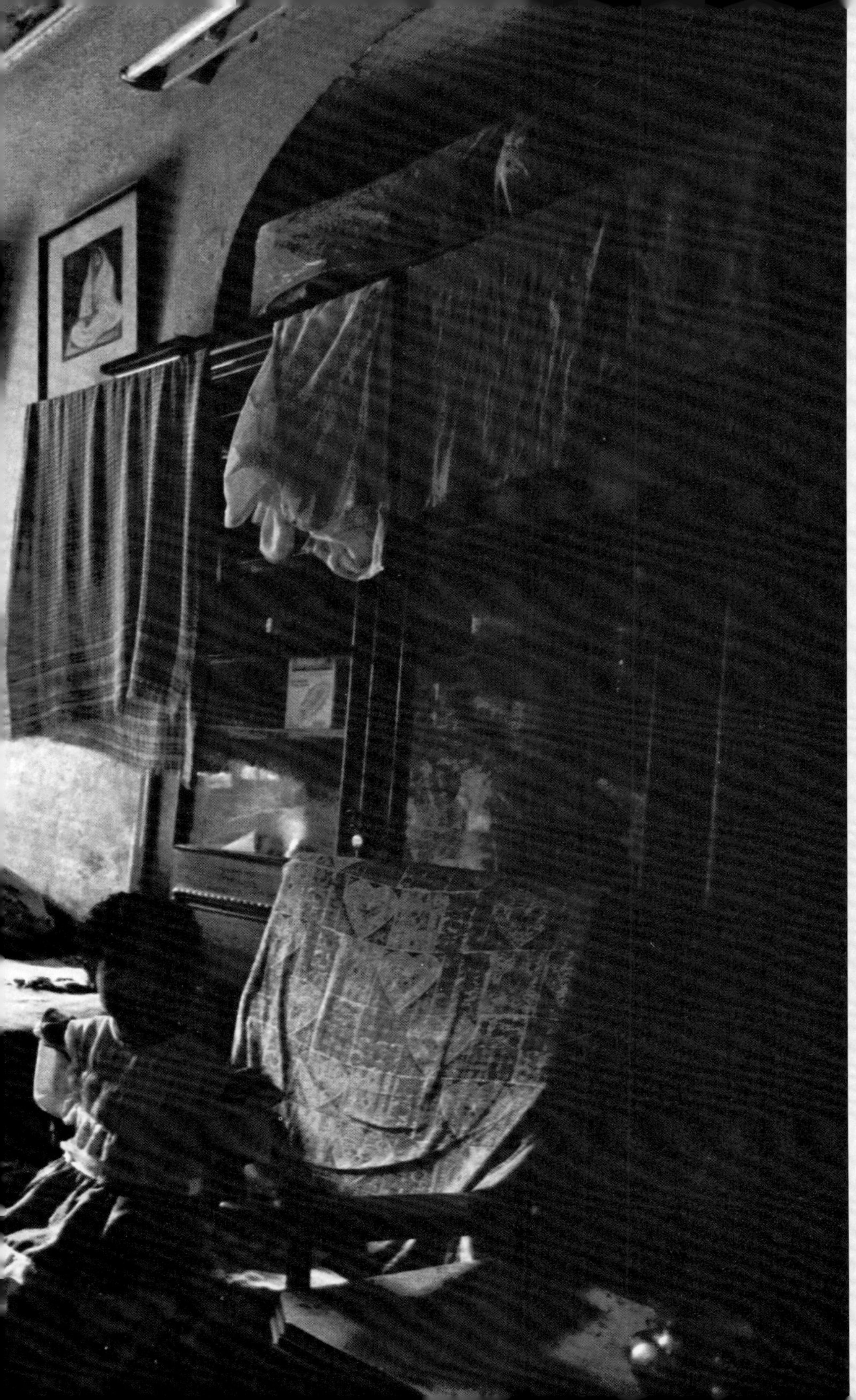

Ordinary lives

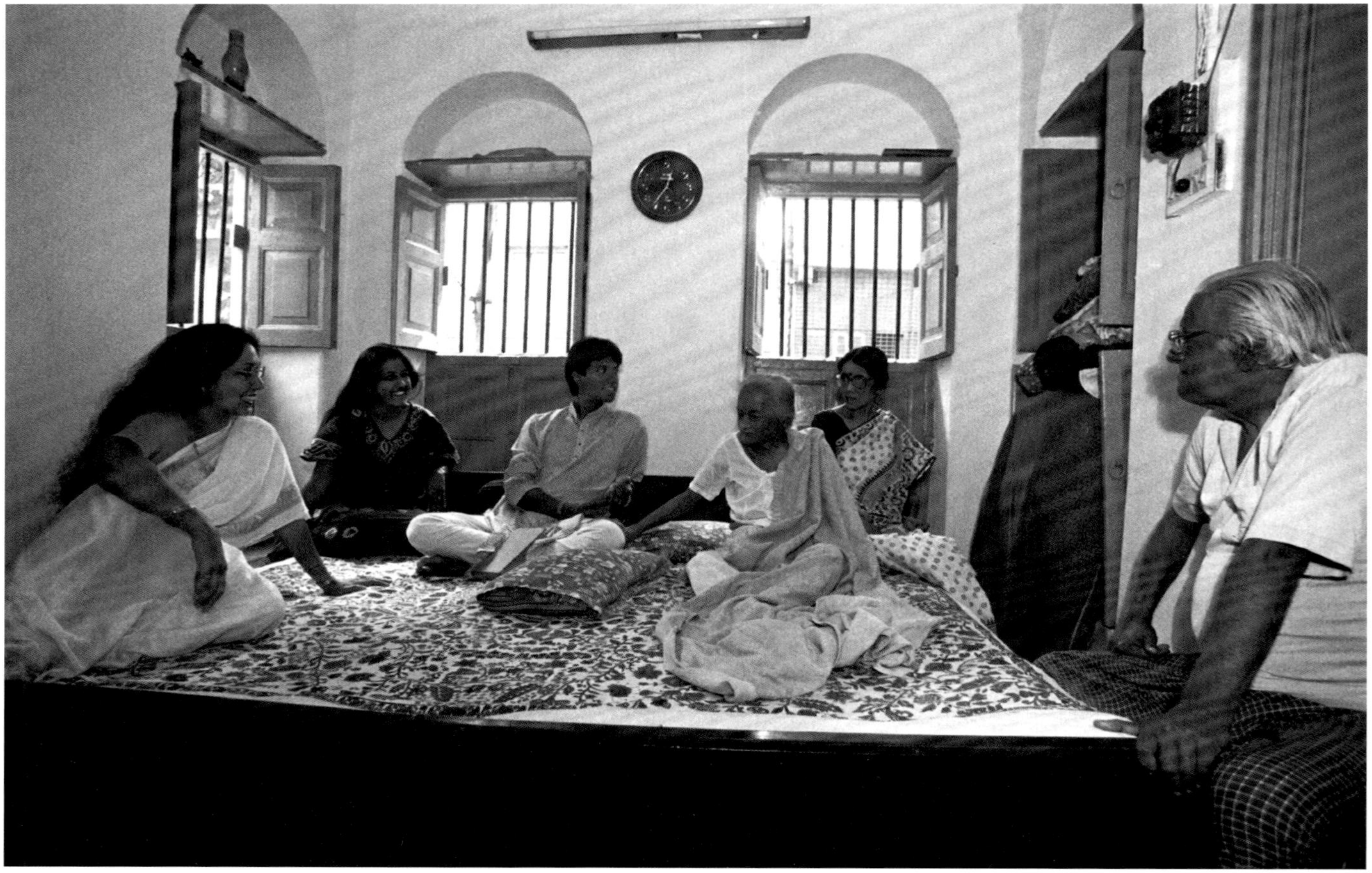

Family tree

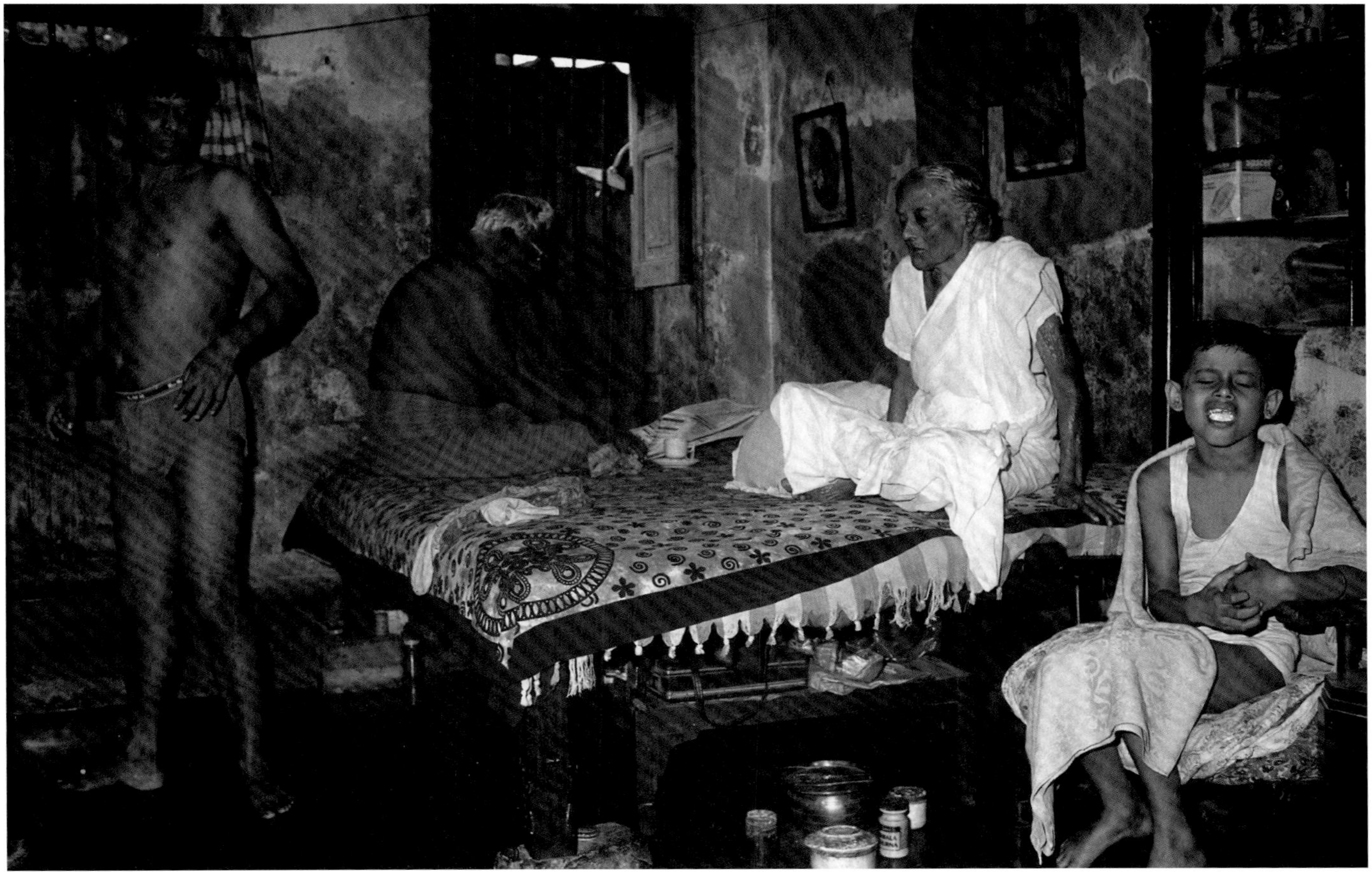

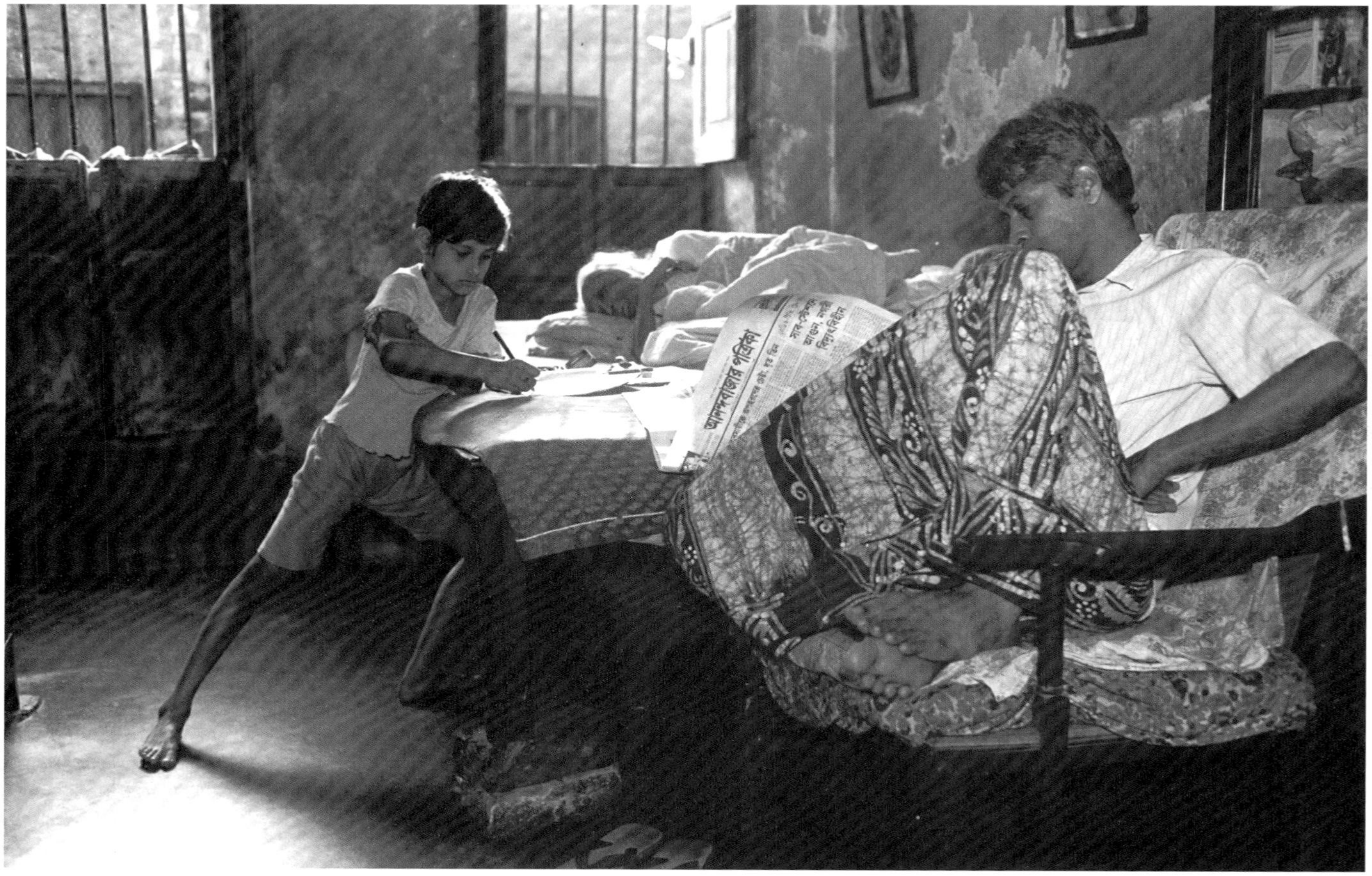

Apurba's brother Amal with Teesta and Muni

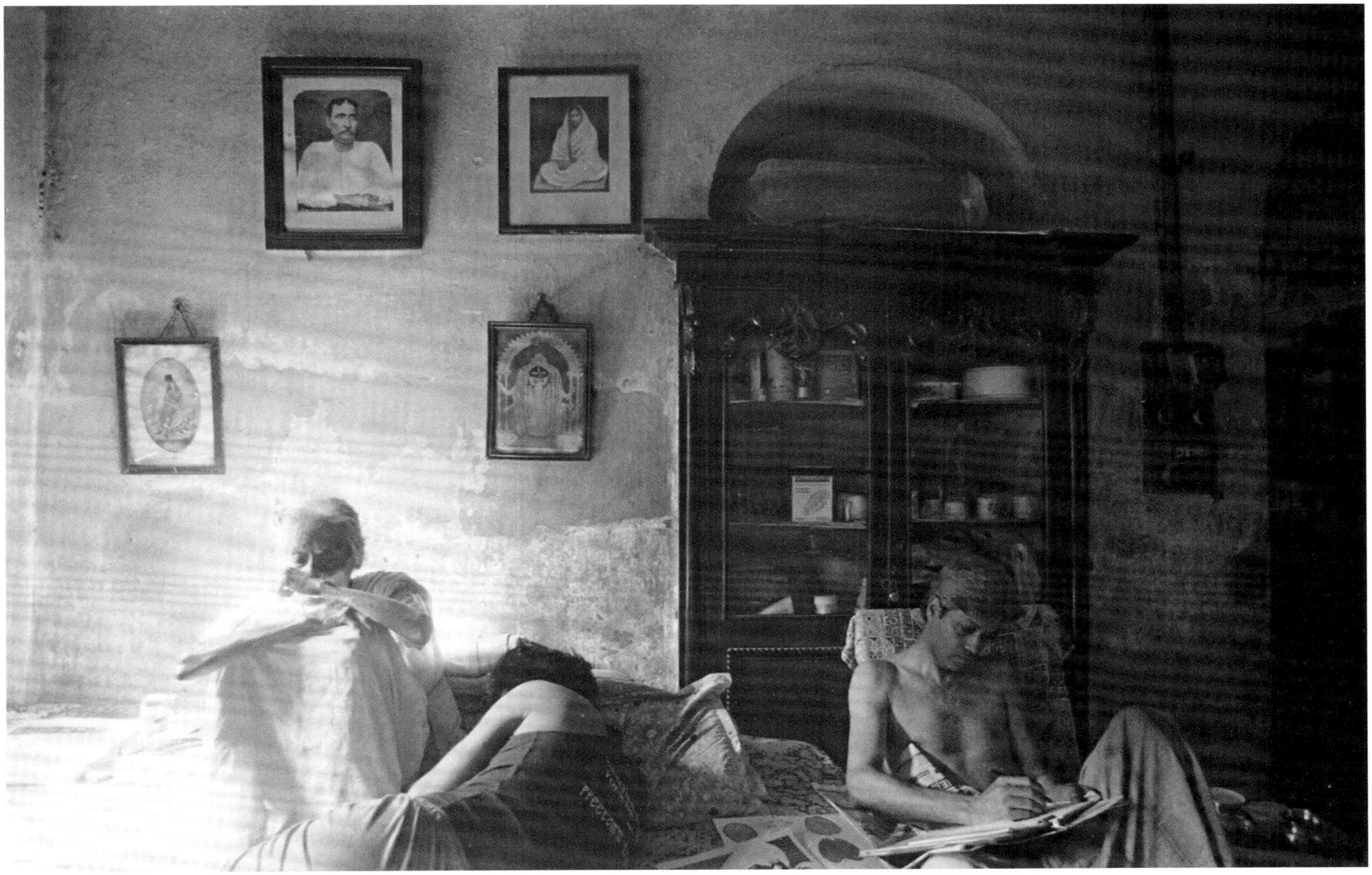

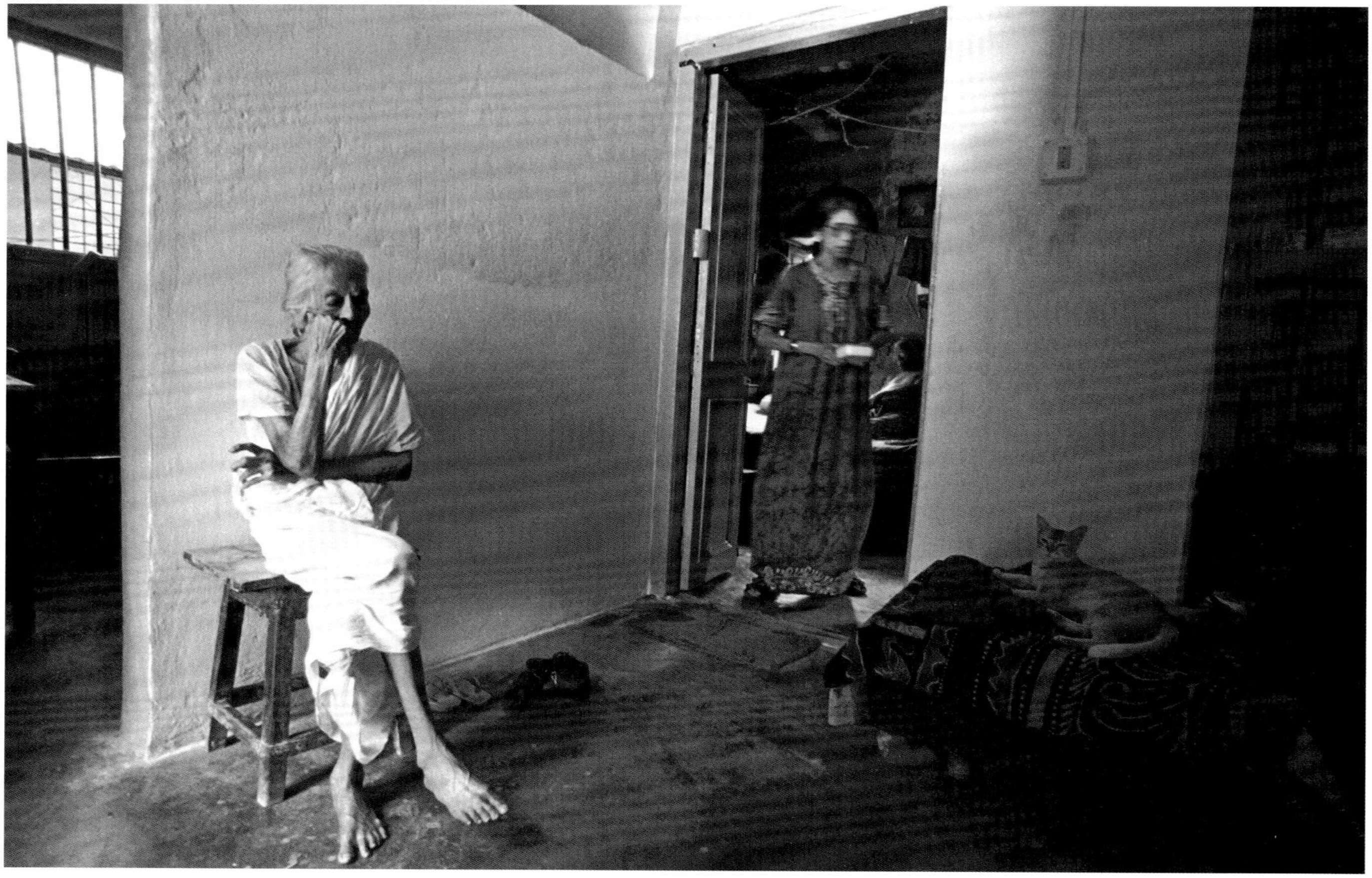

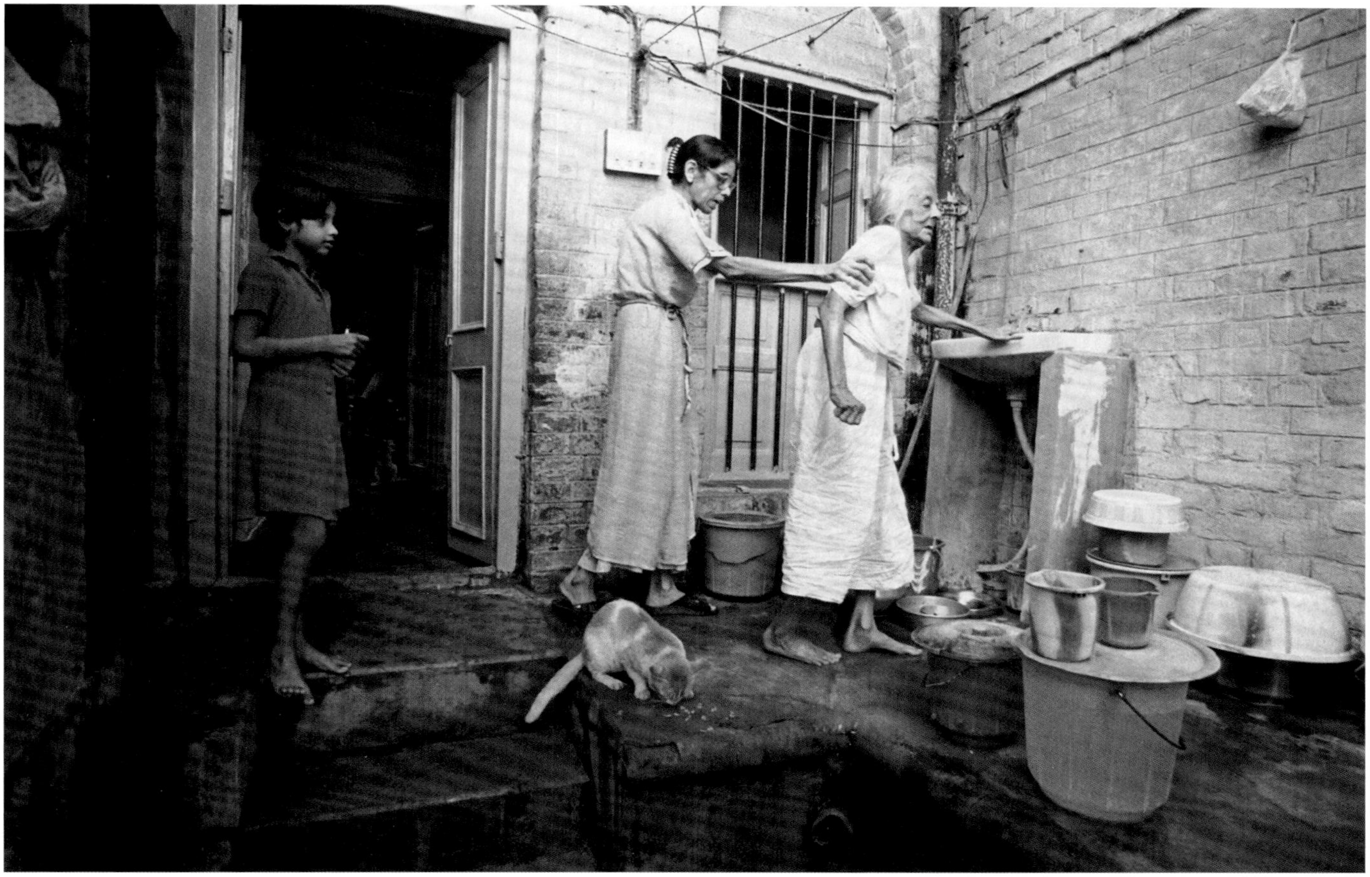

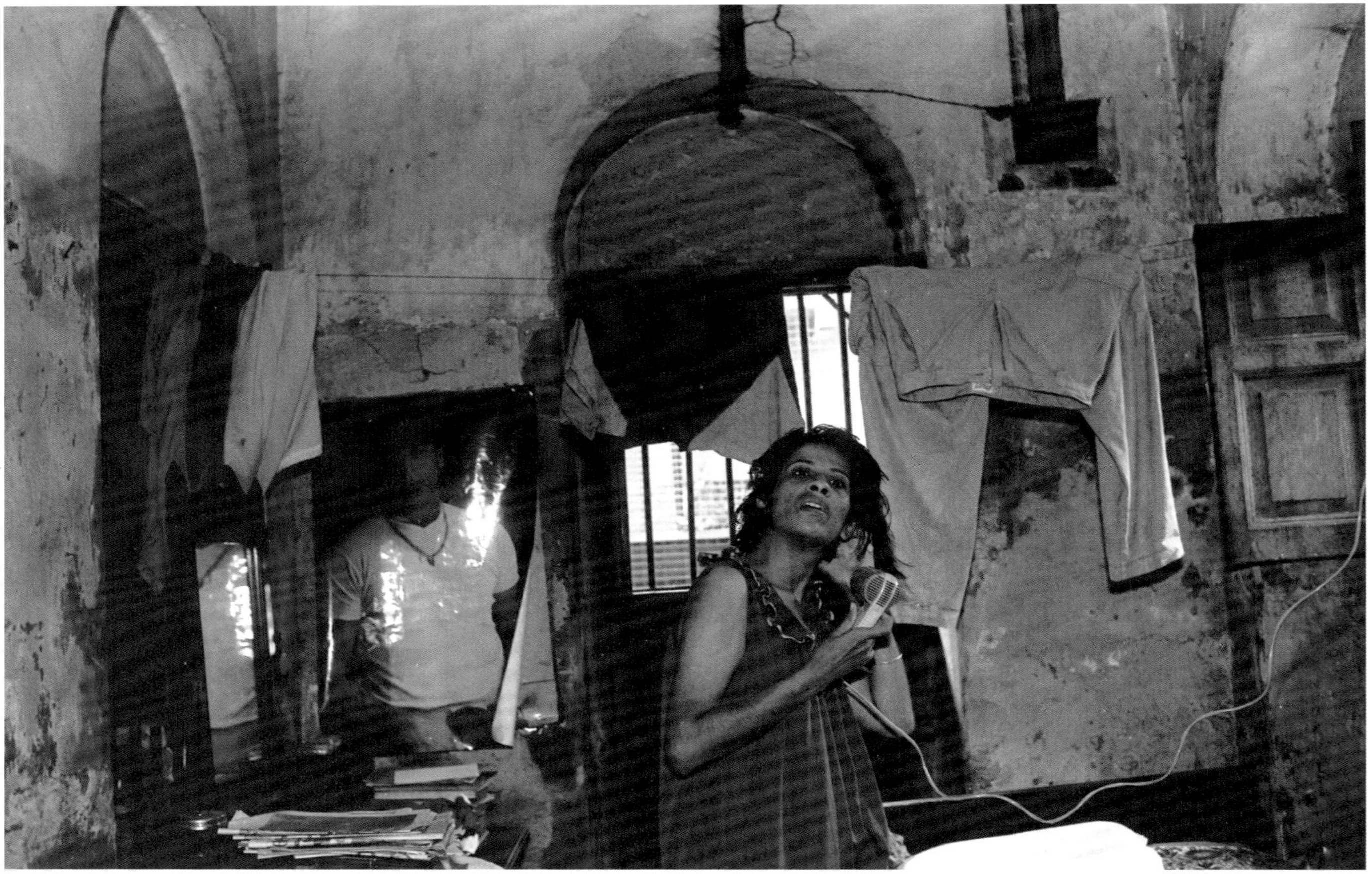

Padmini

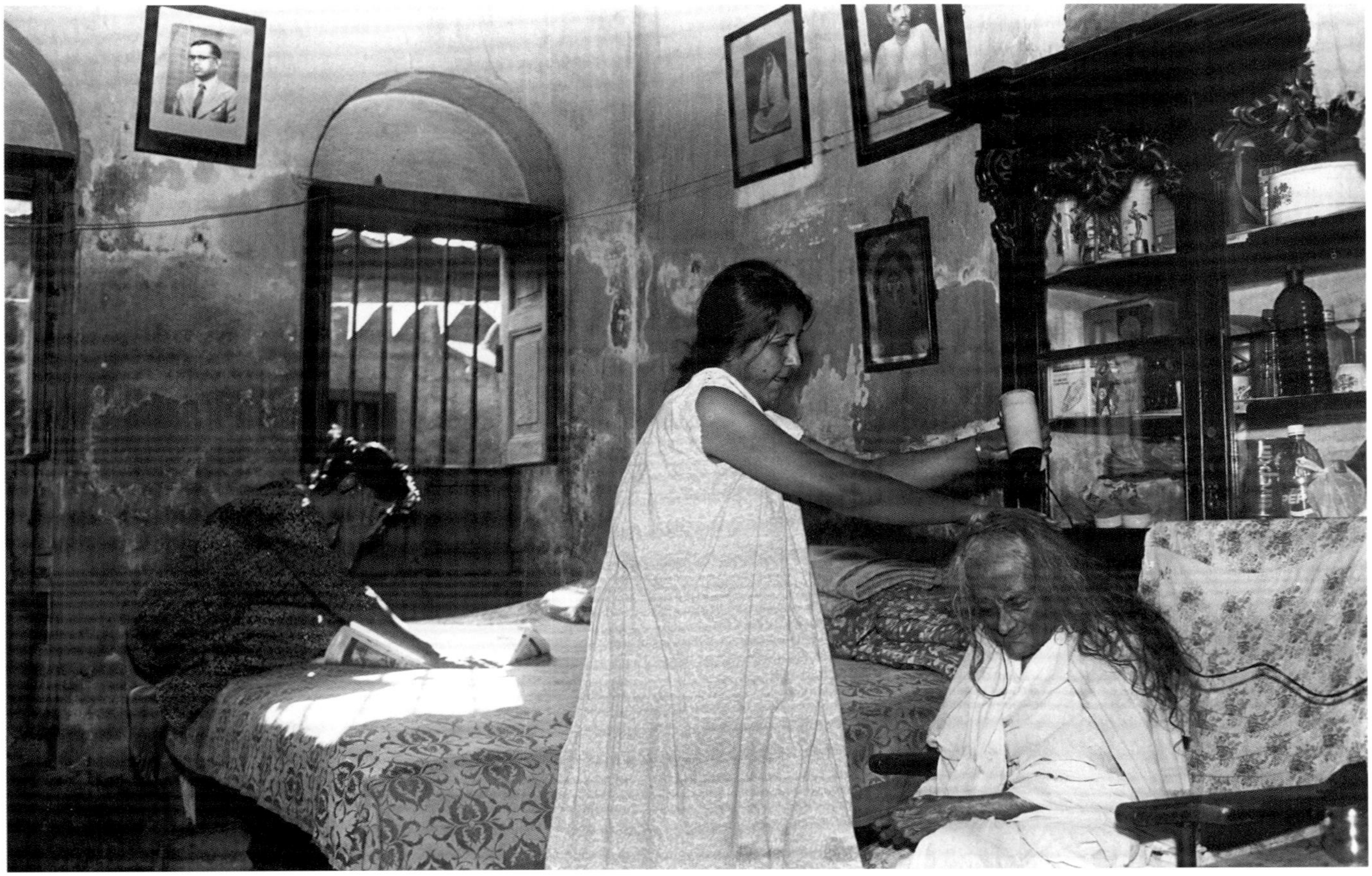

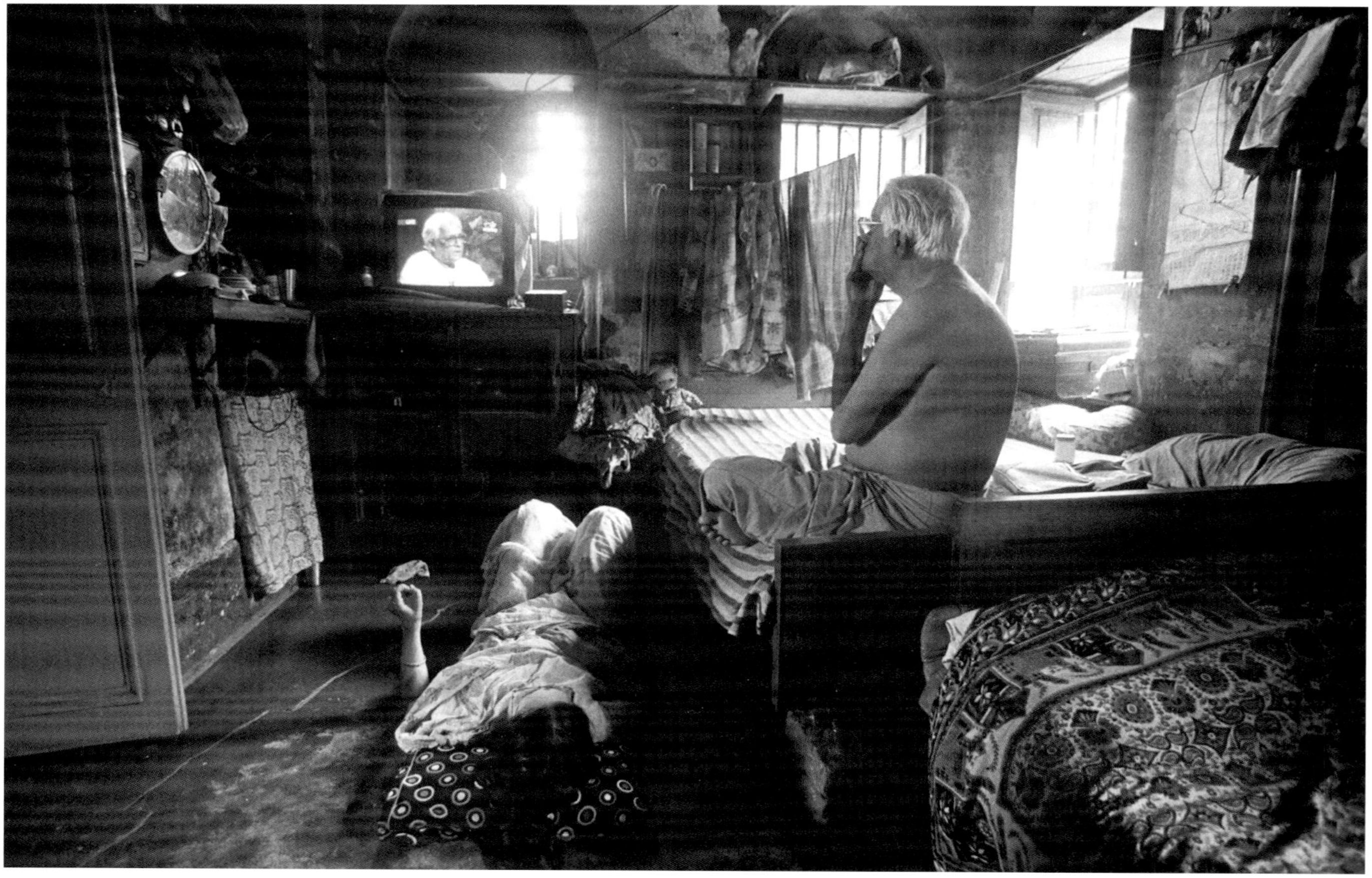

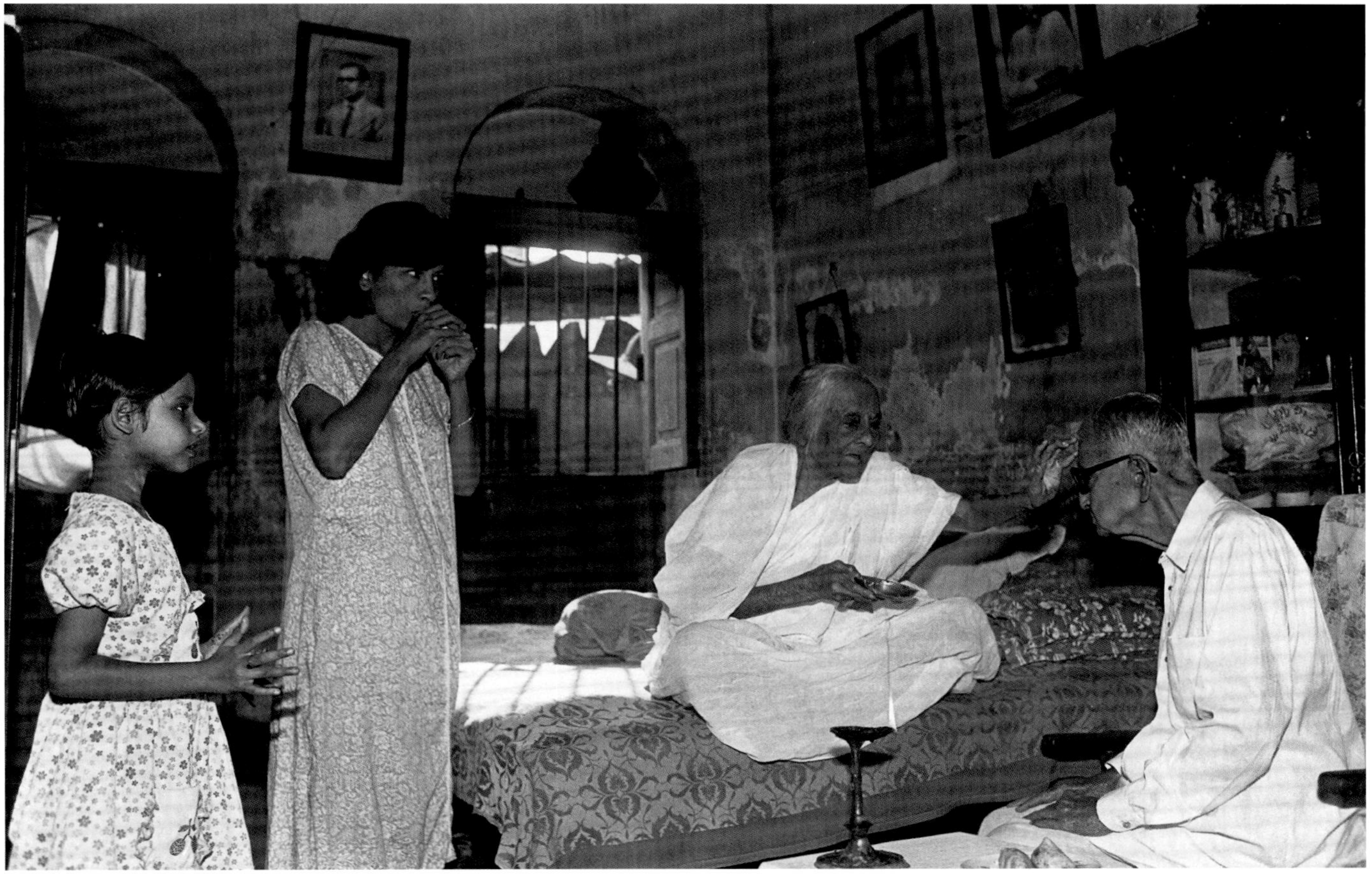

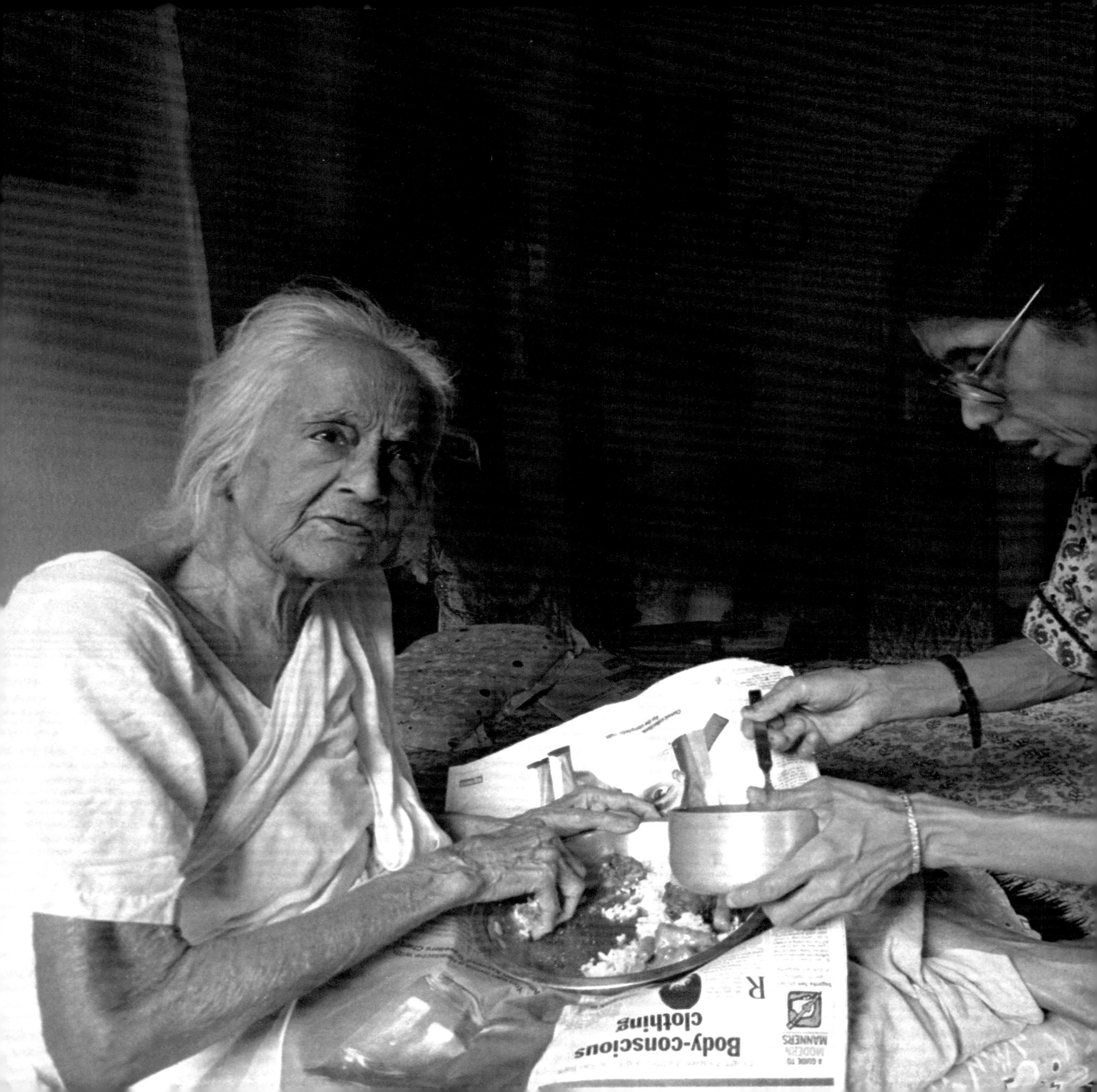
Body-conscious
clothing
A GUIDE TO
MODERN
MANNERS

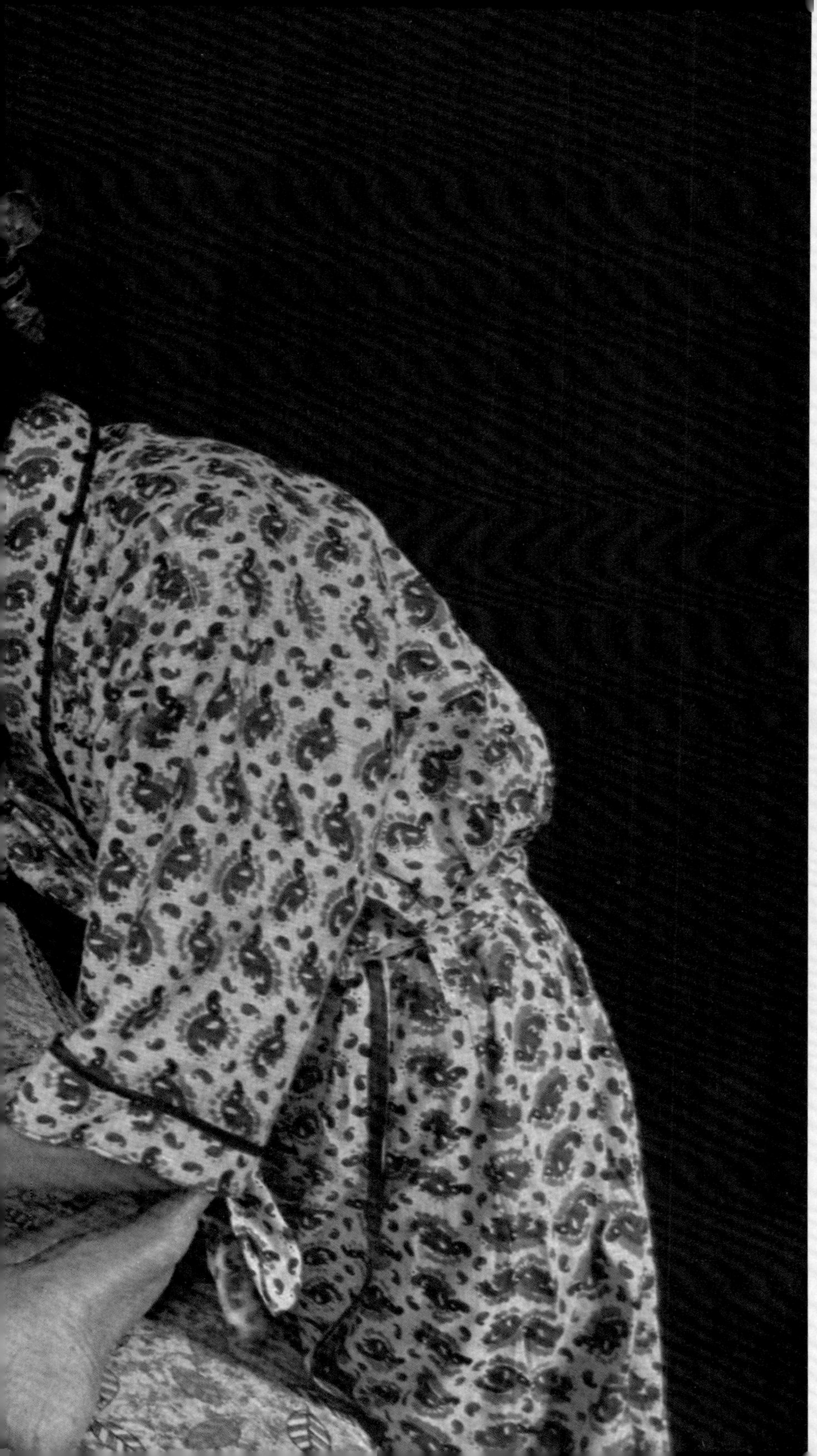

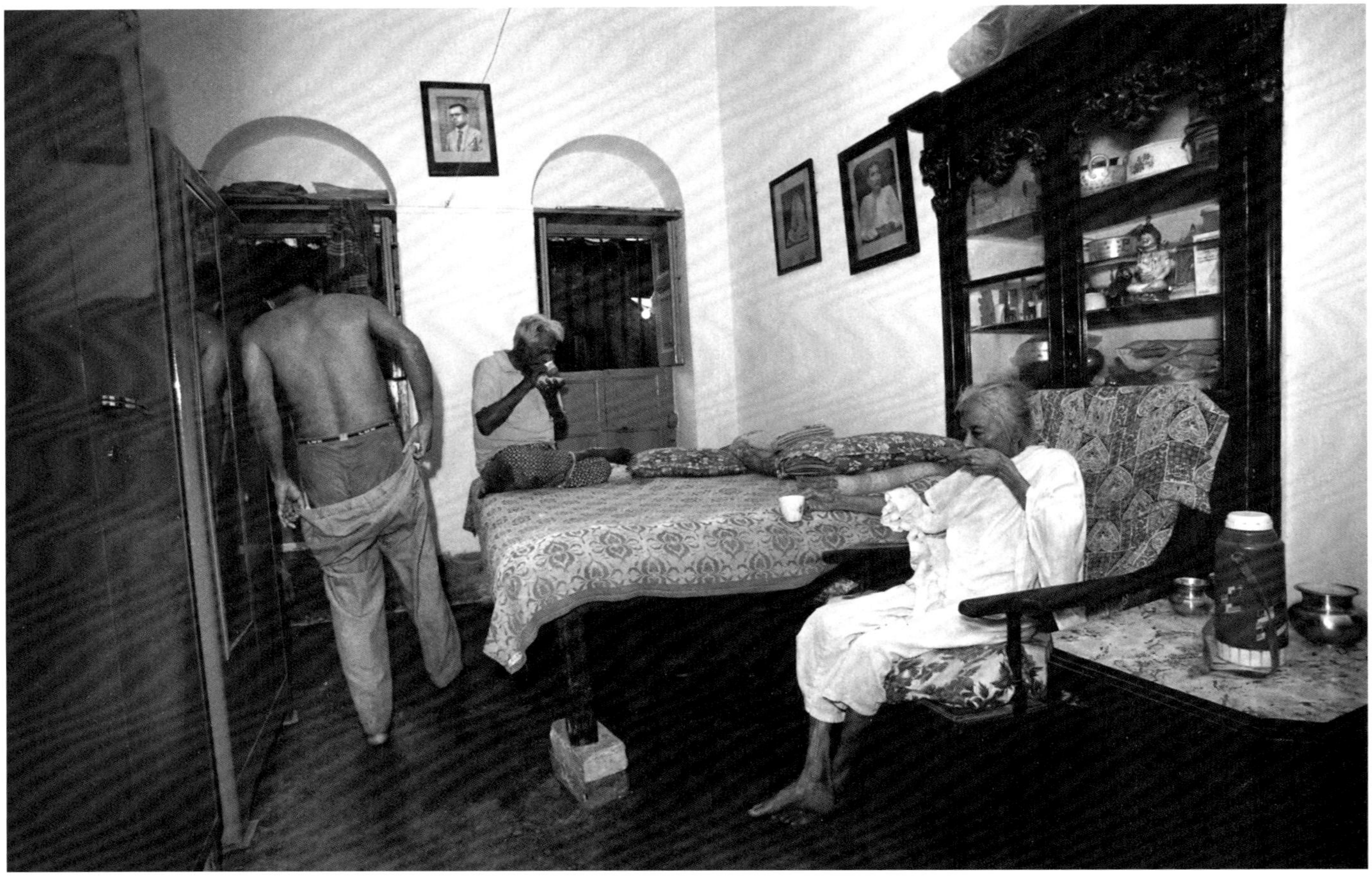

Becoming a fly on the wall

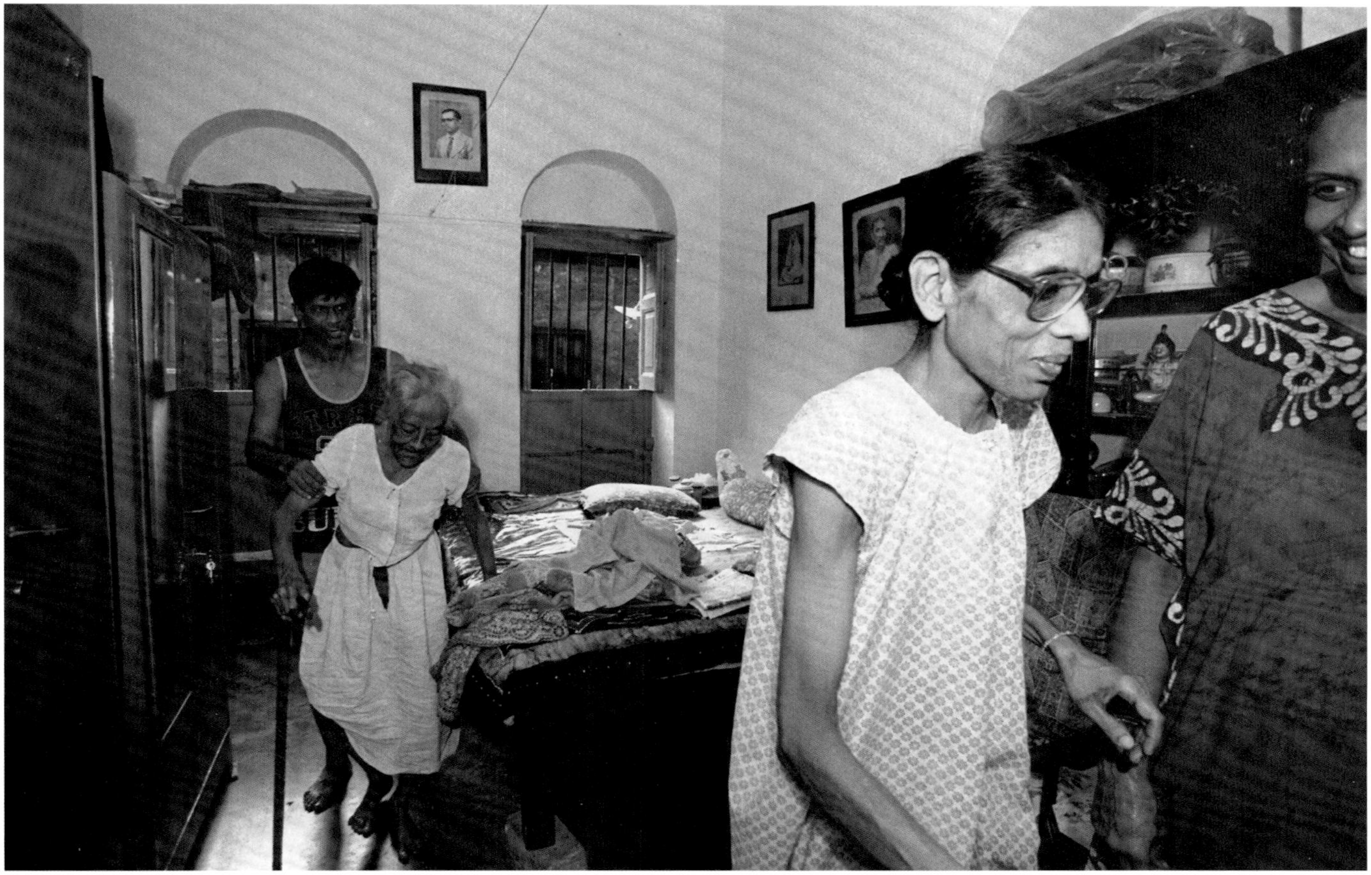

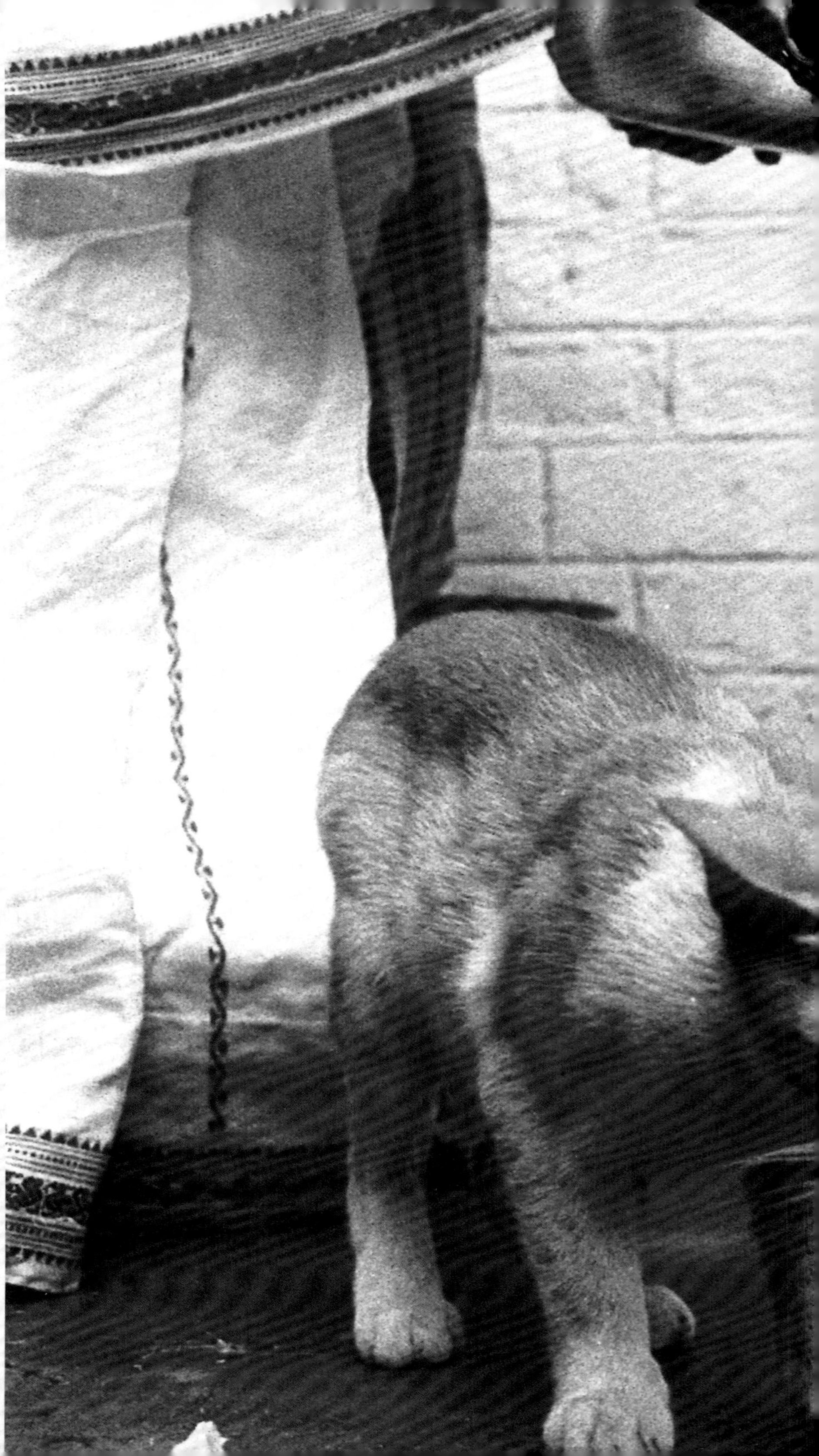

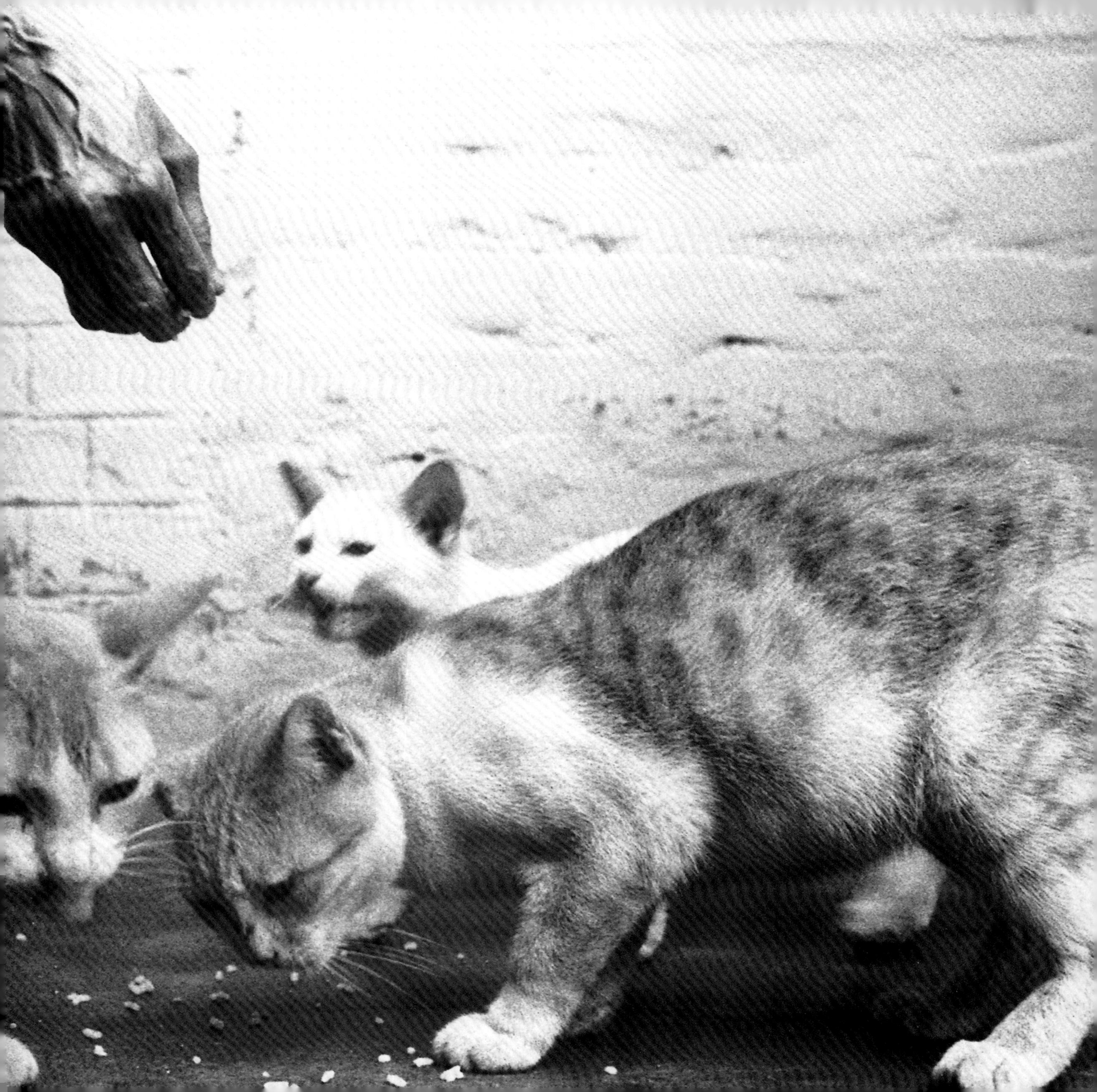

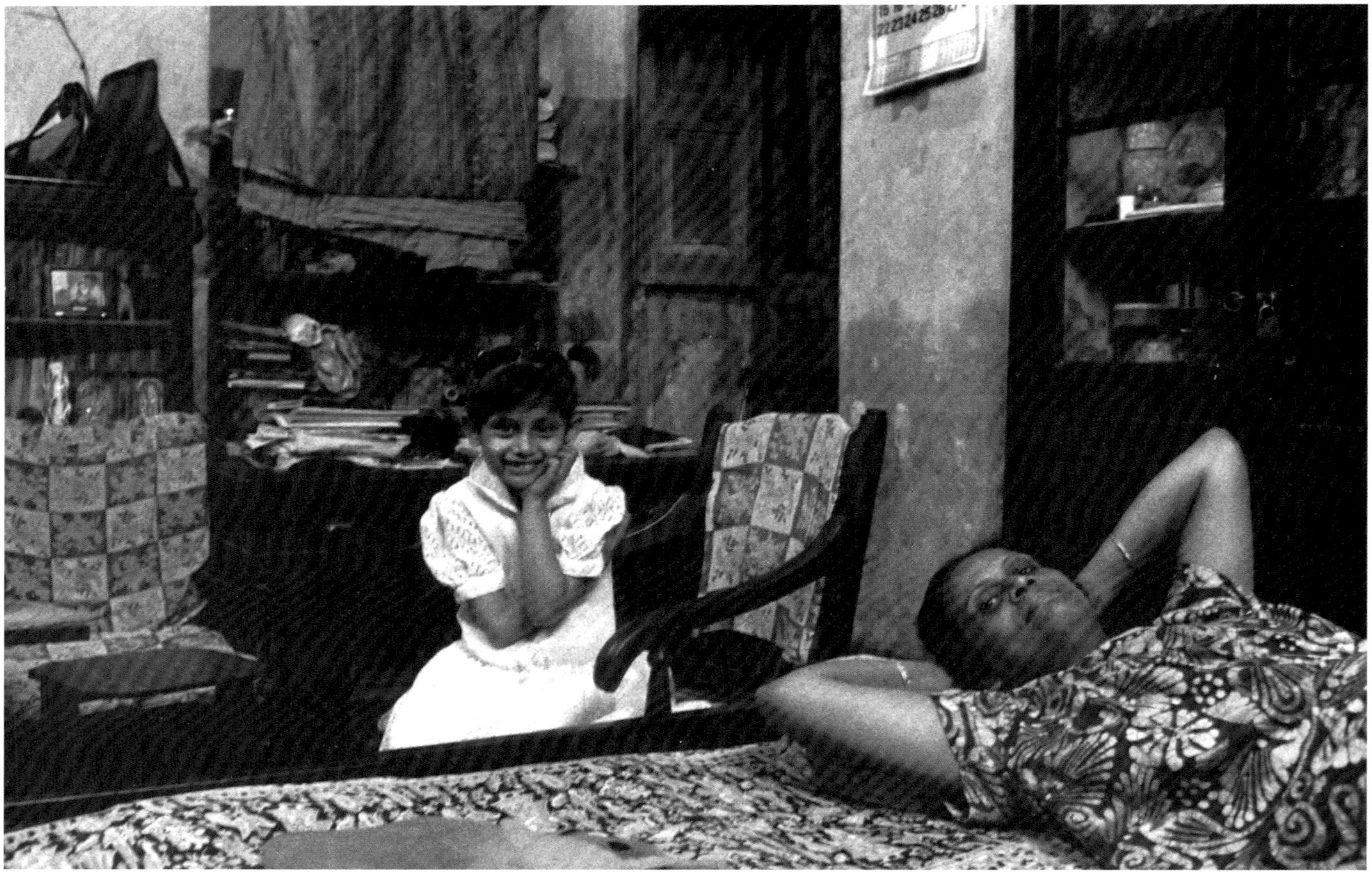

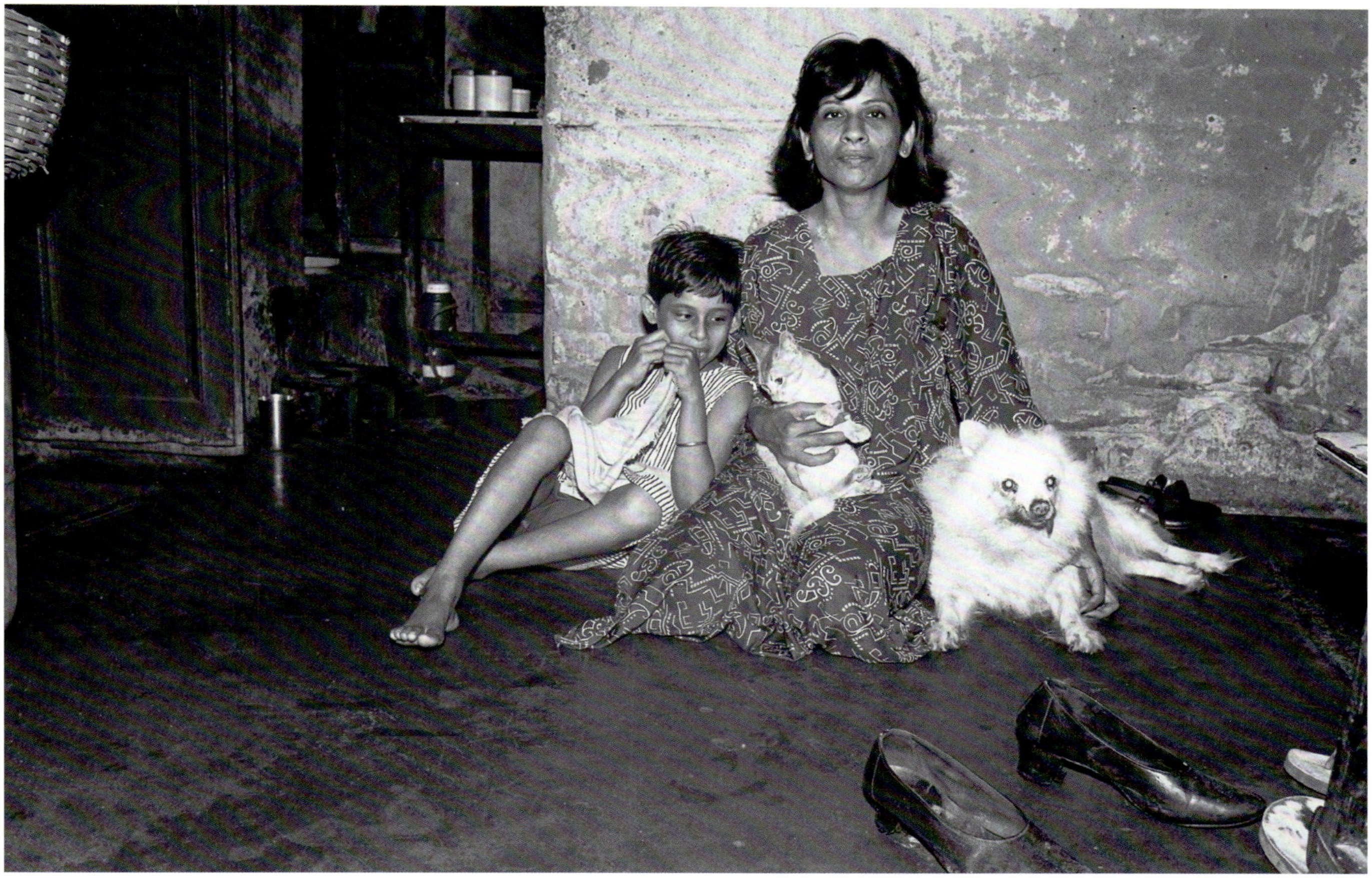

Truth is but a simple thing

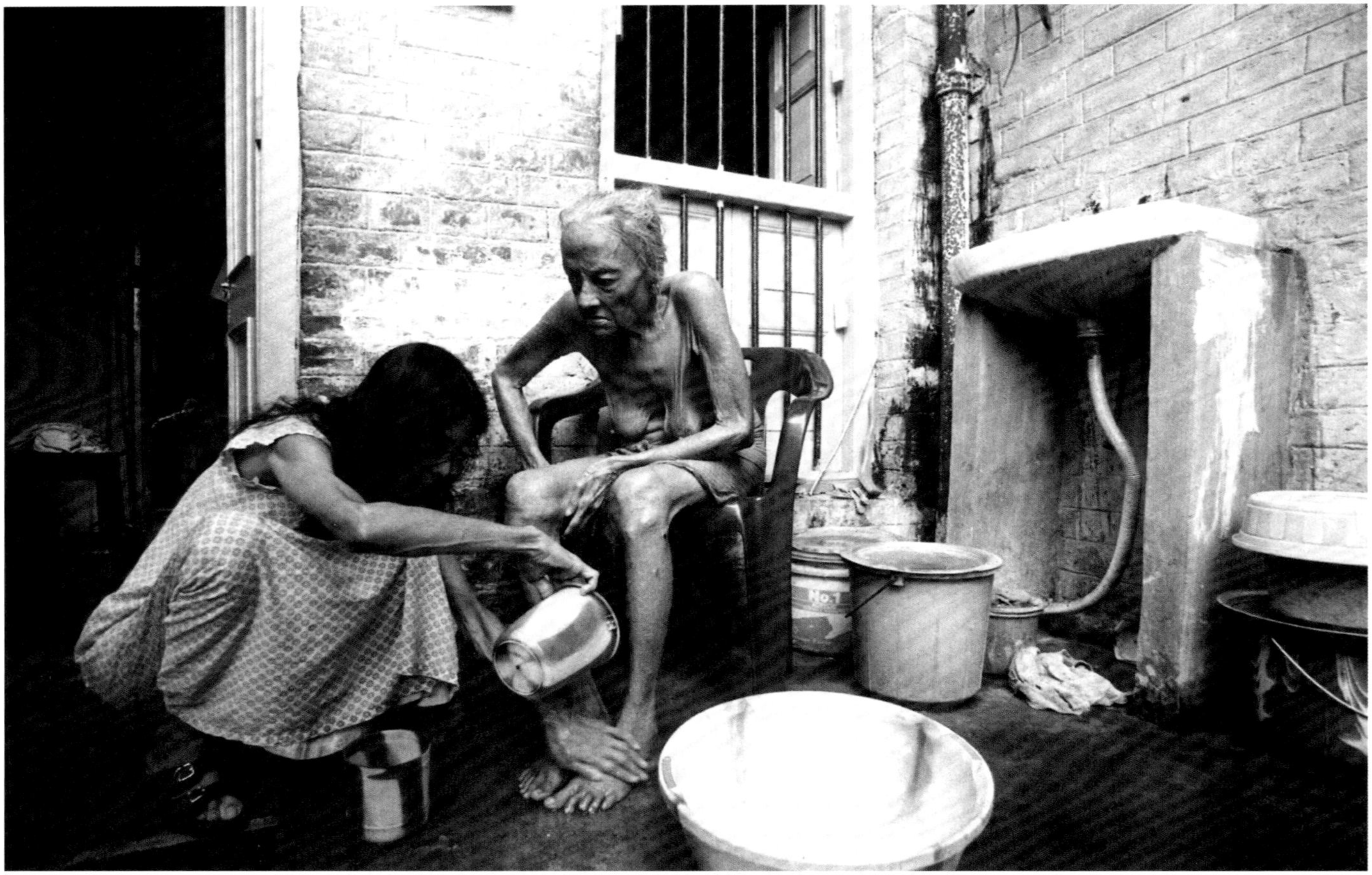

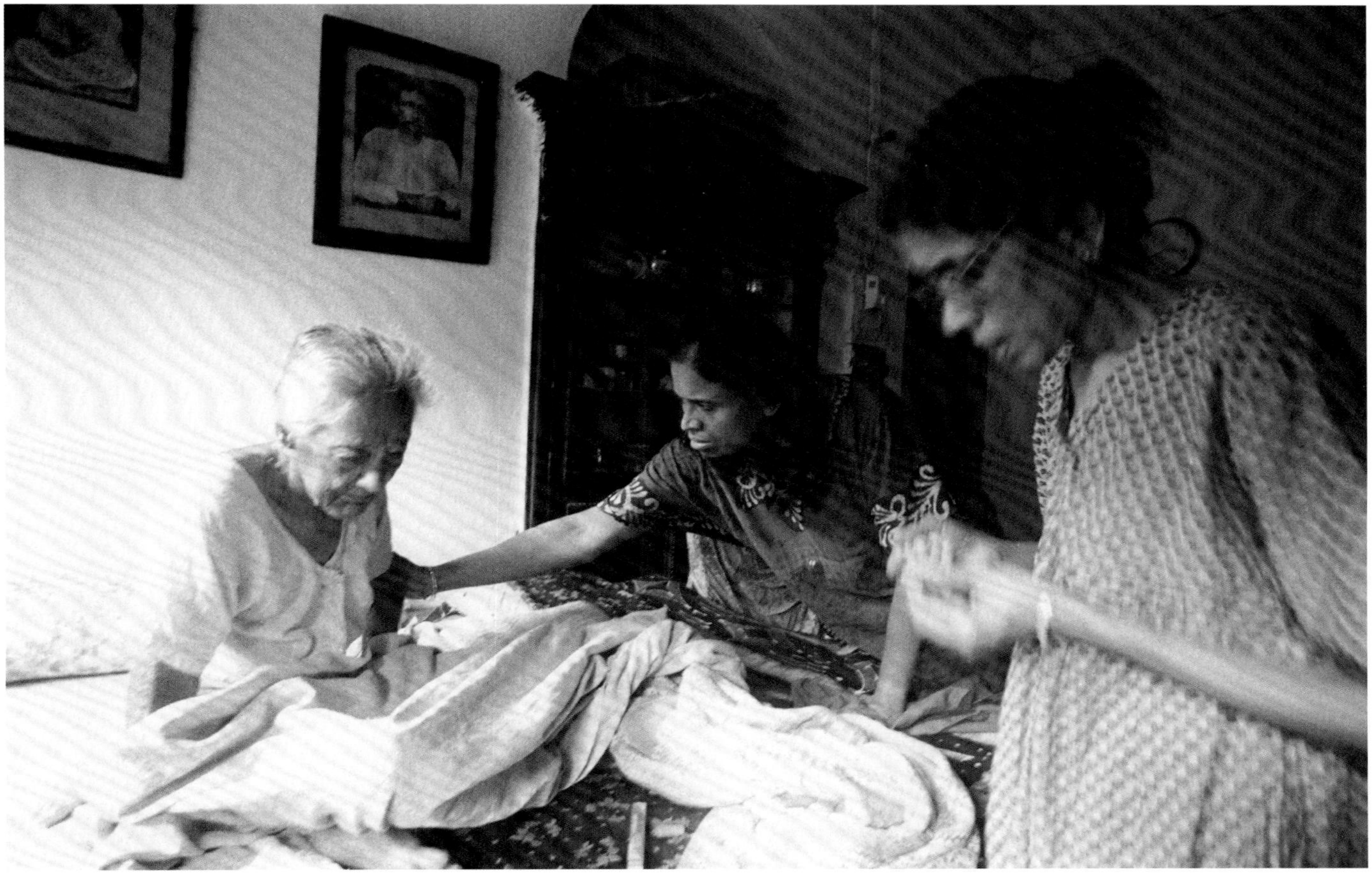

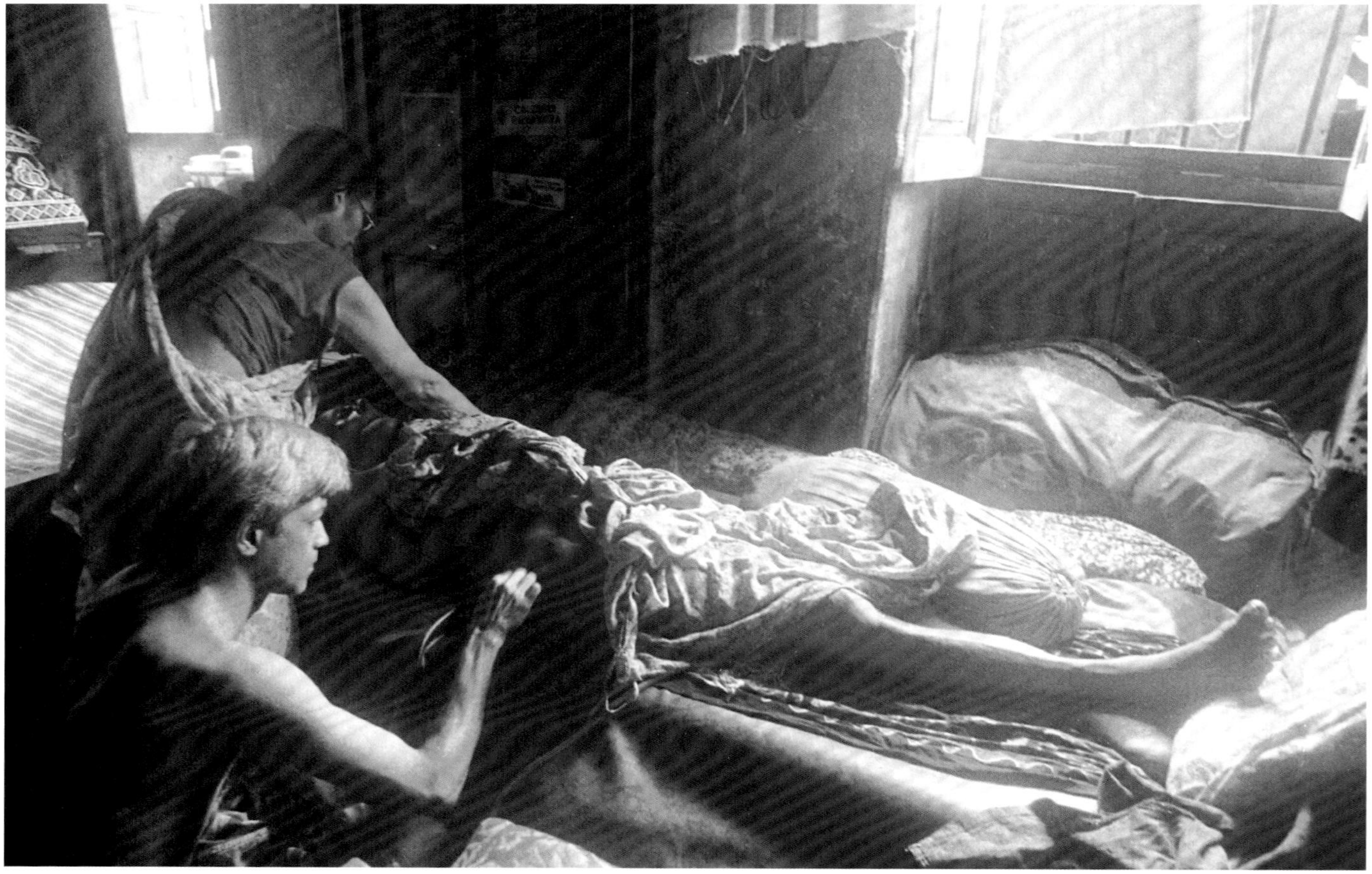

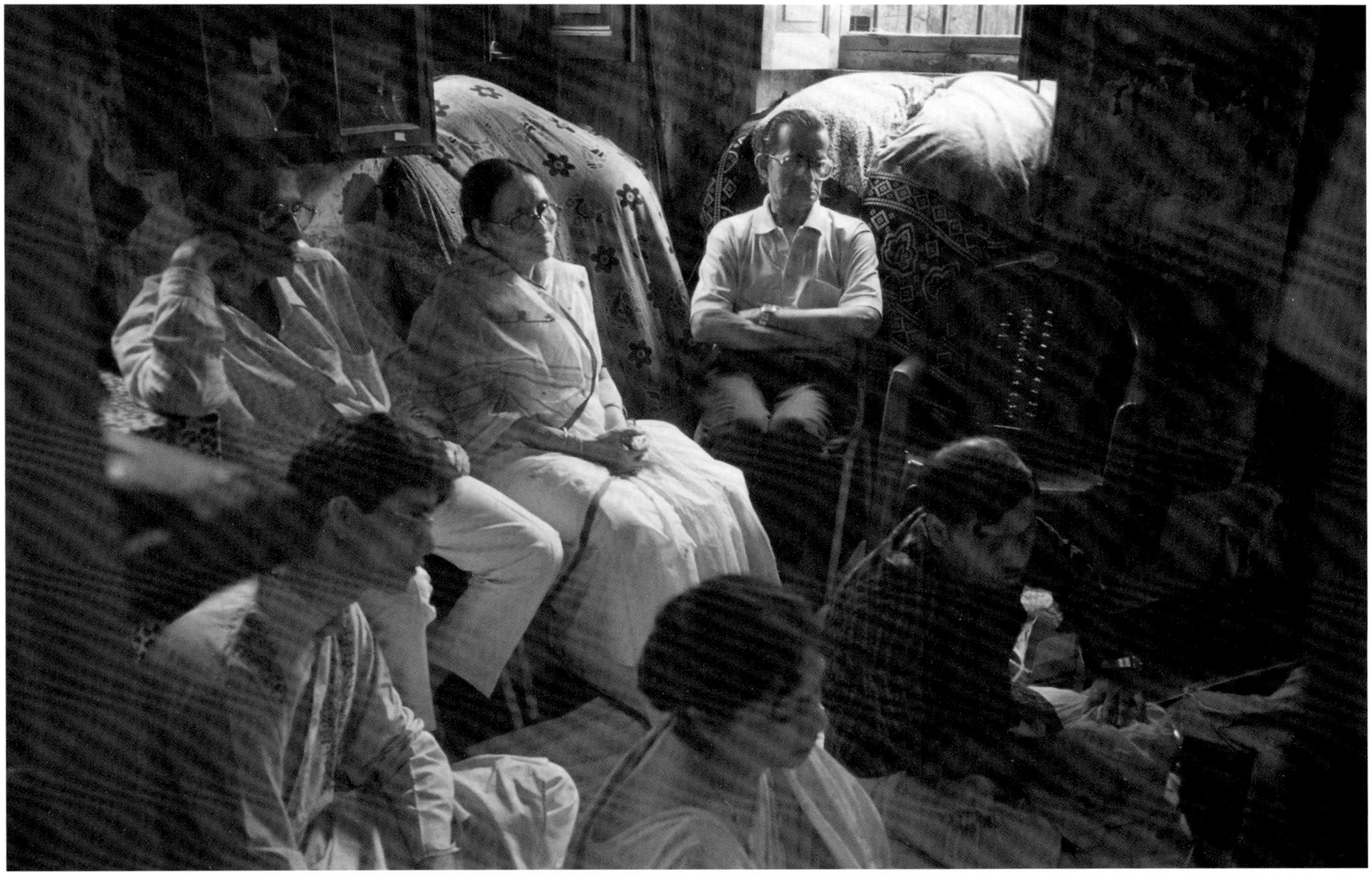

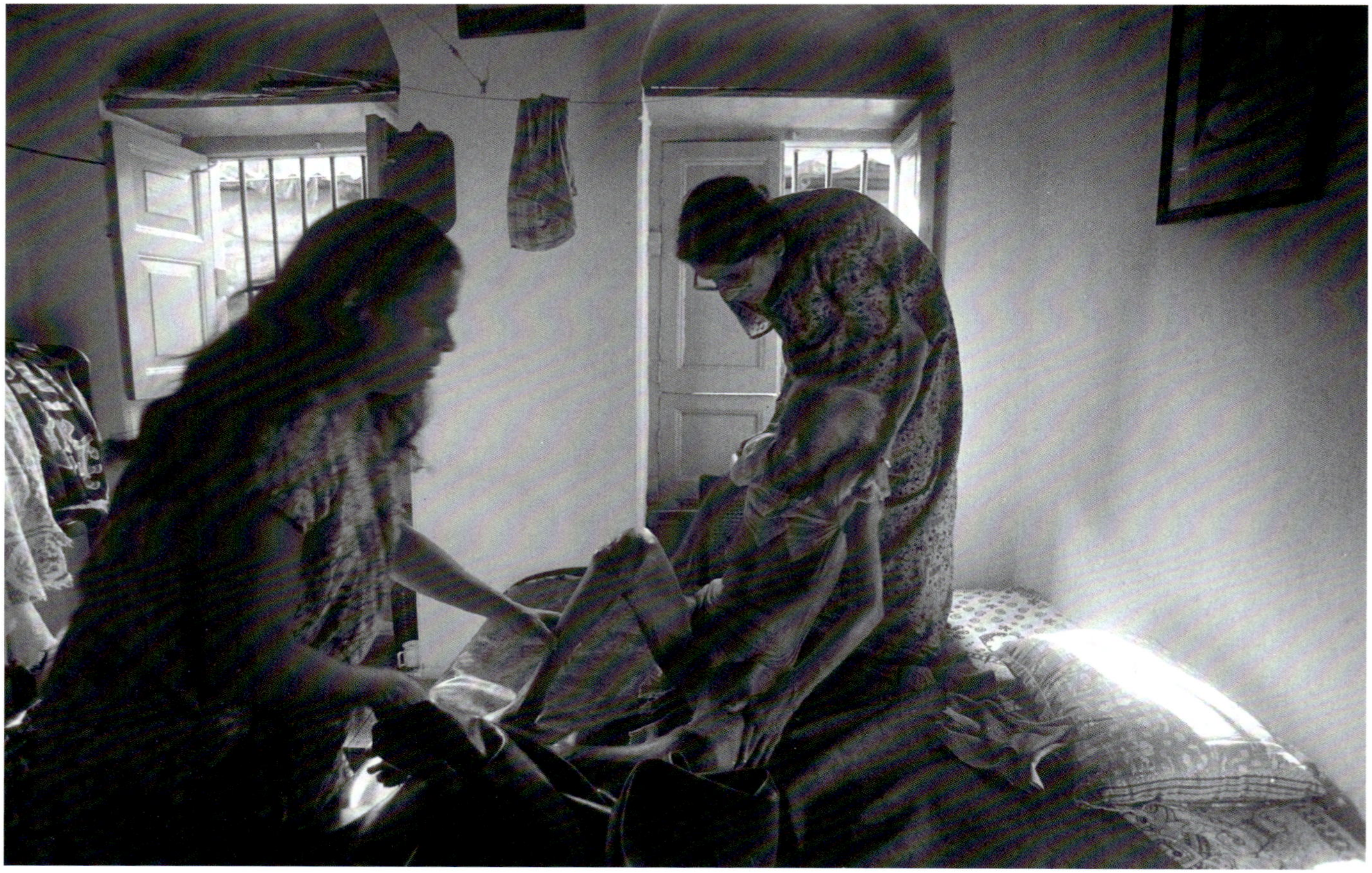

Muni with her two daughters–Manju and Leena

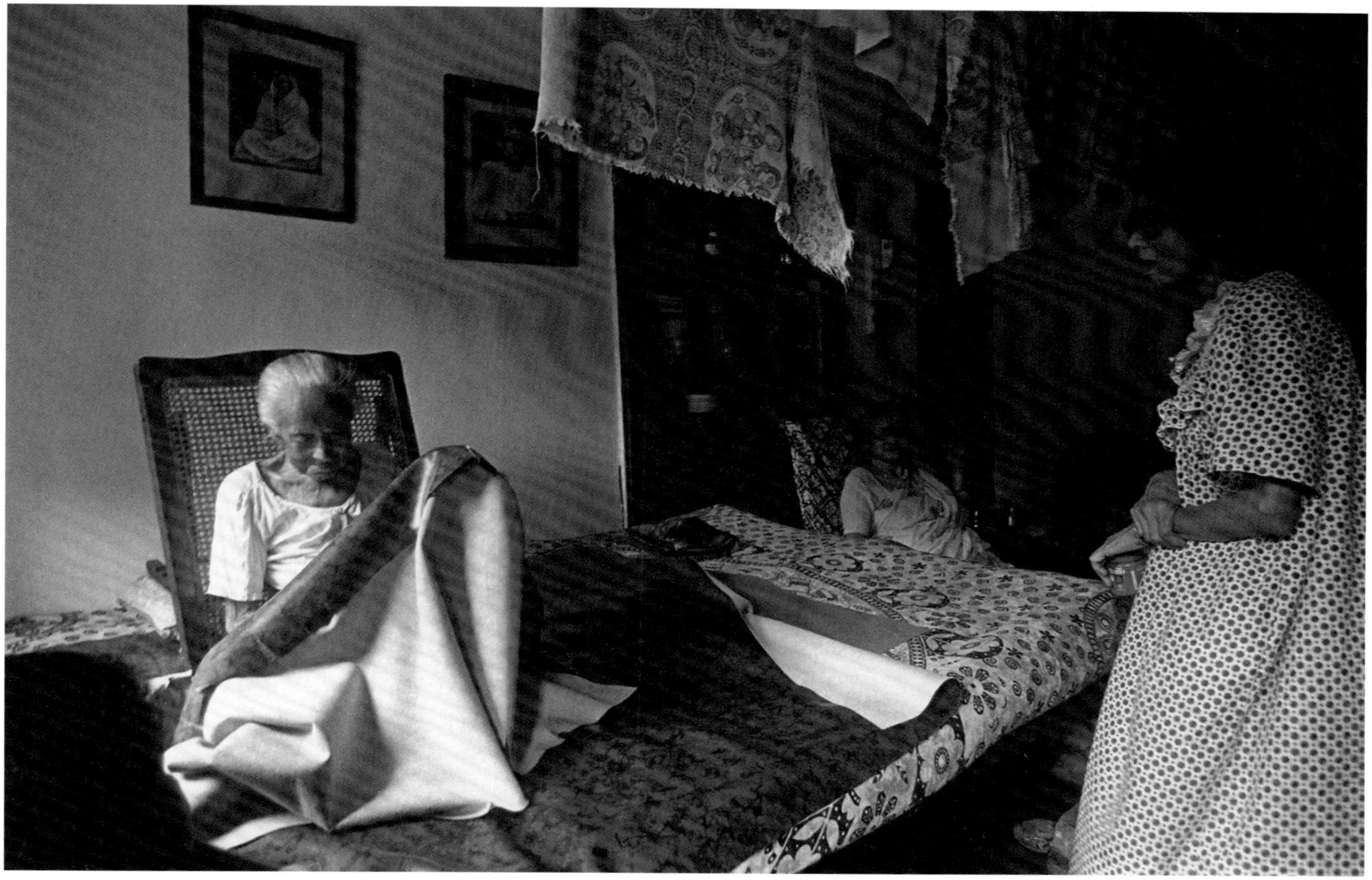

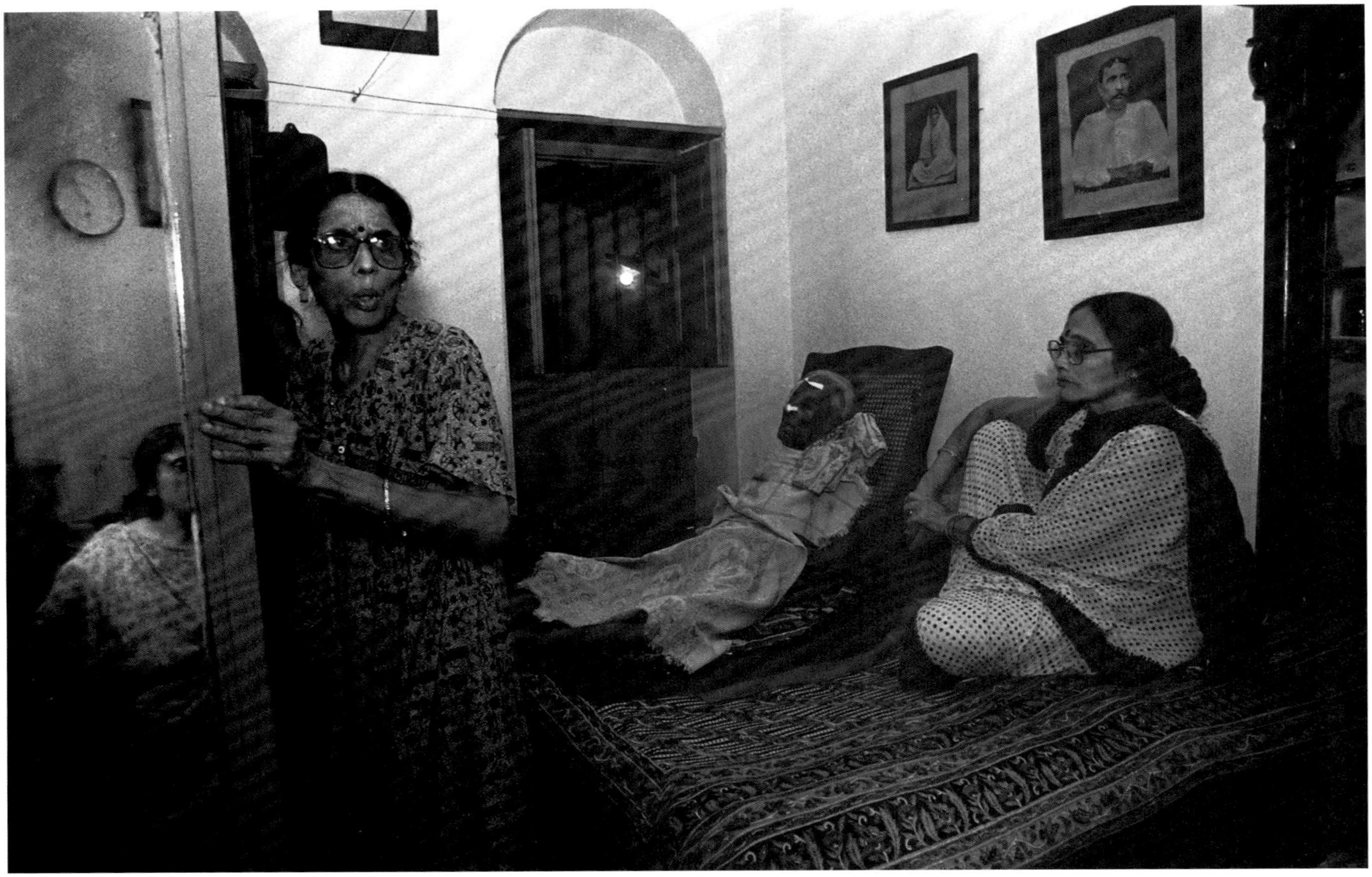

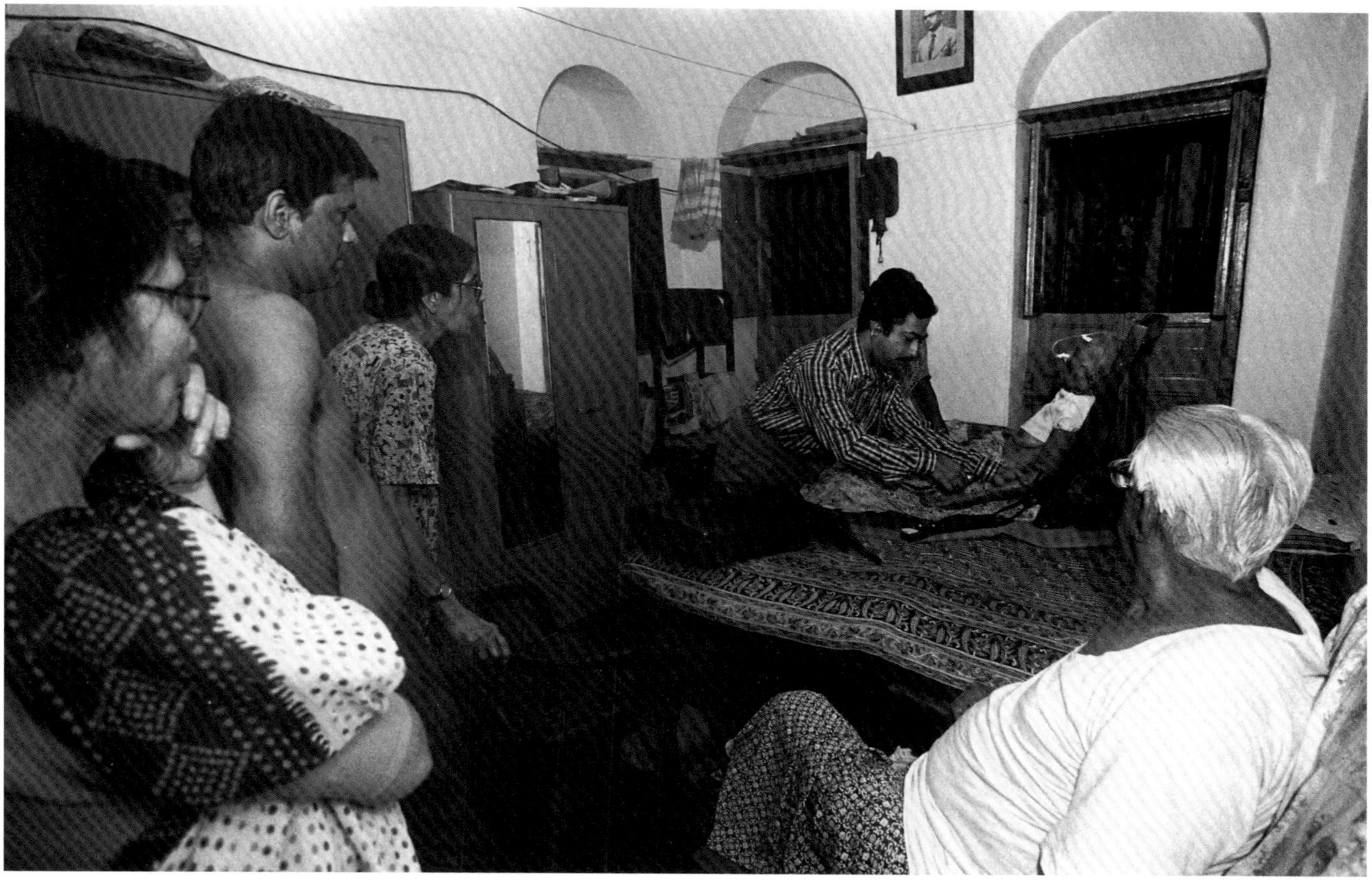

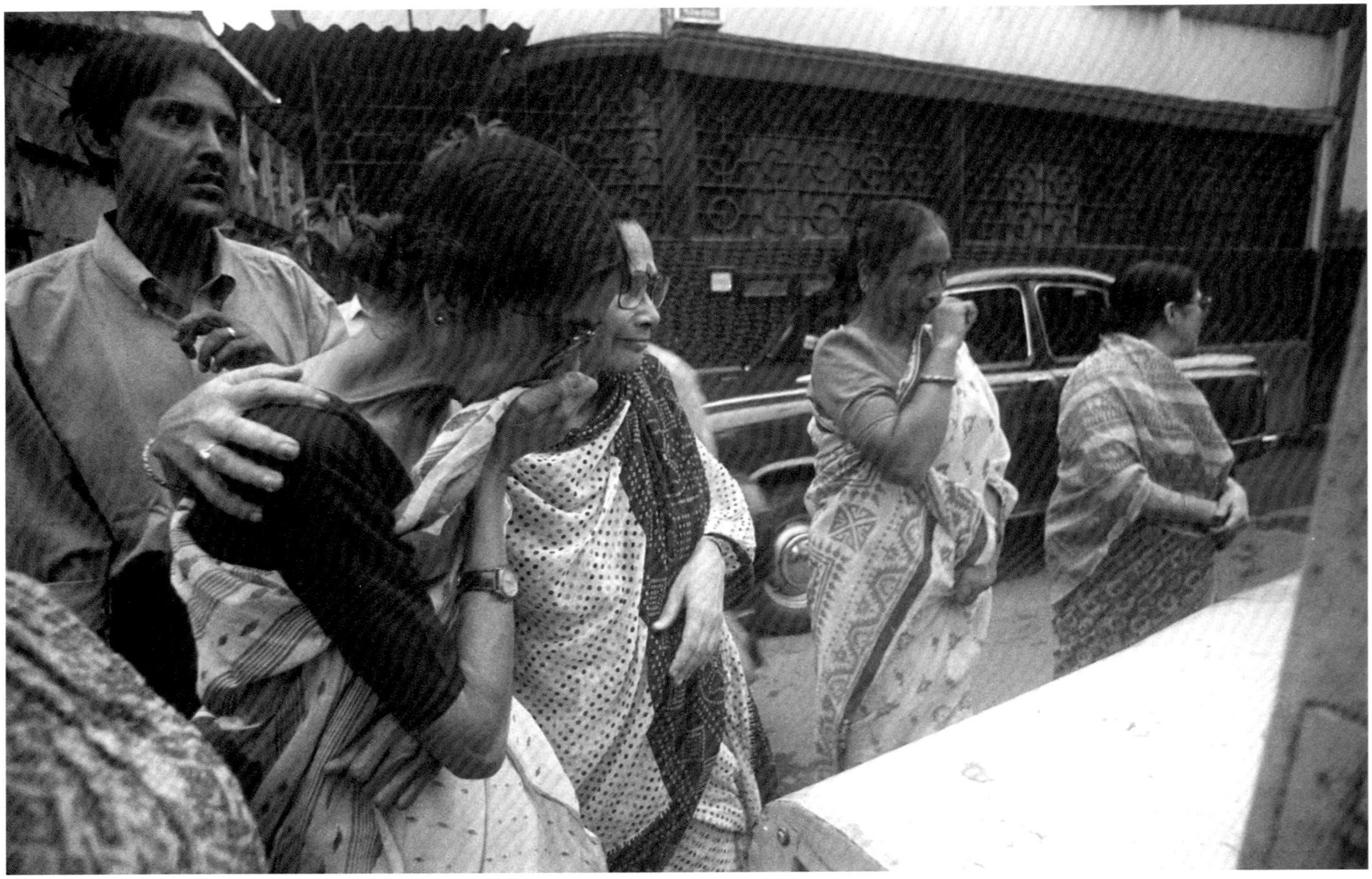

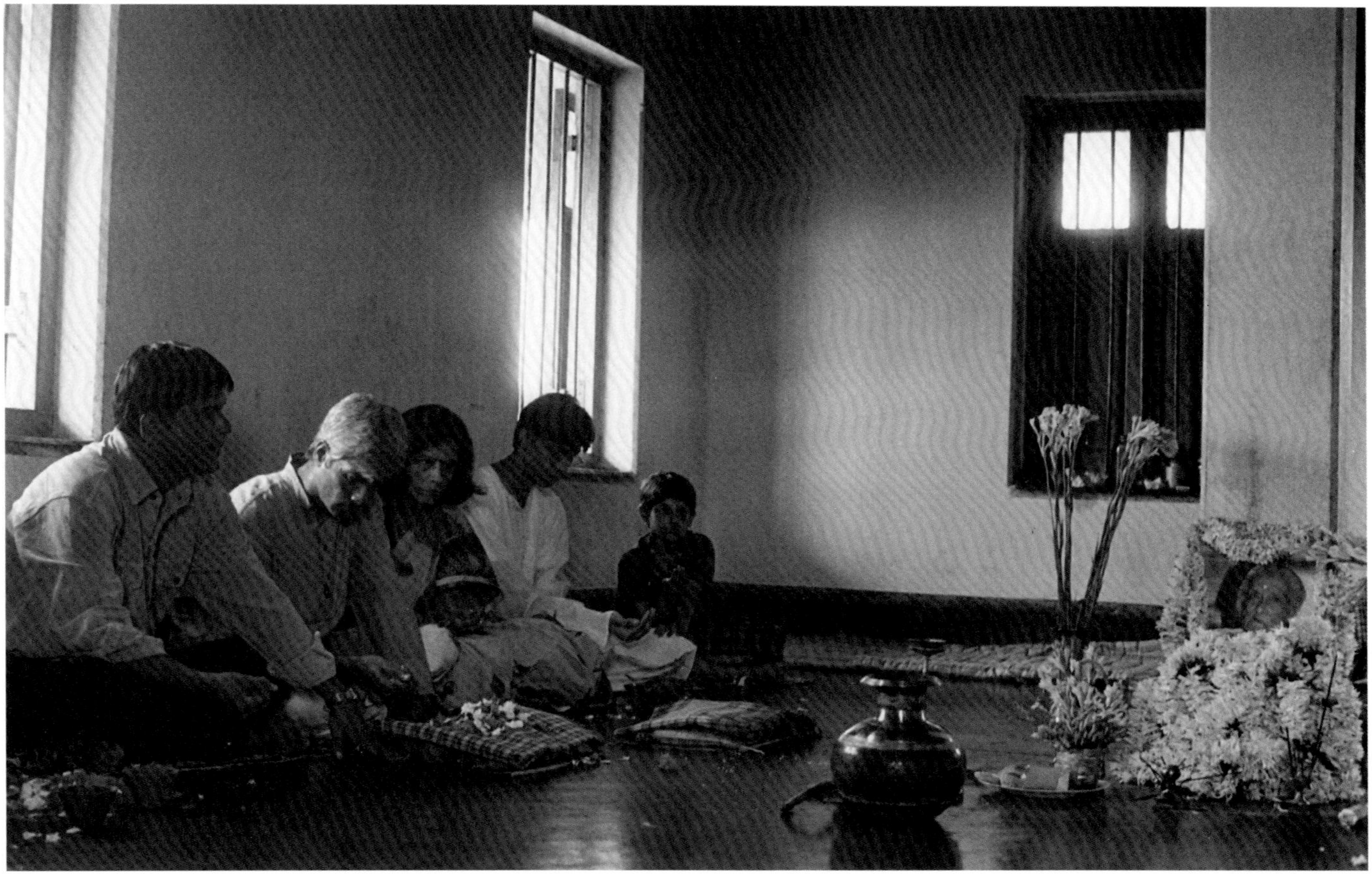

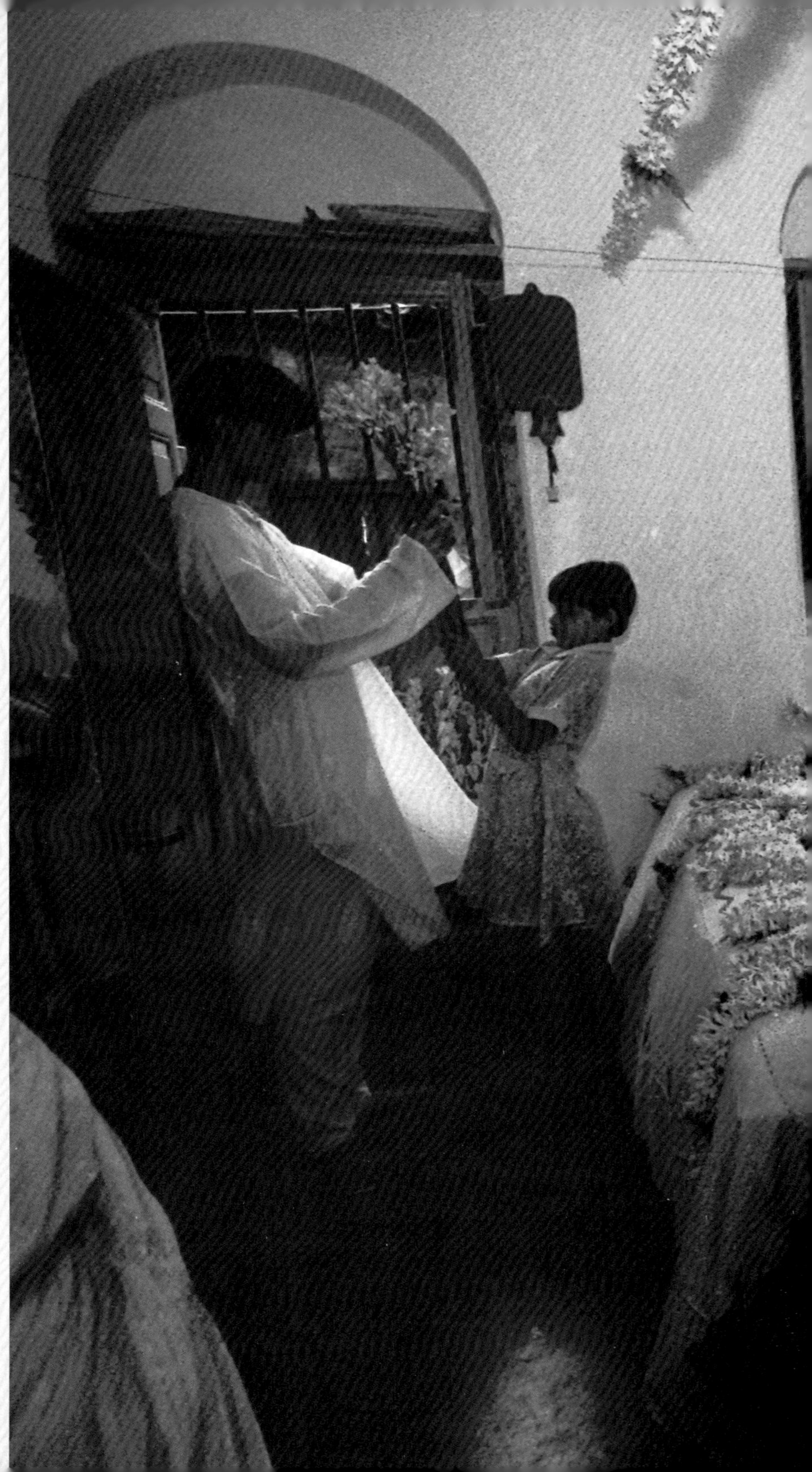

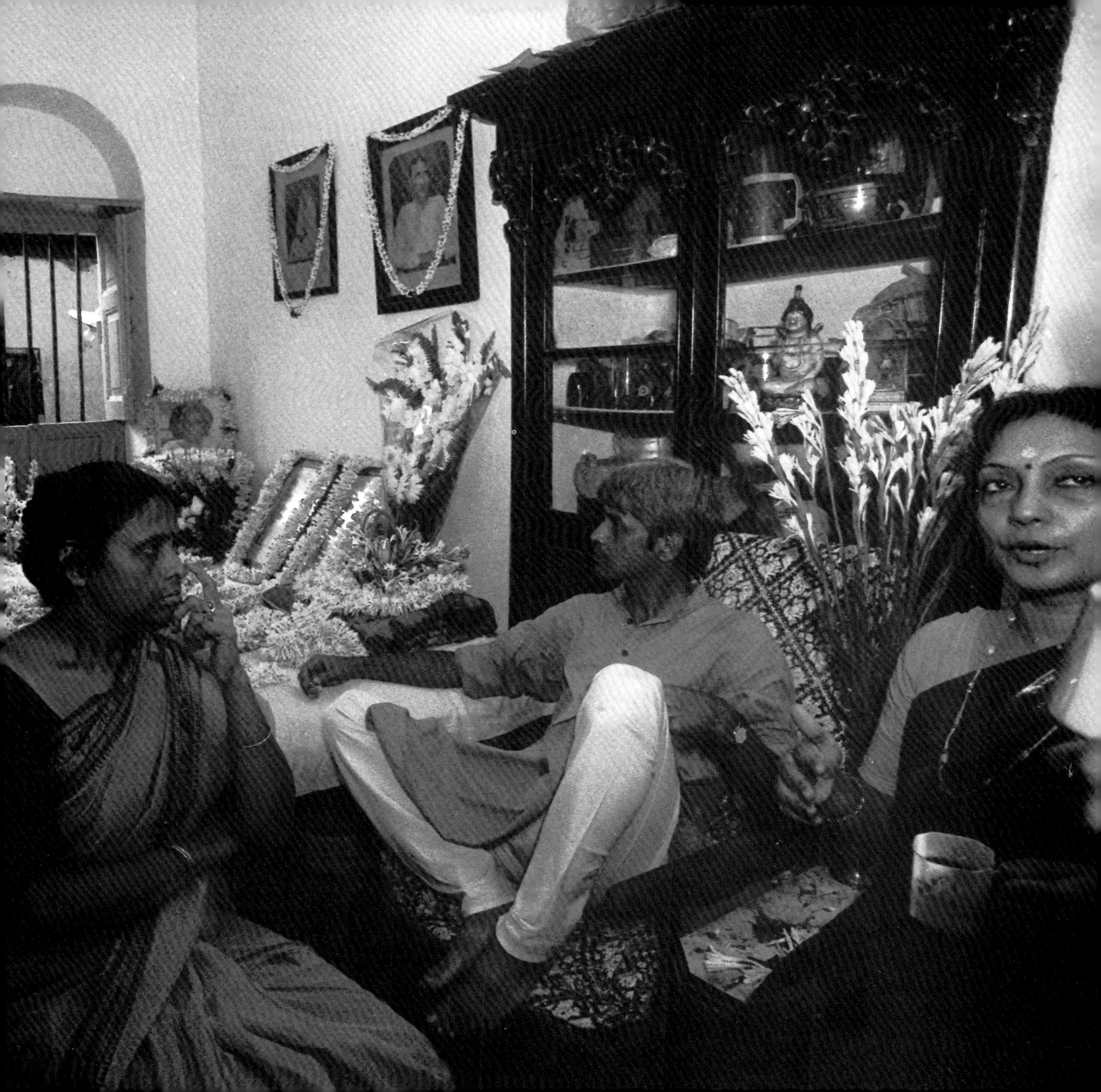

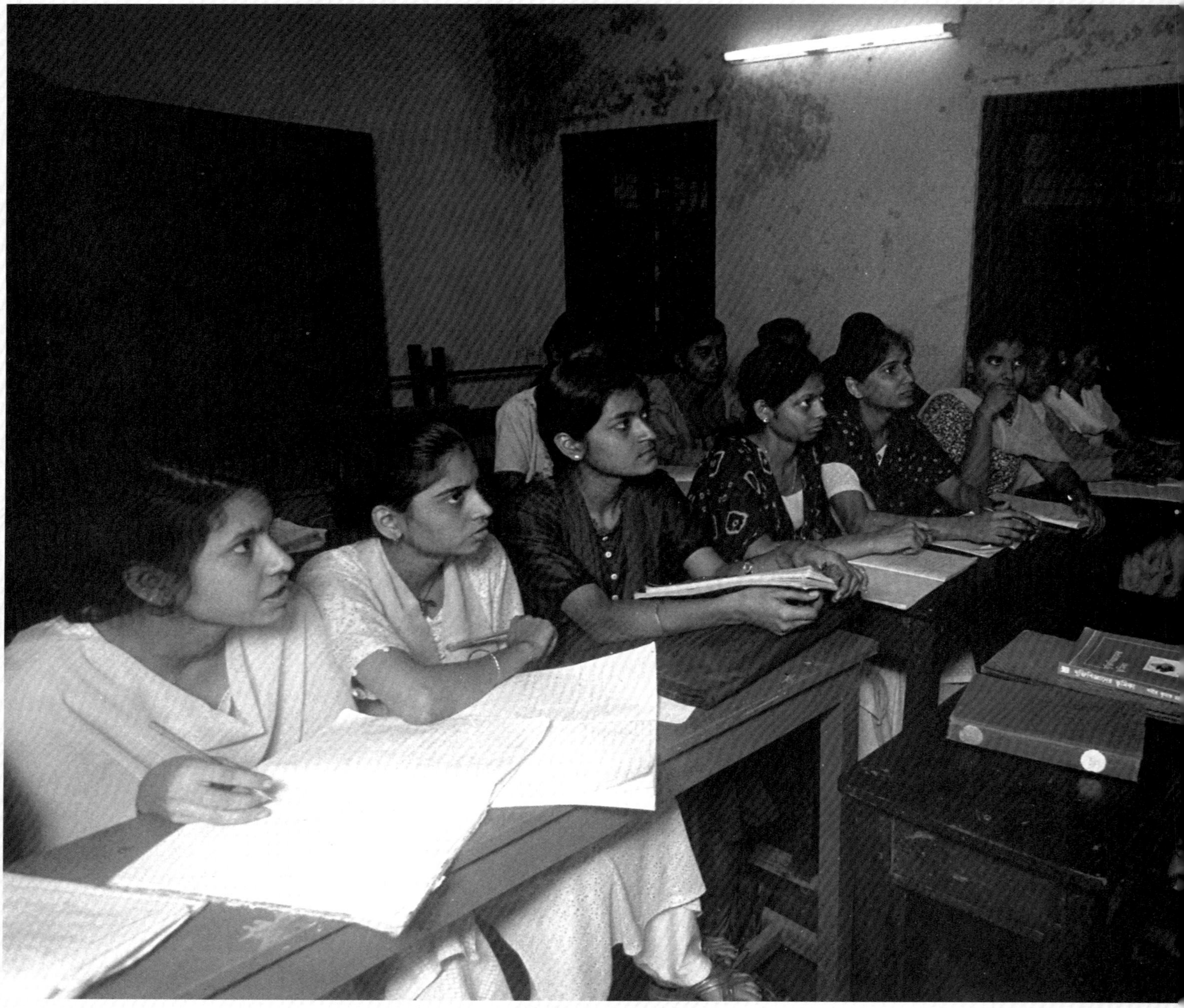

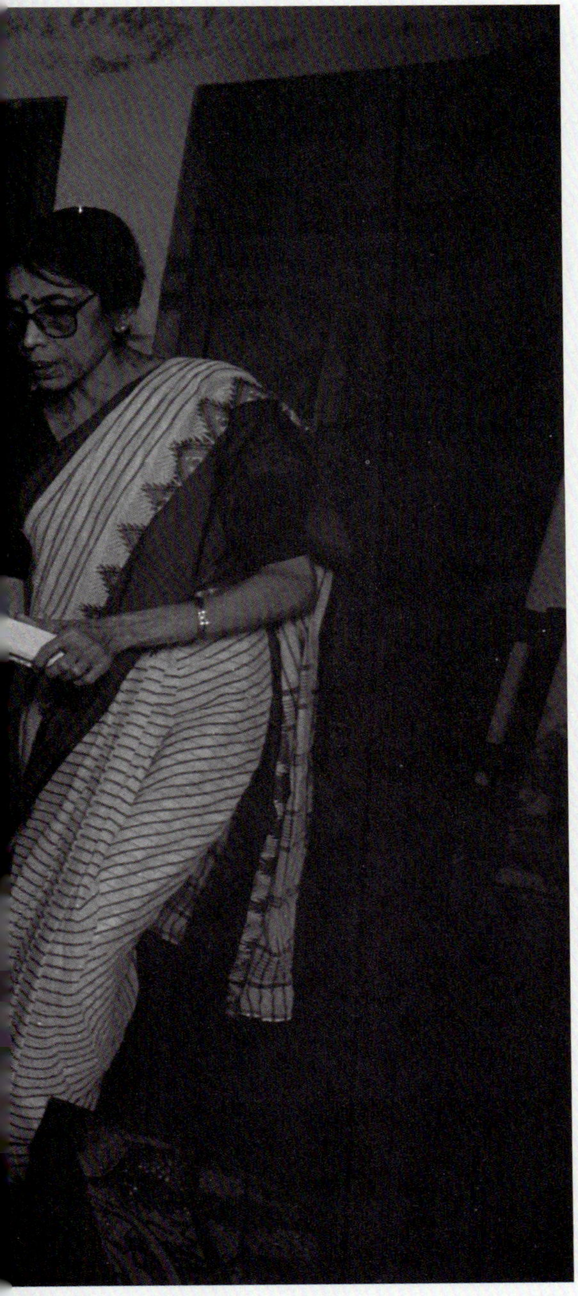

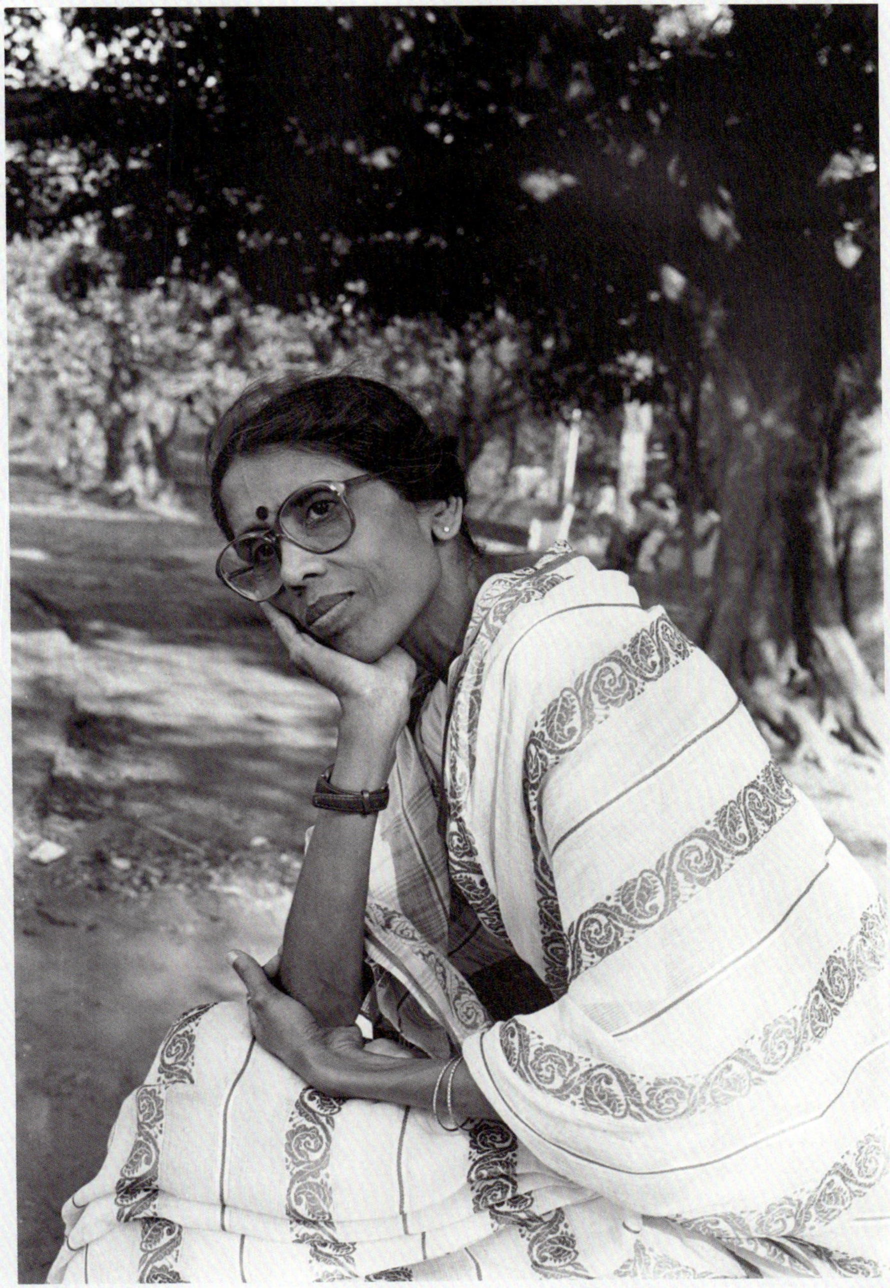

Manju Chatterjee, lecturer in philosophy

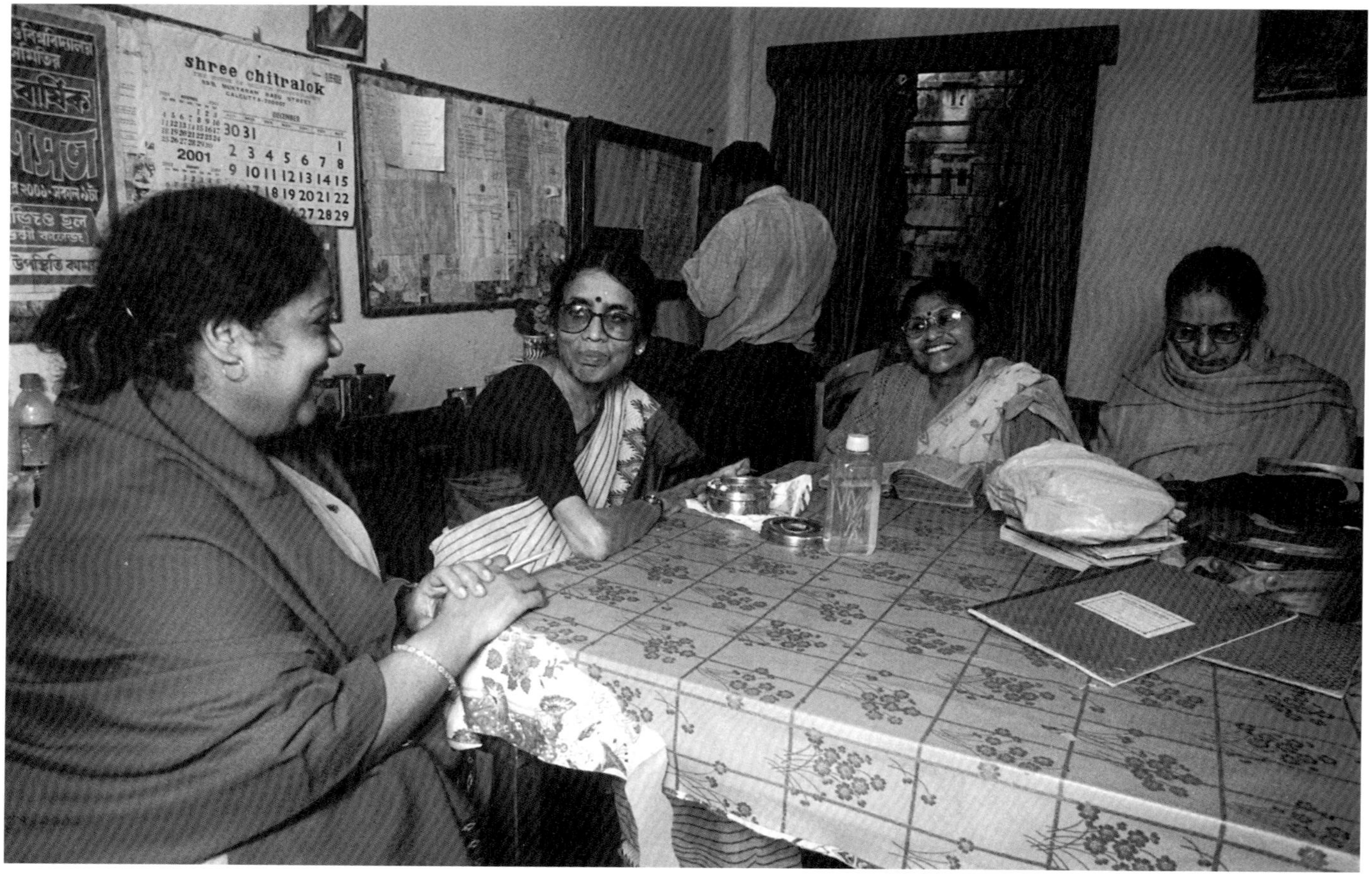
shree chitralok
2001
30 31
1
2 3 4 5 6 7 8
9 10 11 12 13 14 15

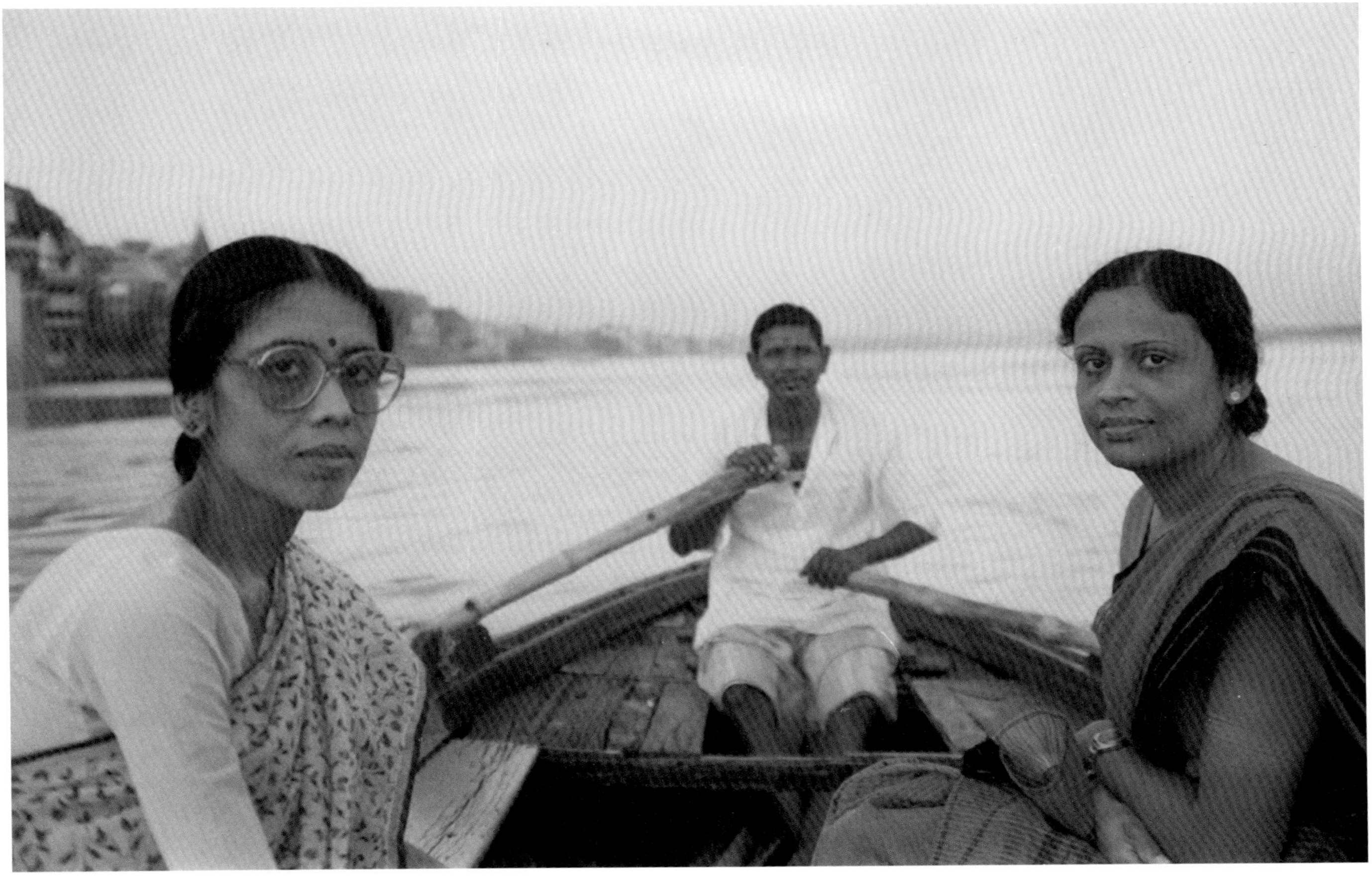

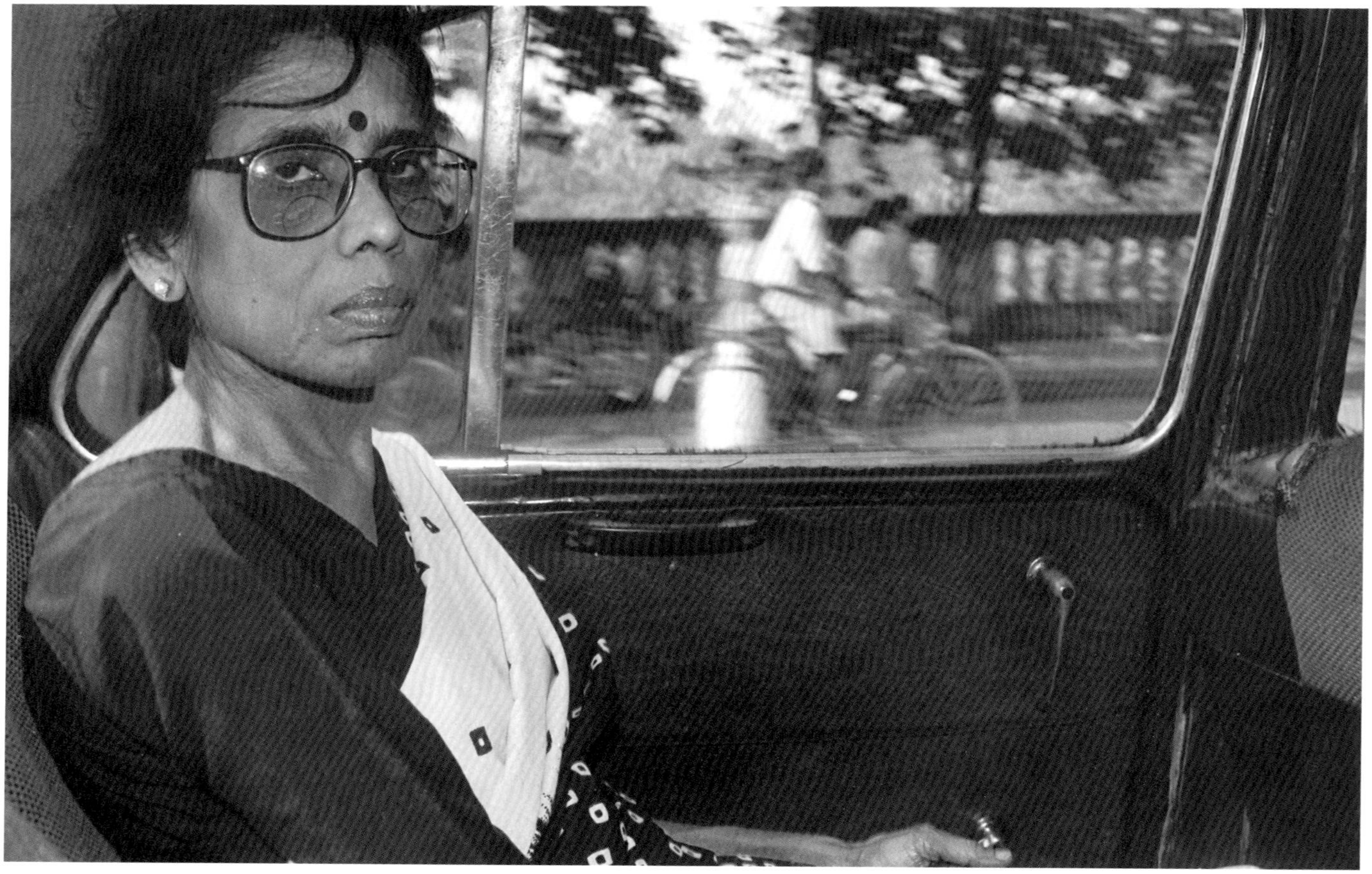

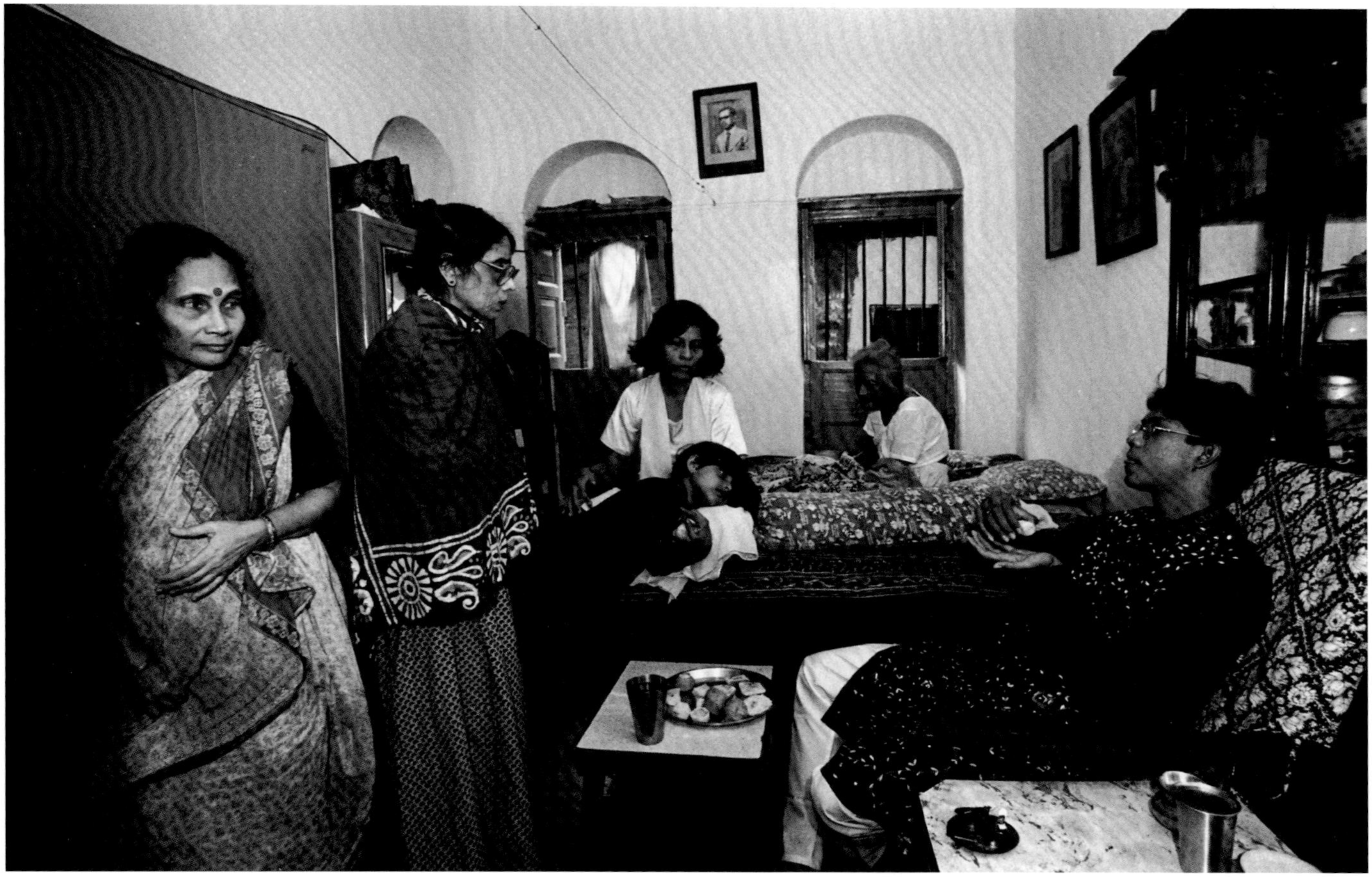

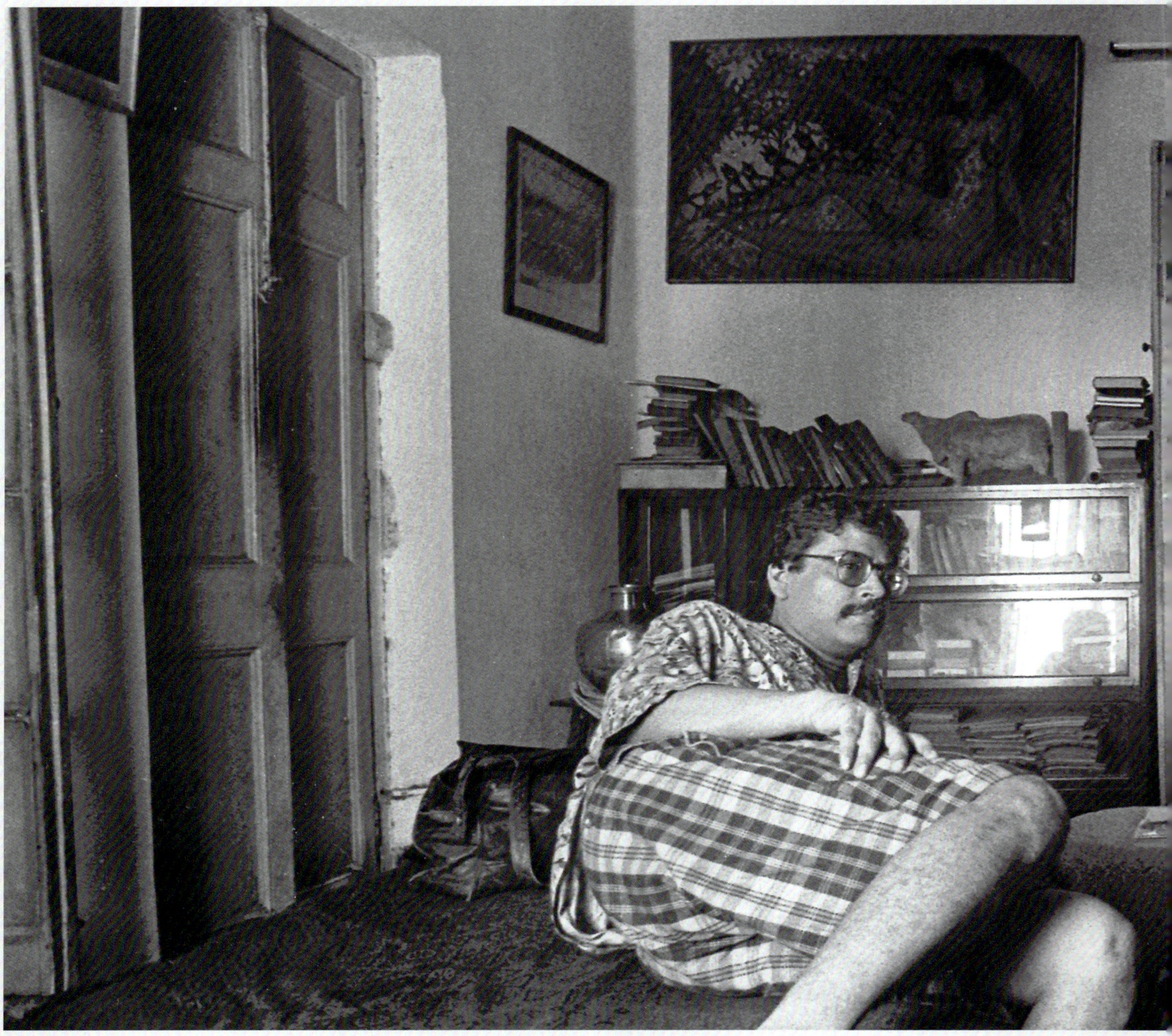

Between the two it was of friendship of minds,
of pain and solitariness

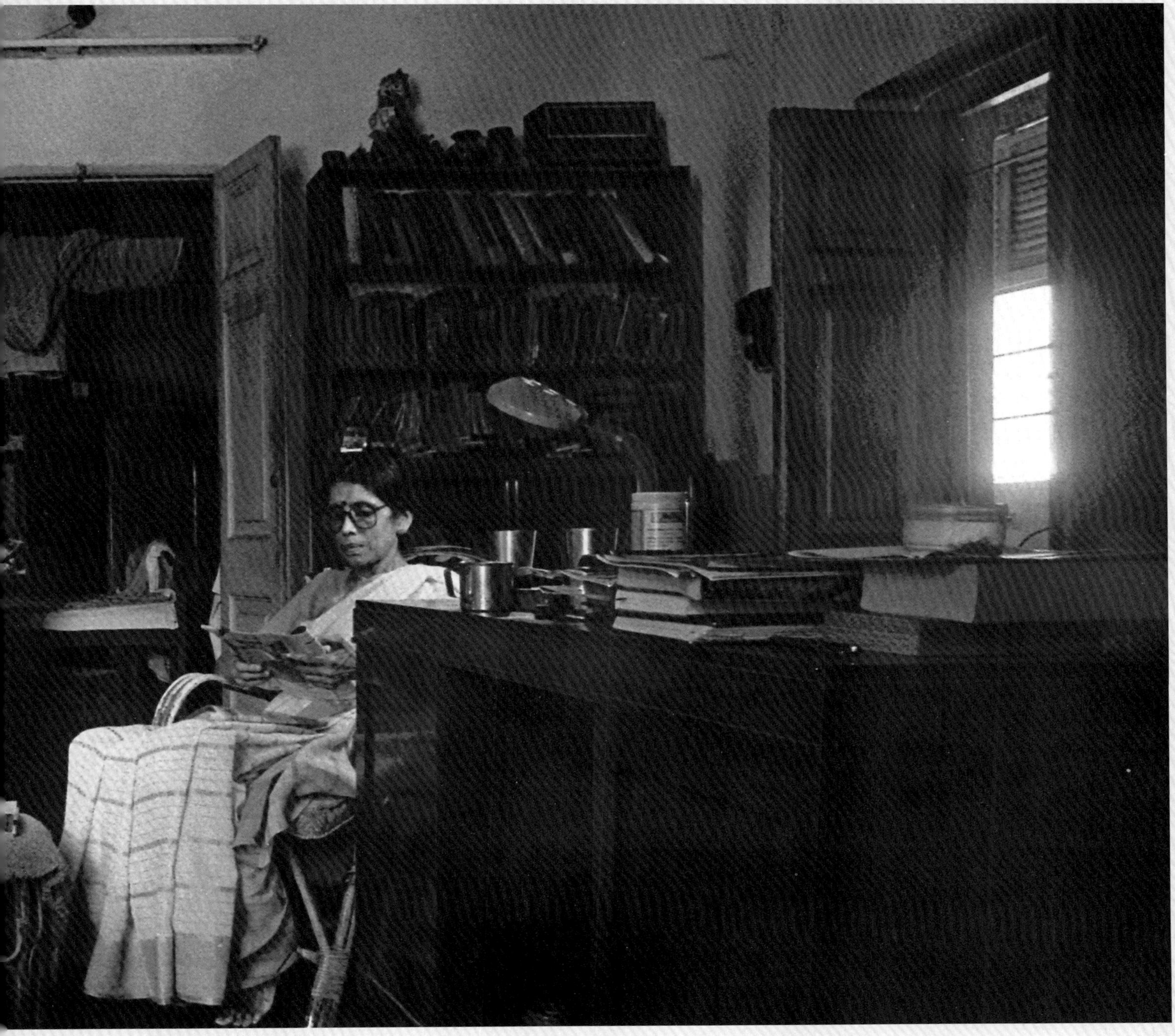

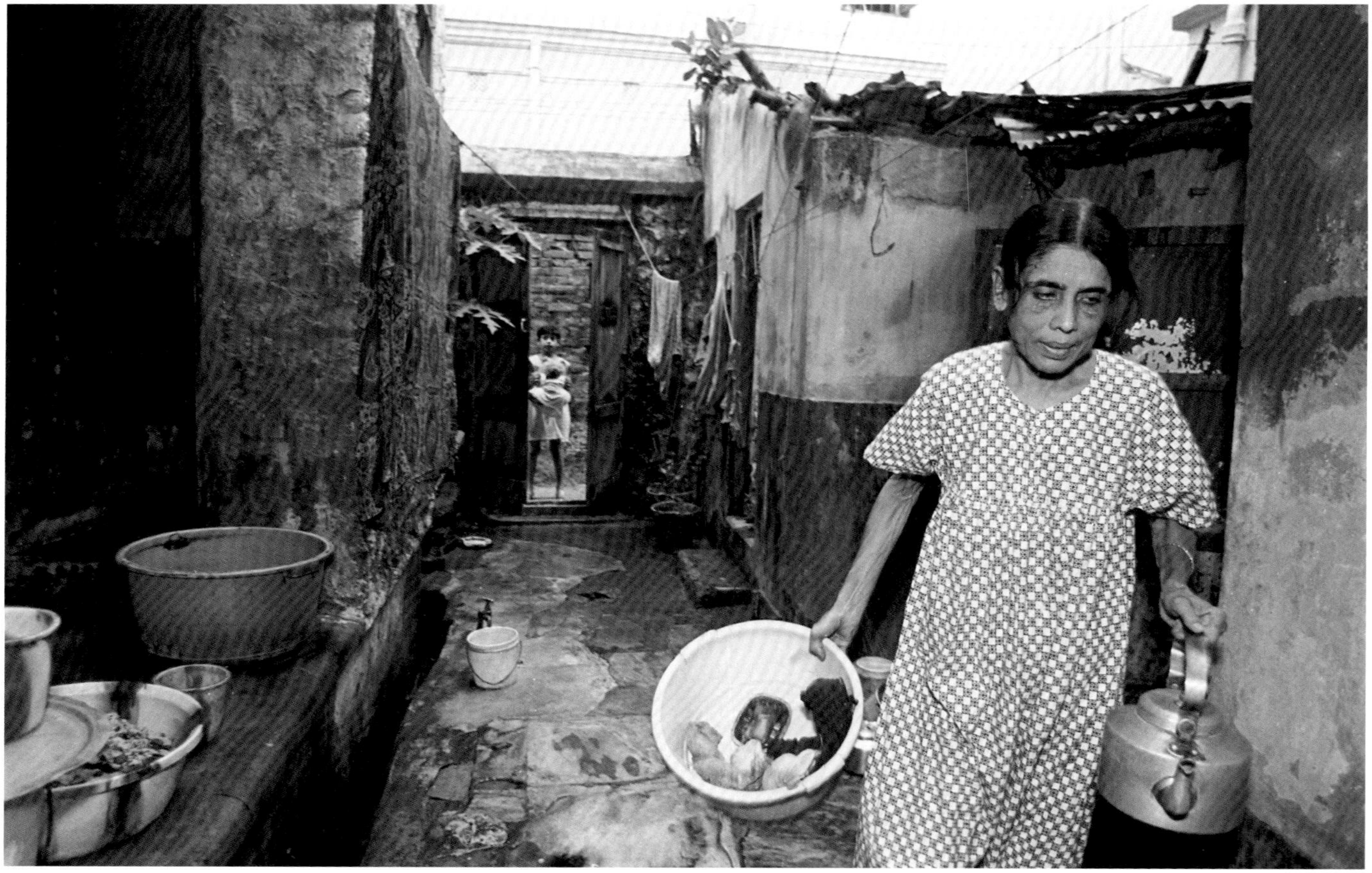

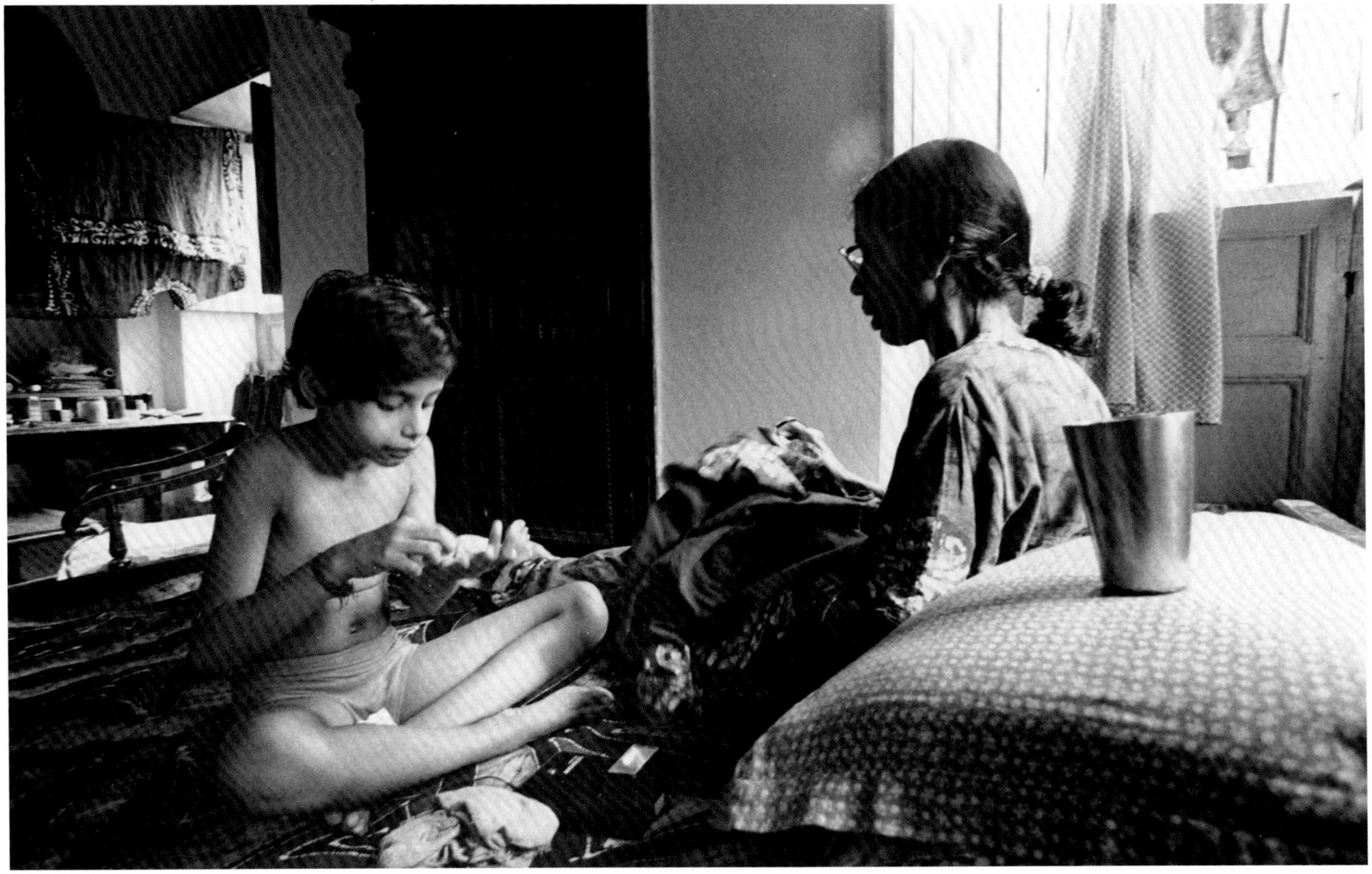

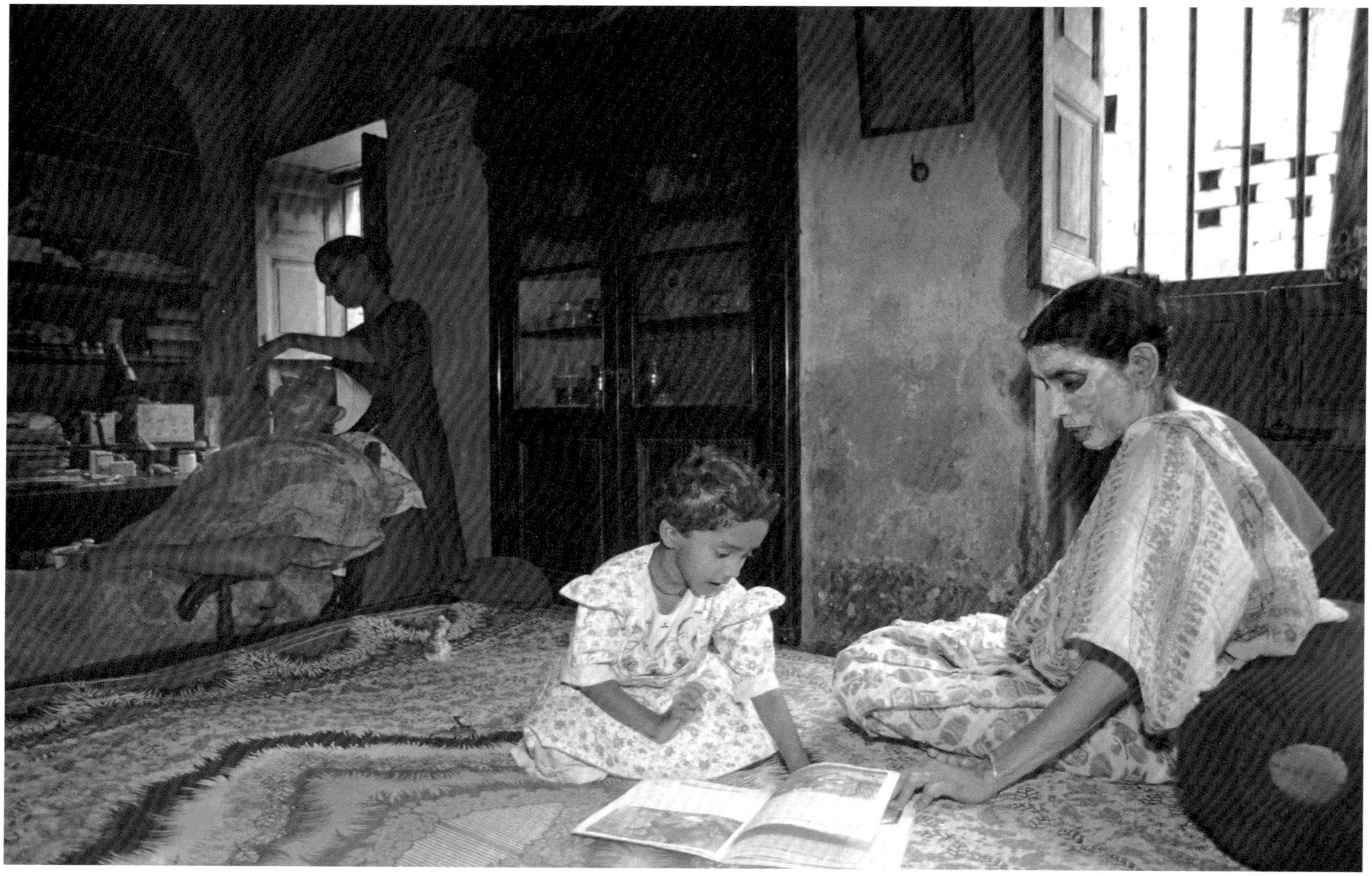

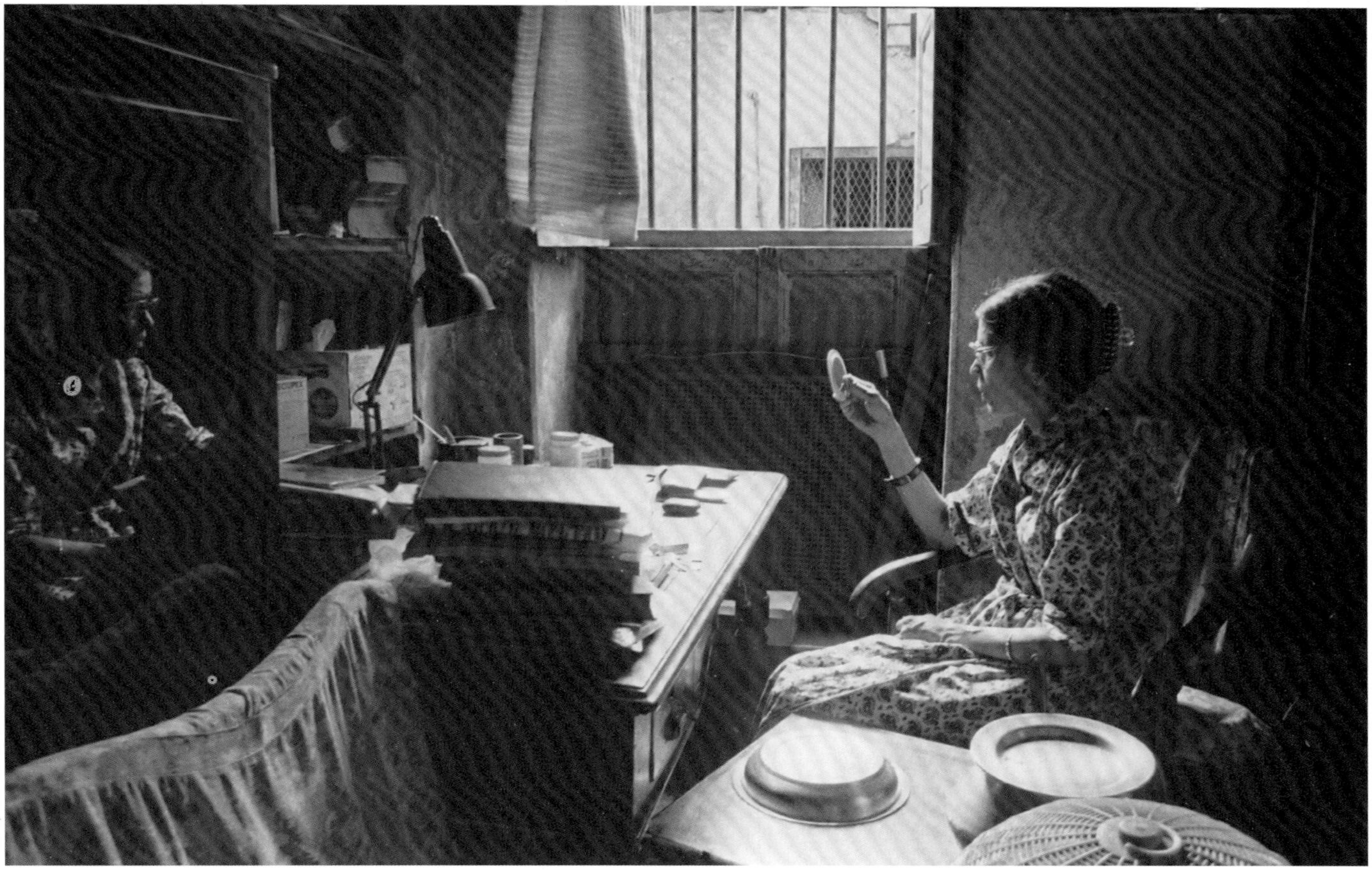

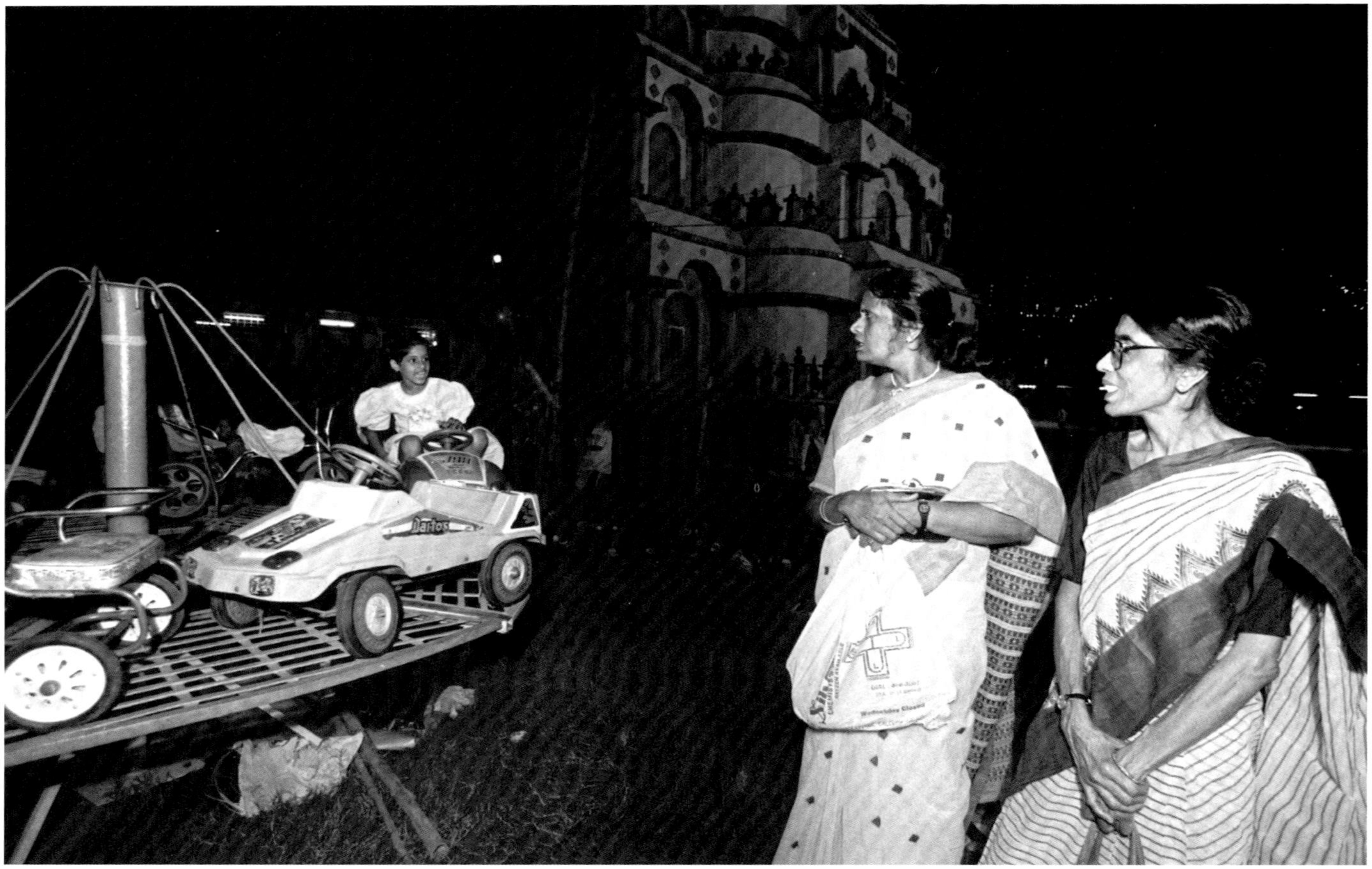

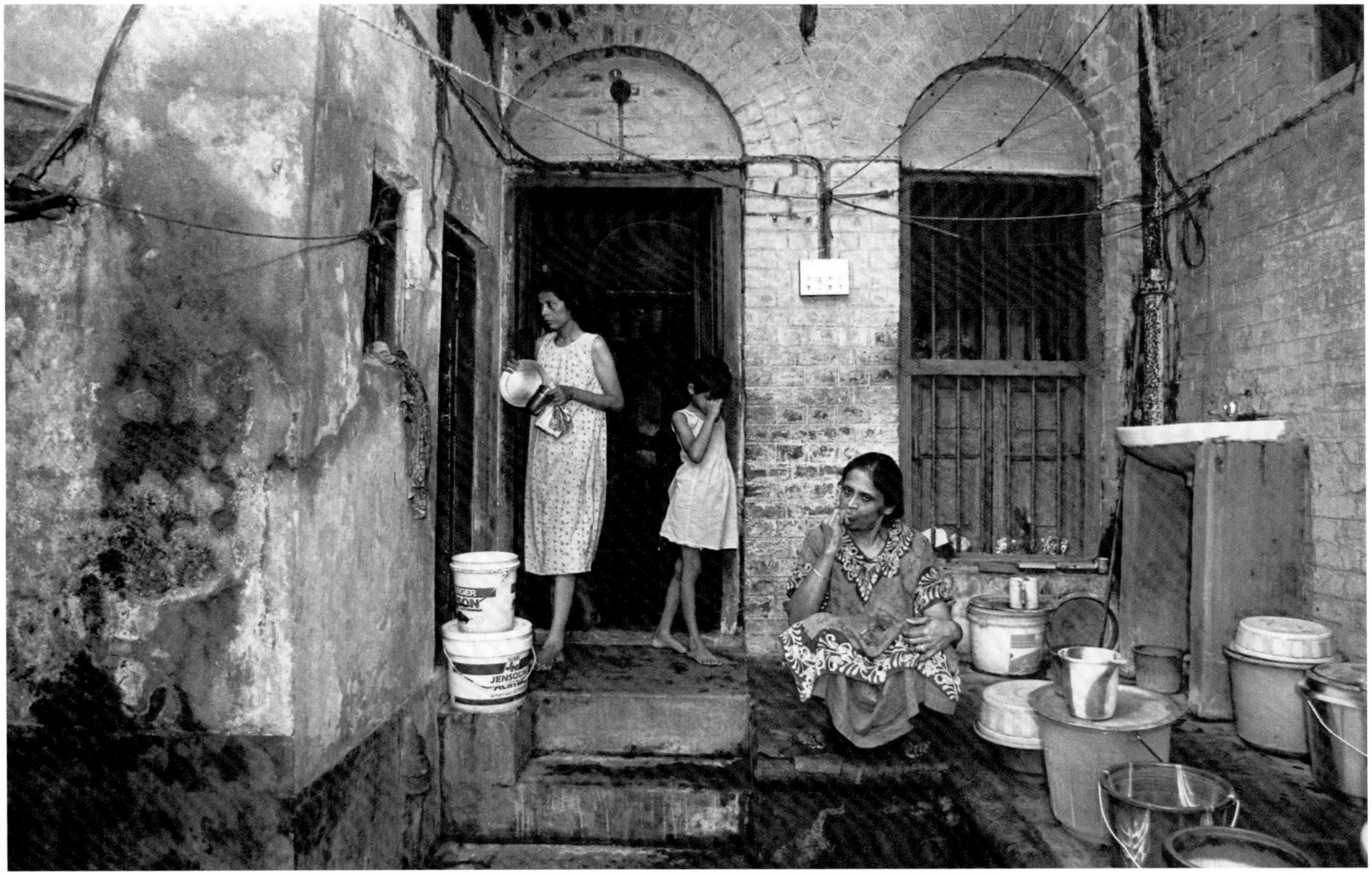

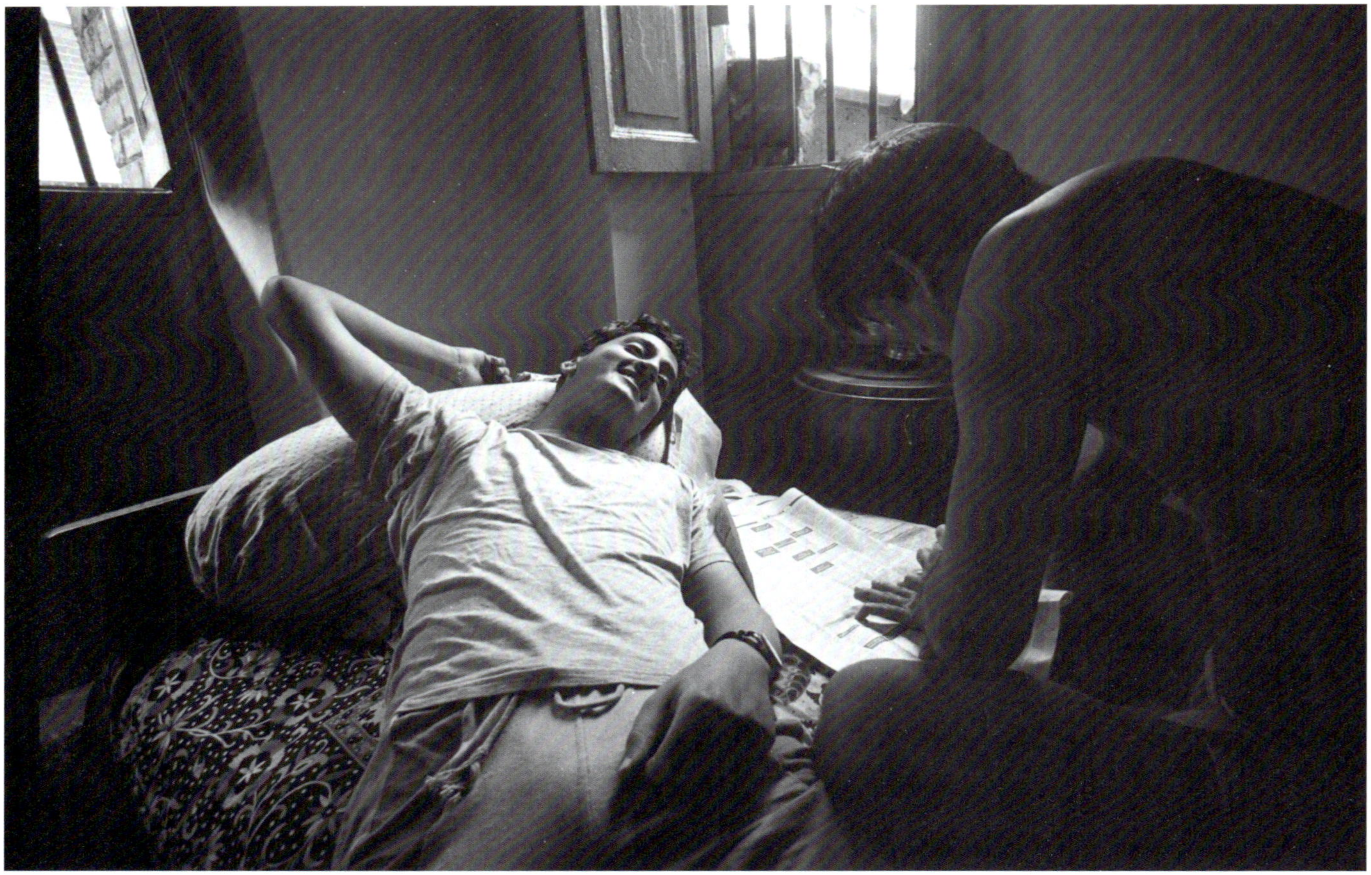

Kalighat afternoon

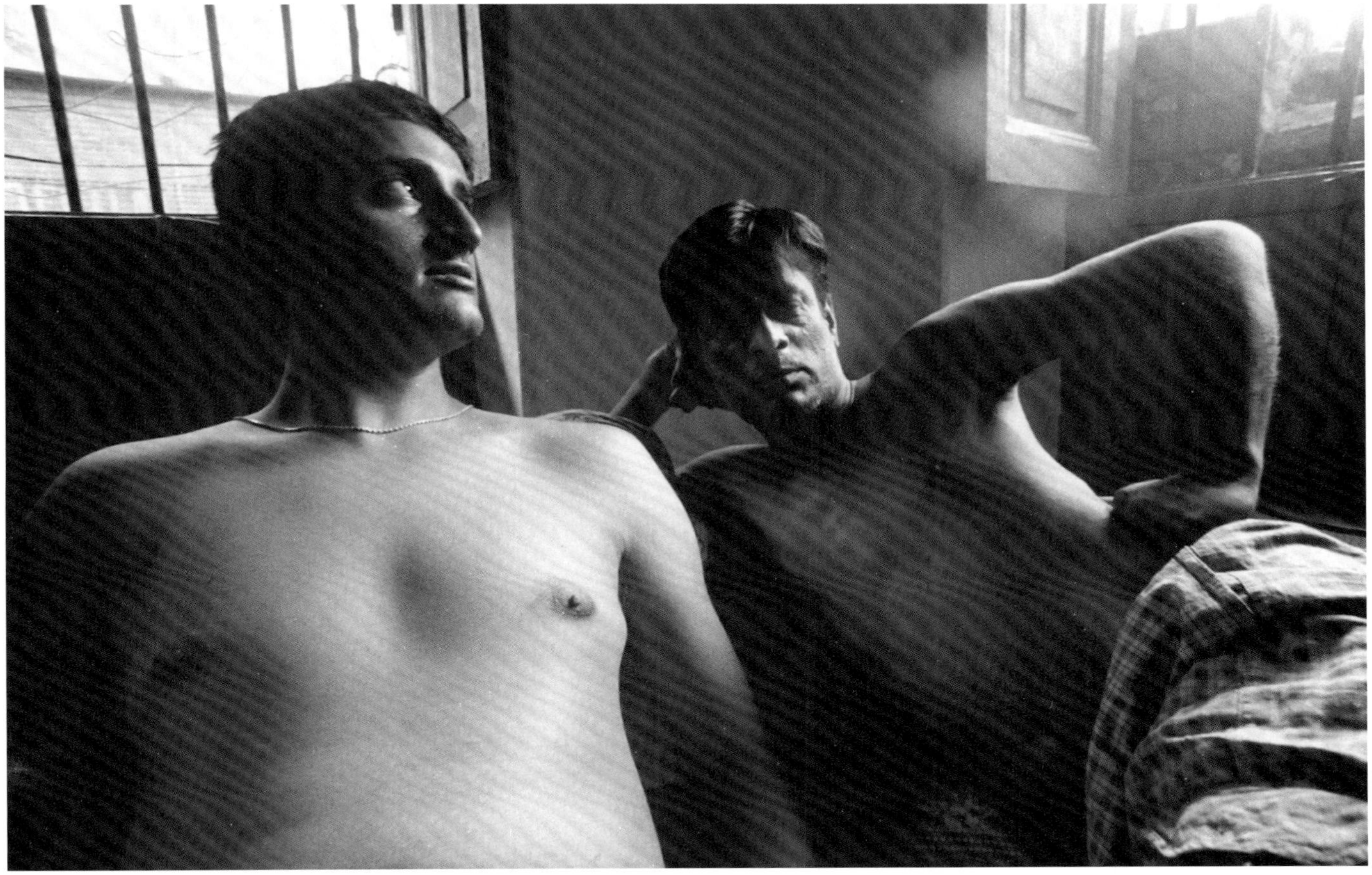

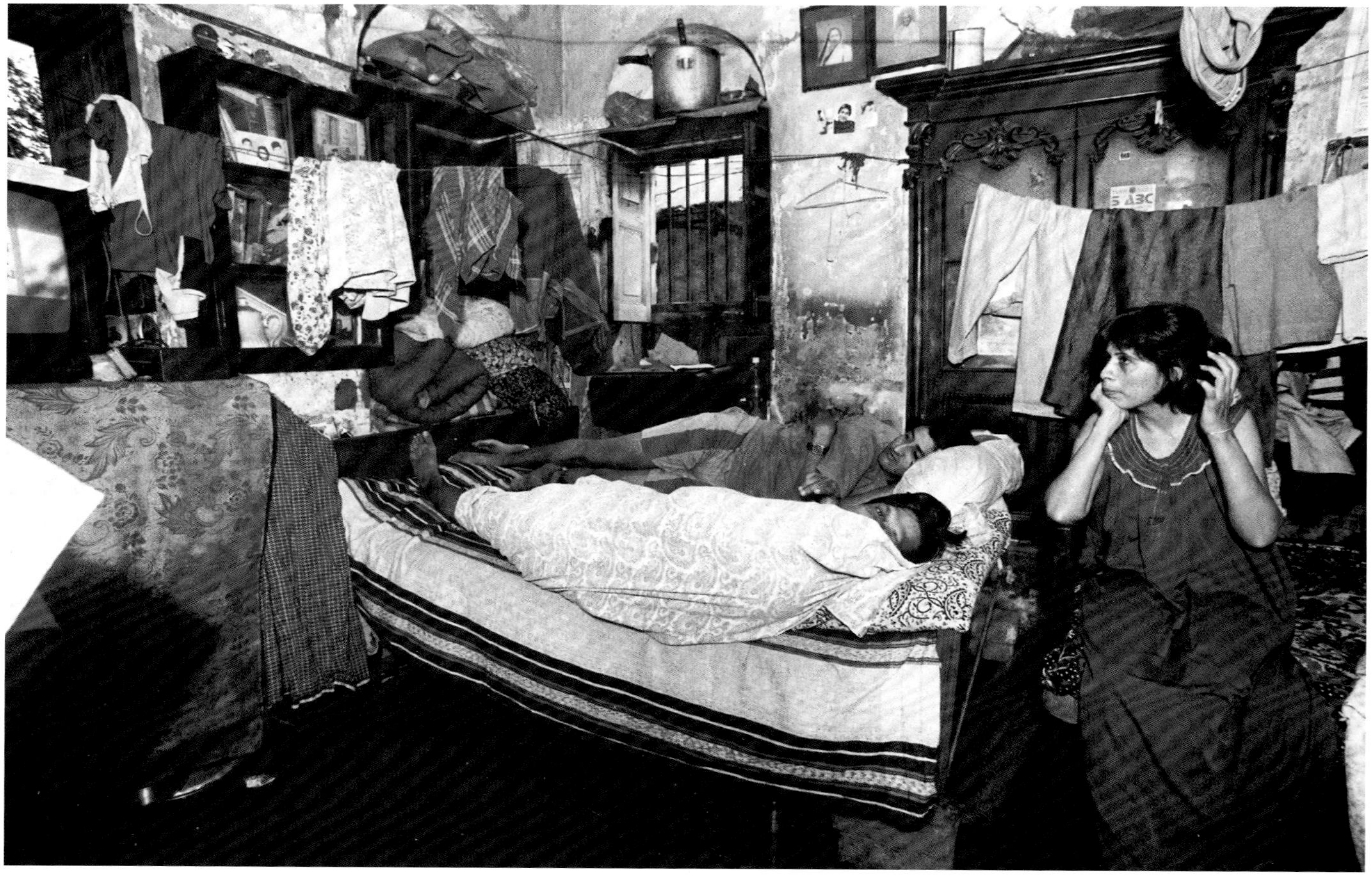

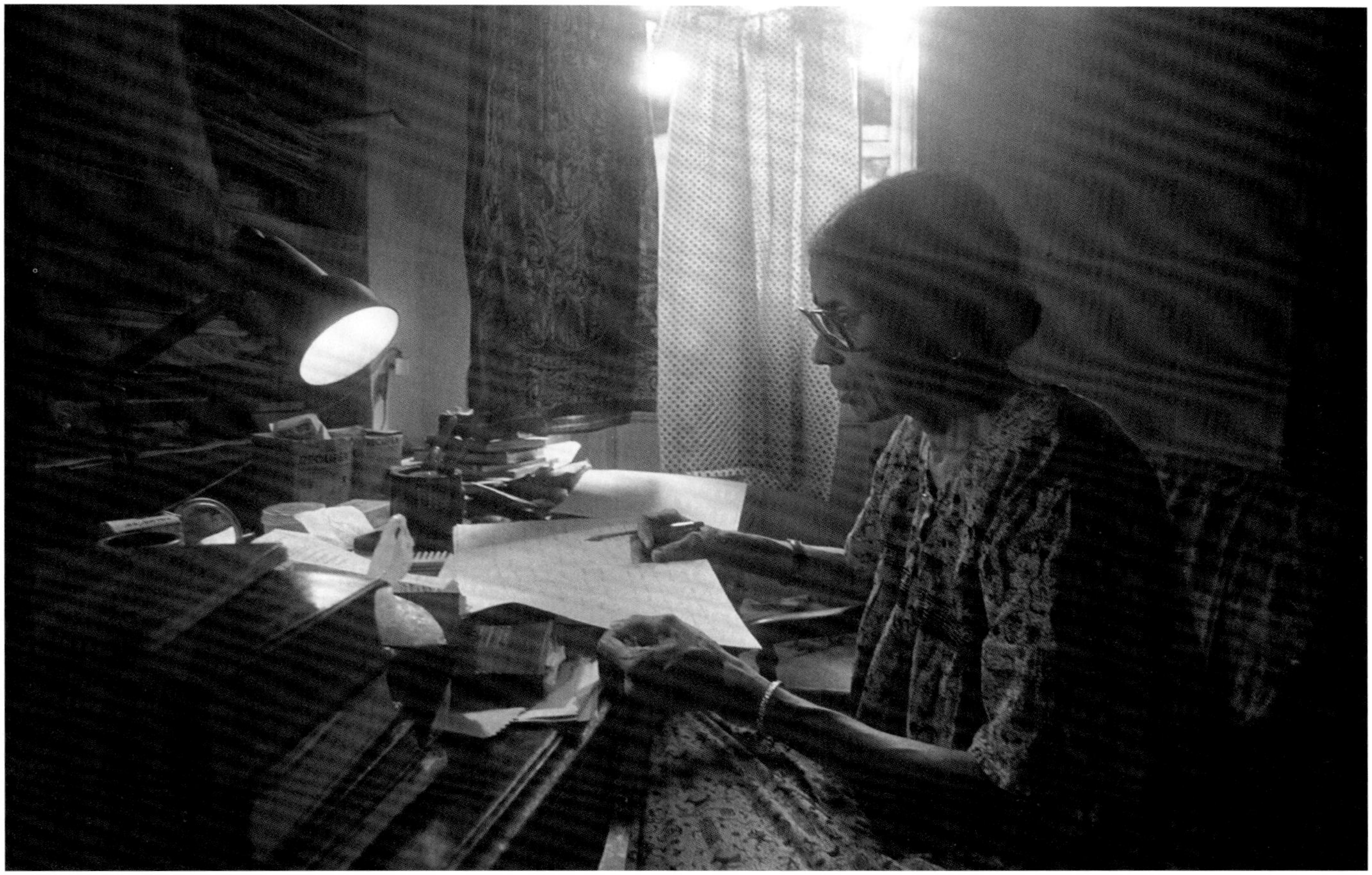

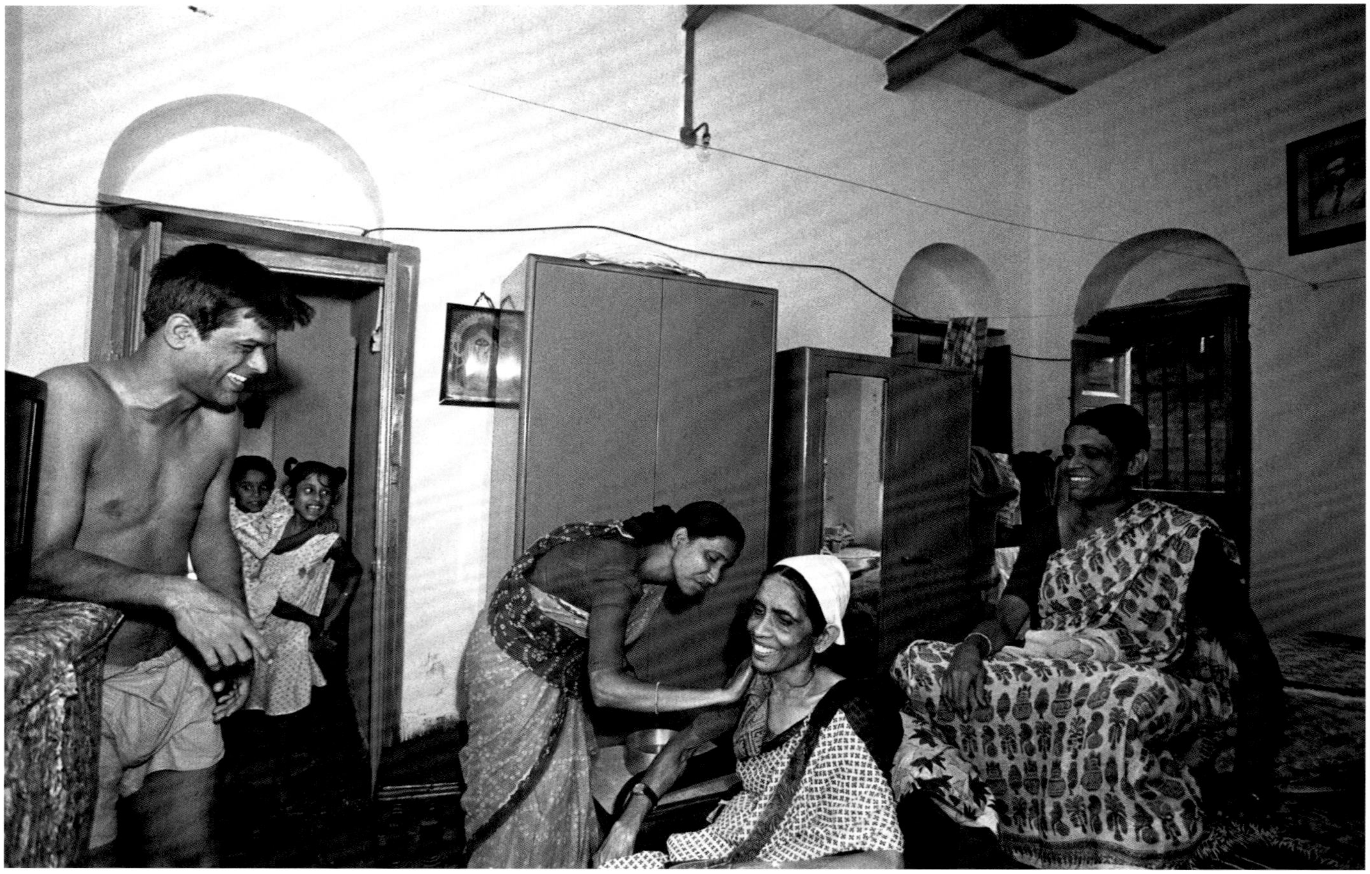

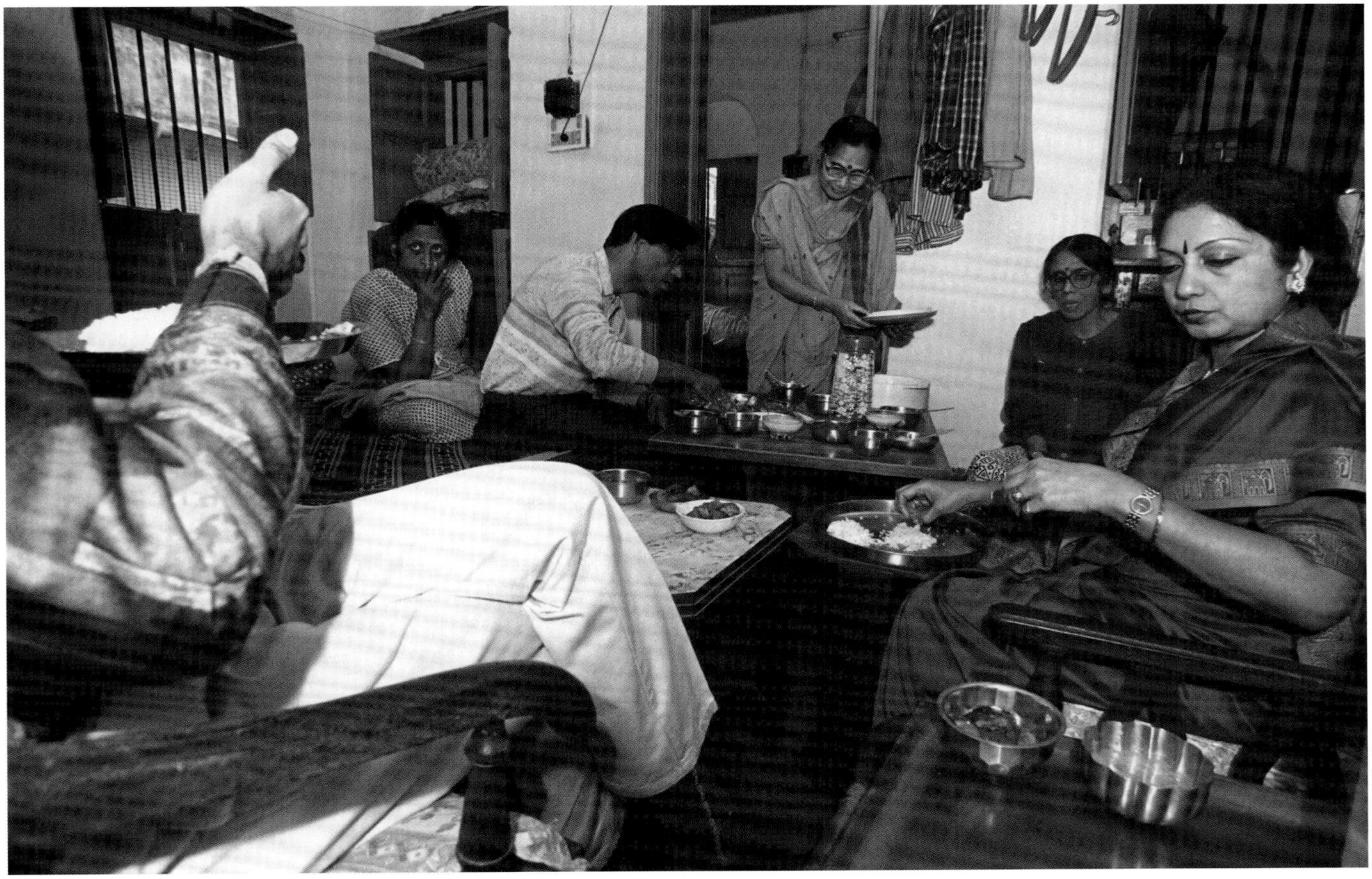

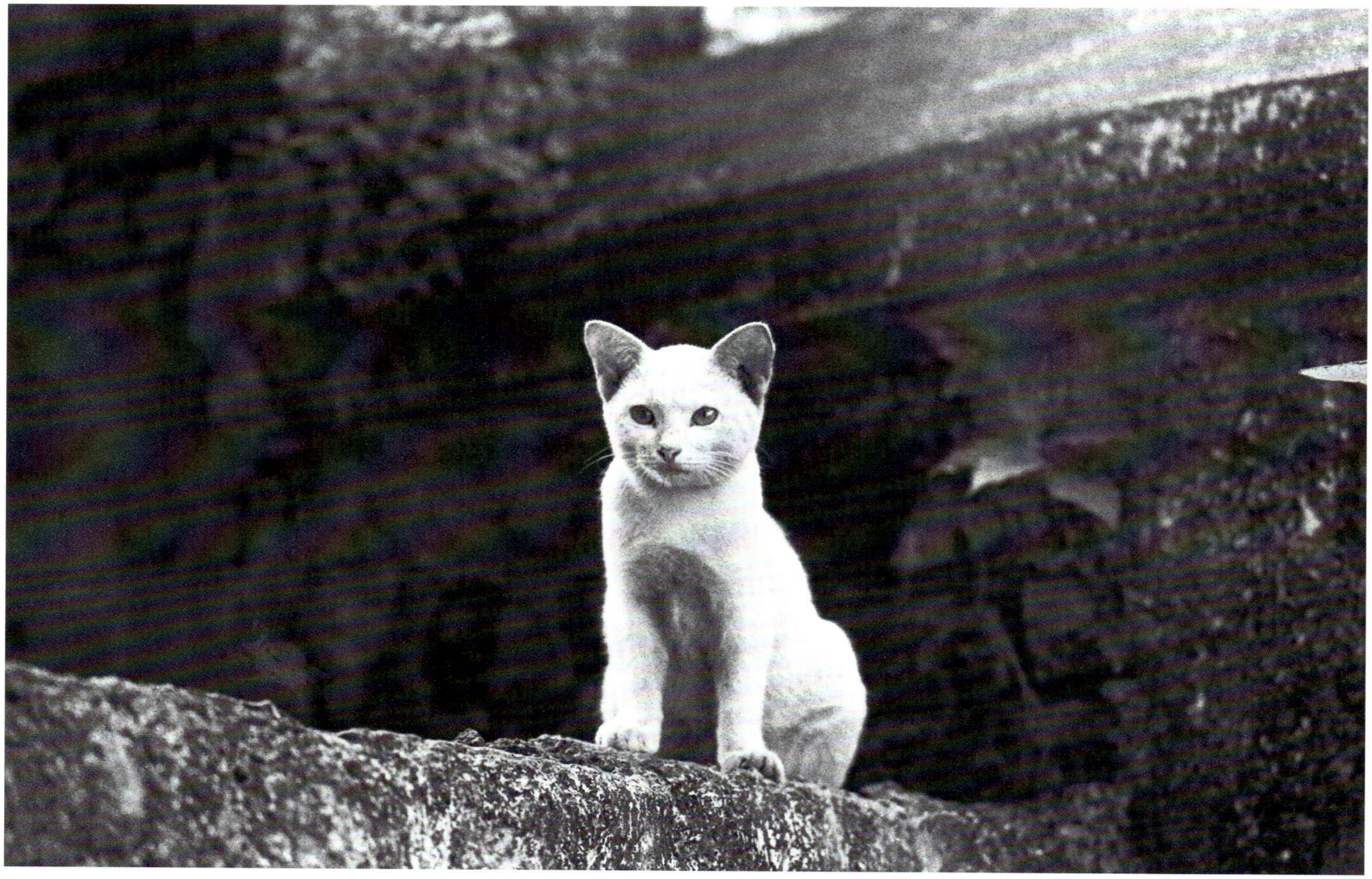

Shadababu–Mr. White–came to live with the Chartterjees

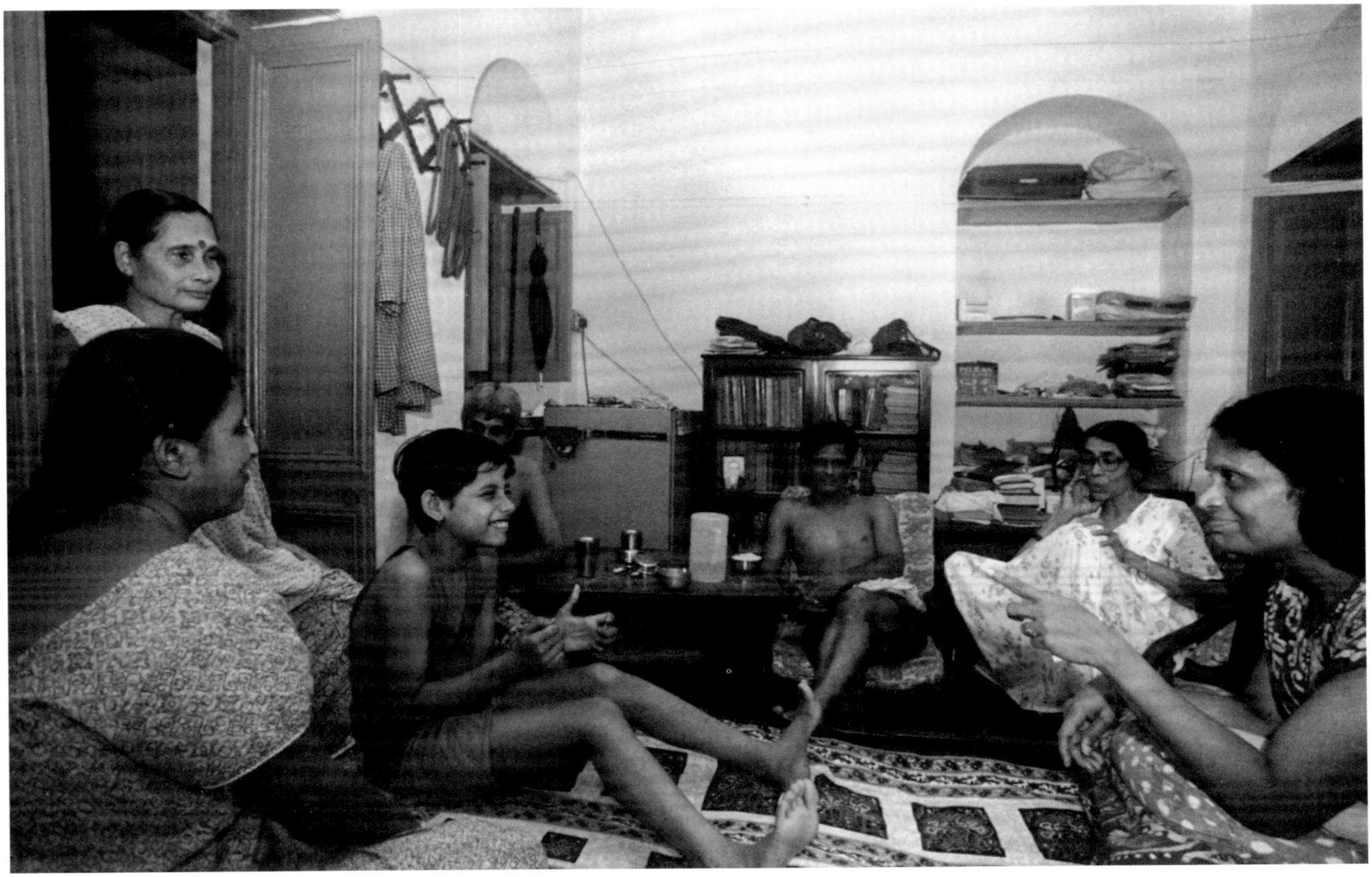

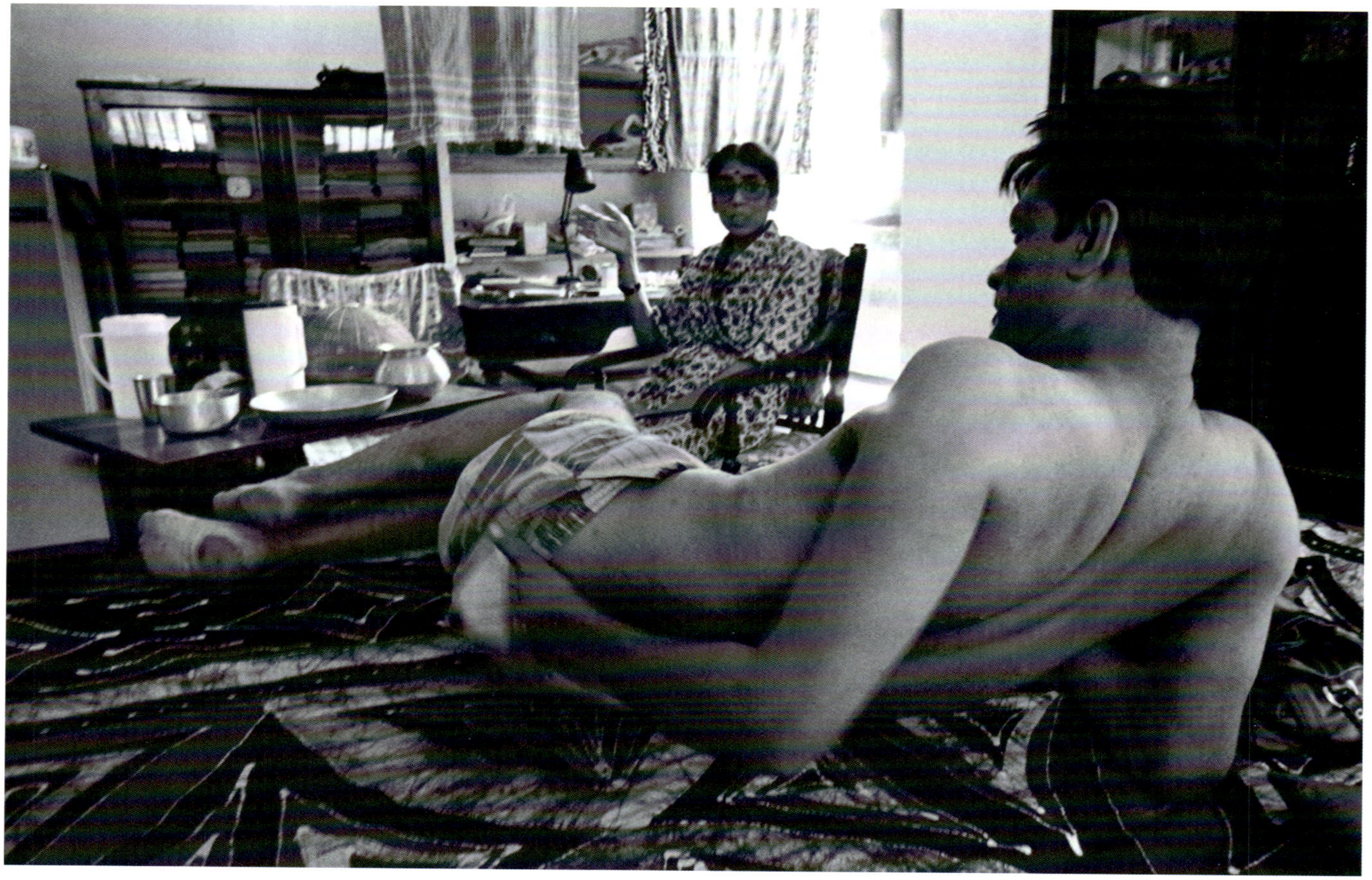

No fear of the camera's disapproval

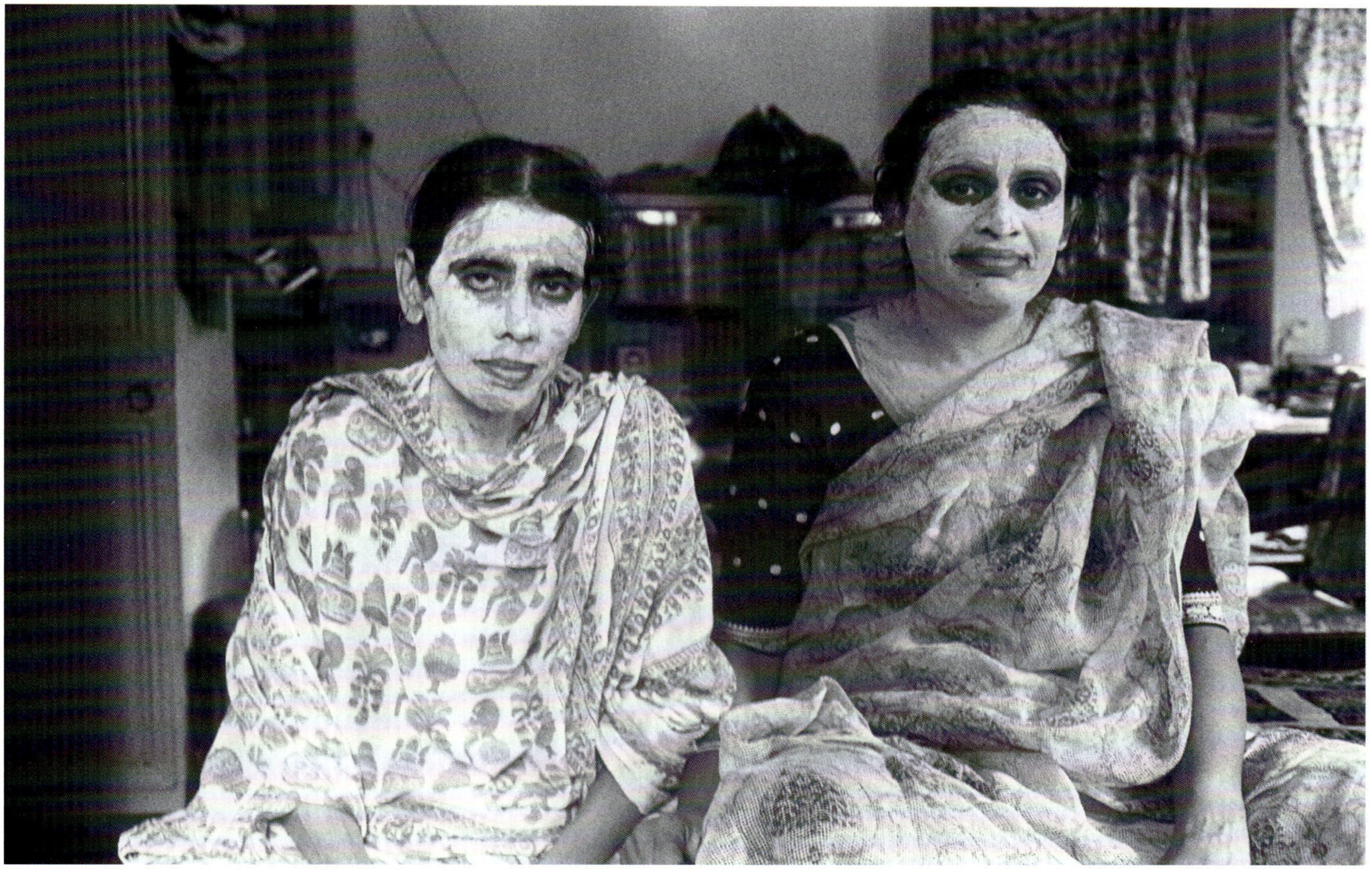

Beauty treatment

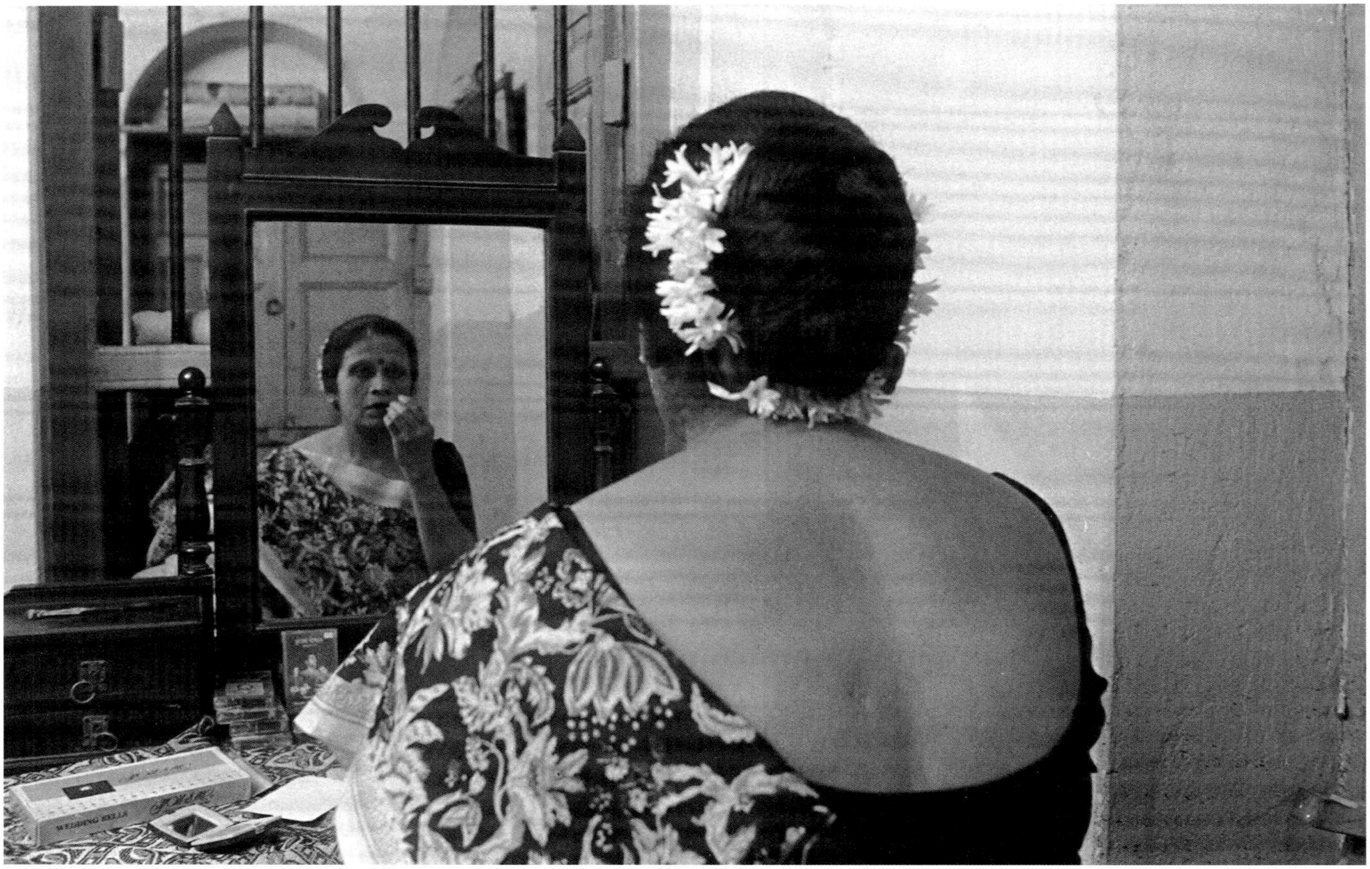
WEDDING BELLS

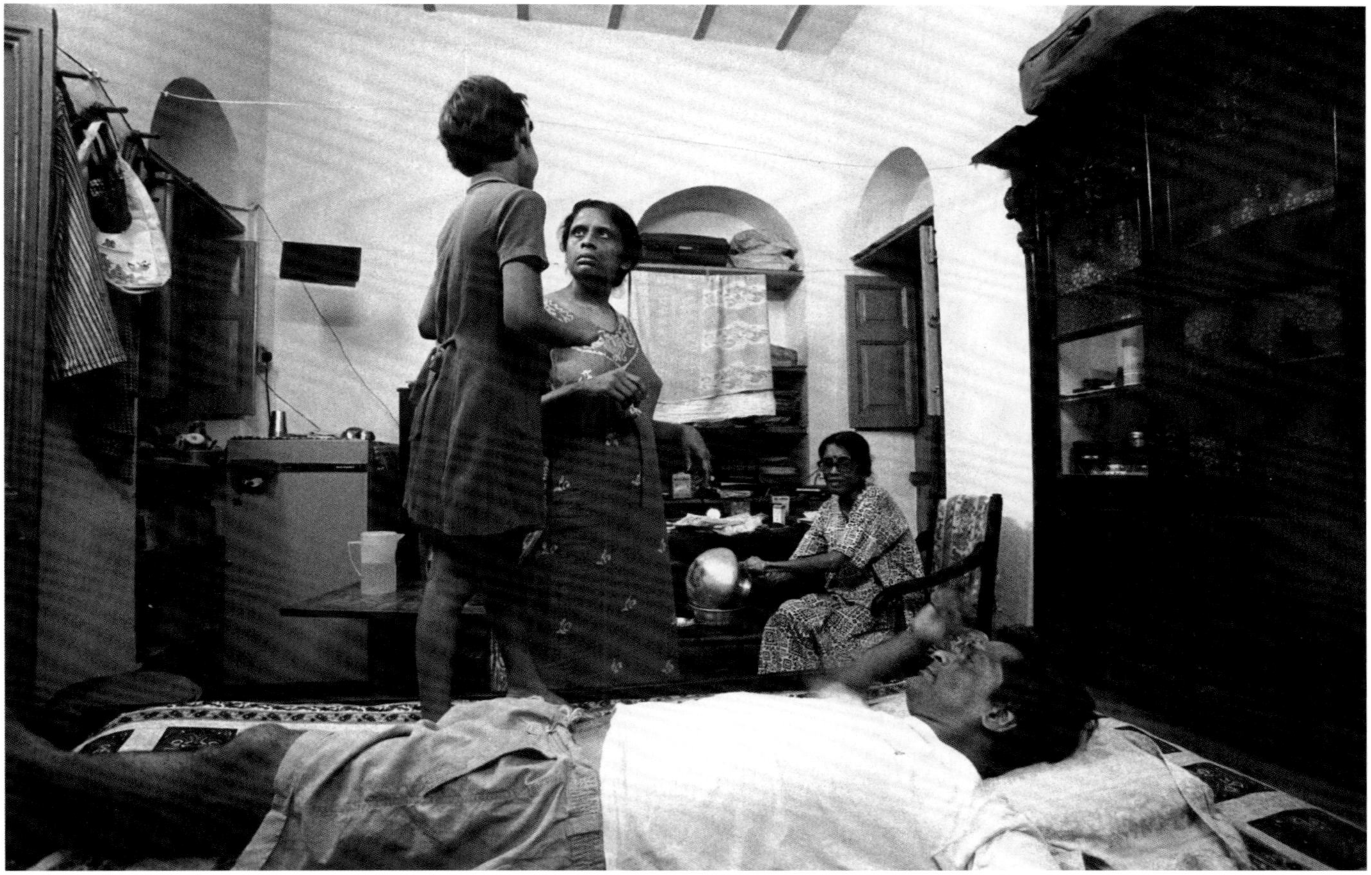

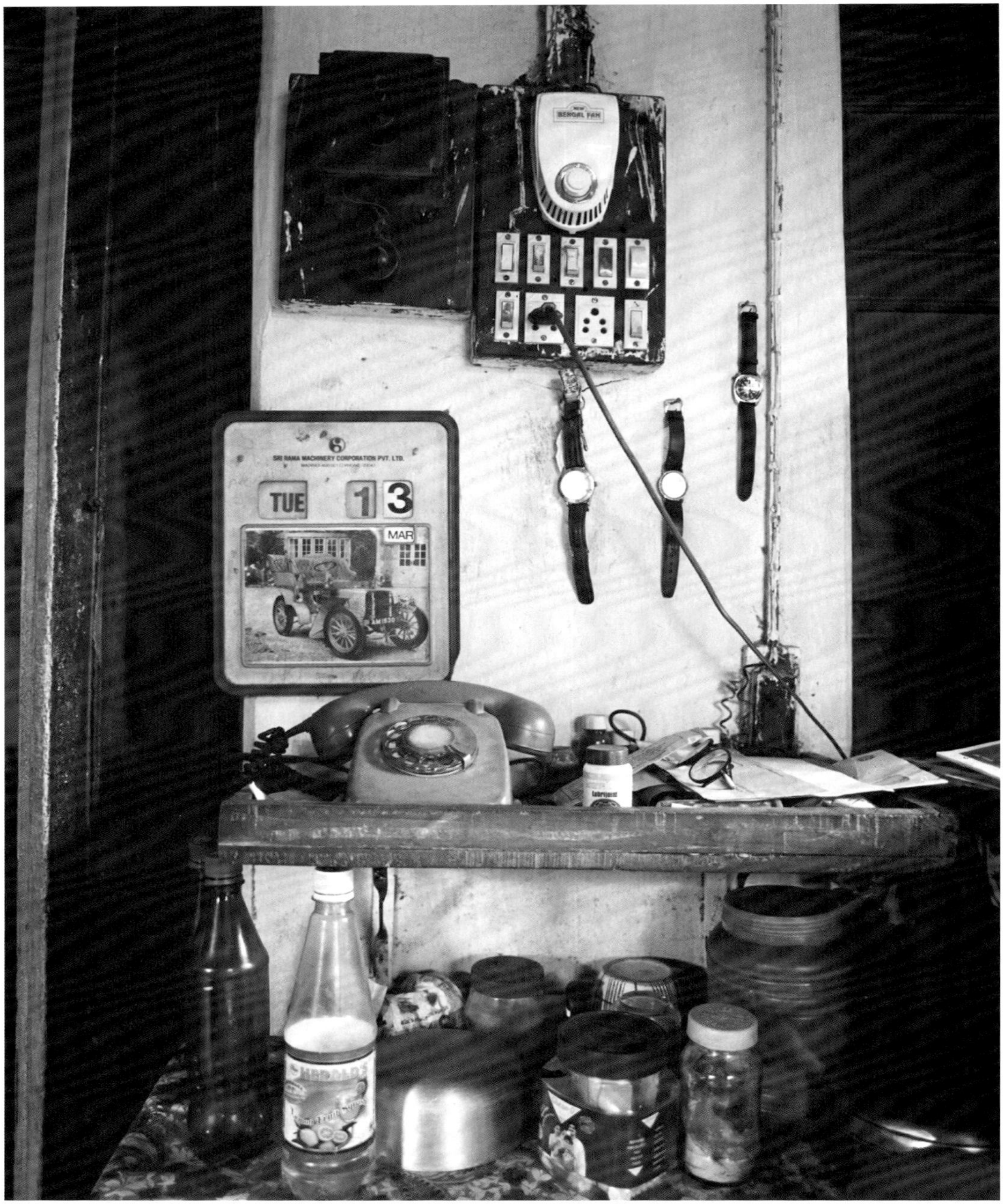
SRI RAMA MACHINERY CORPORATION PVT. LTD.
TUE
13
MAR

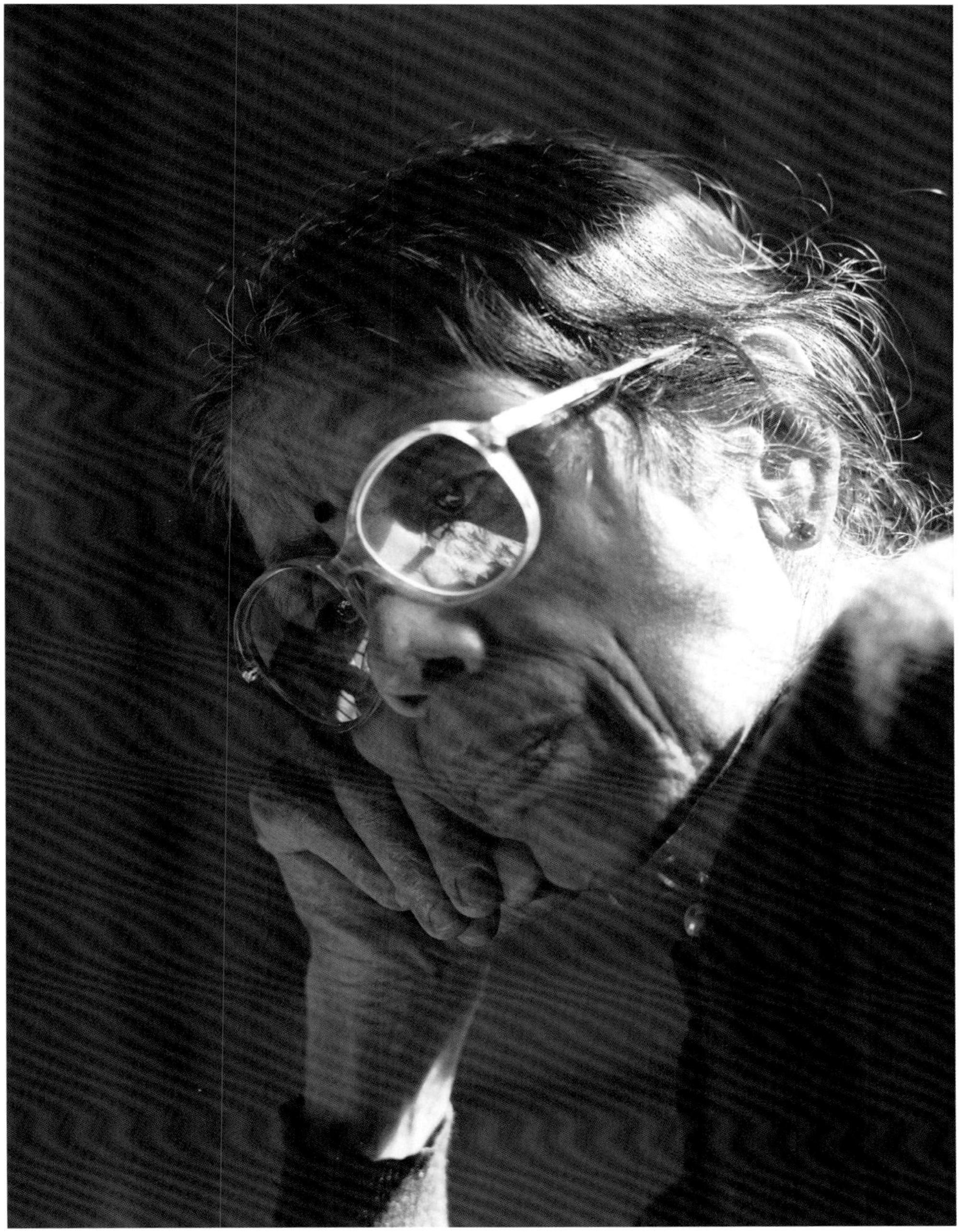

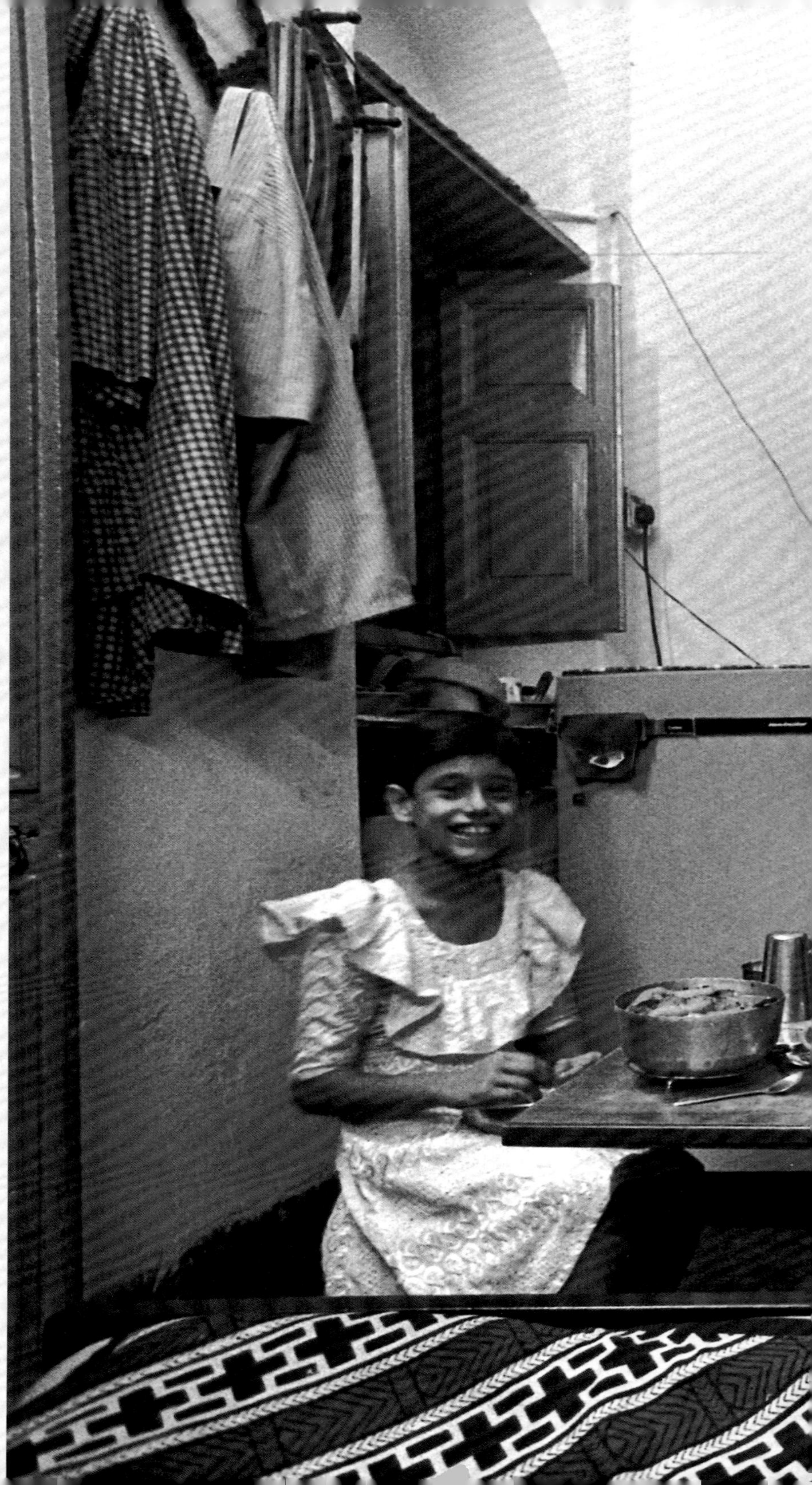

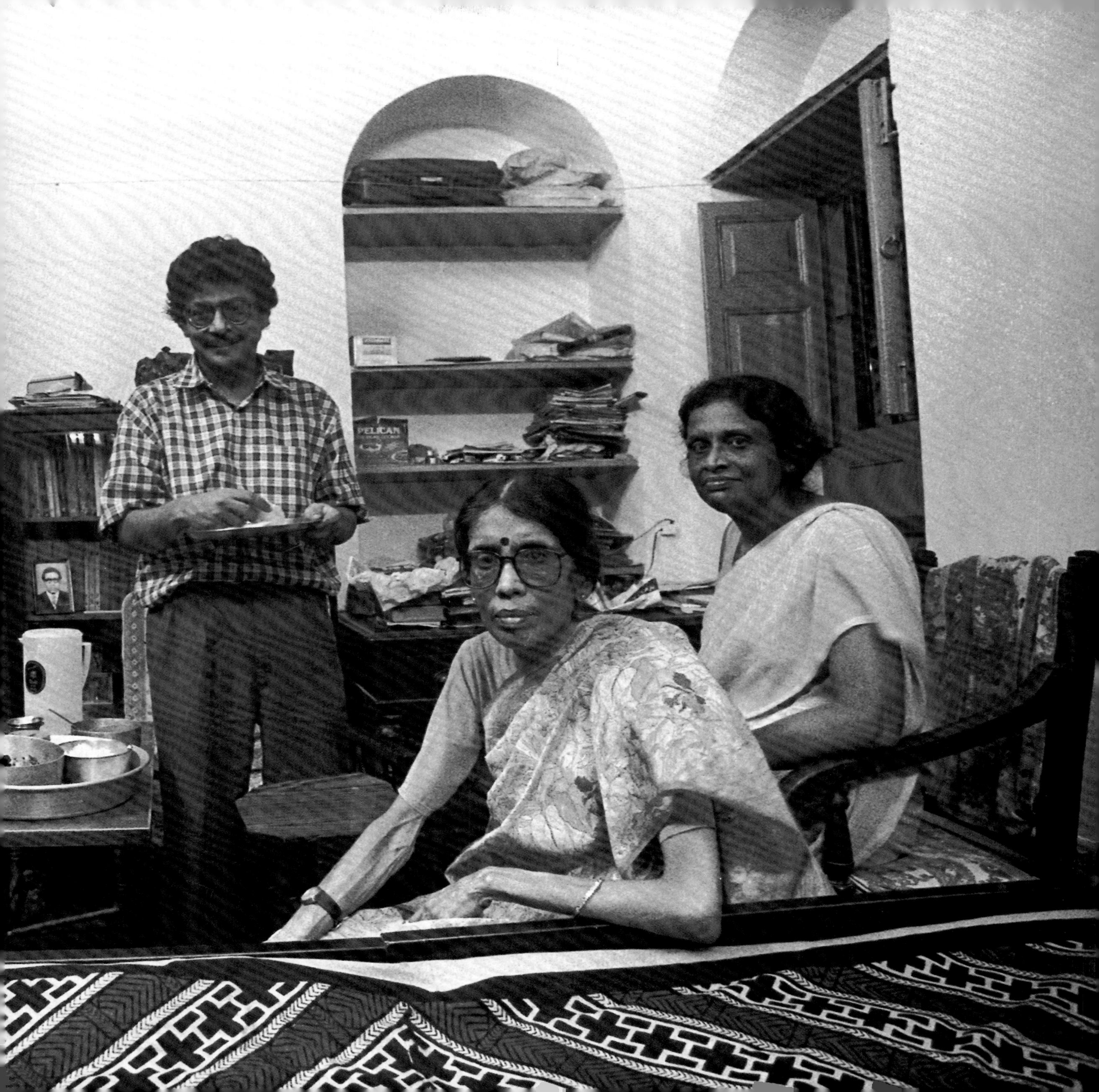
PELICAN

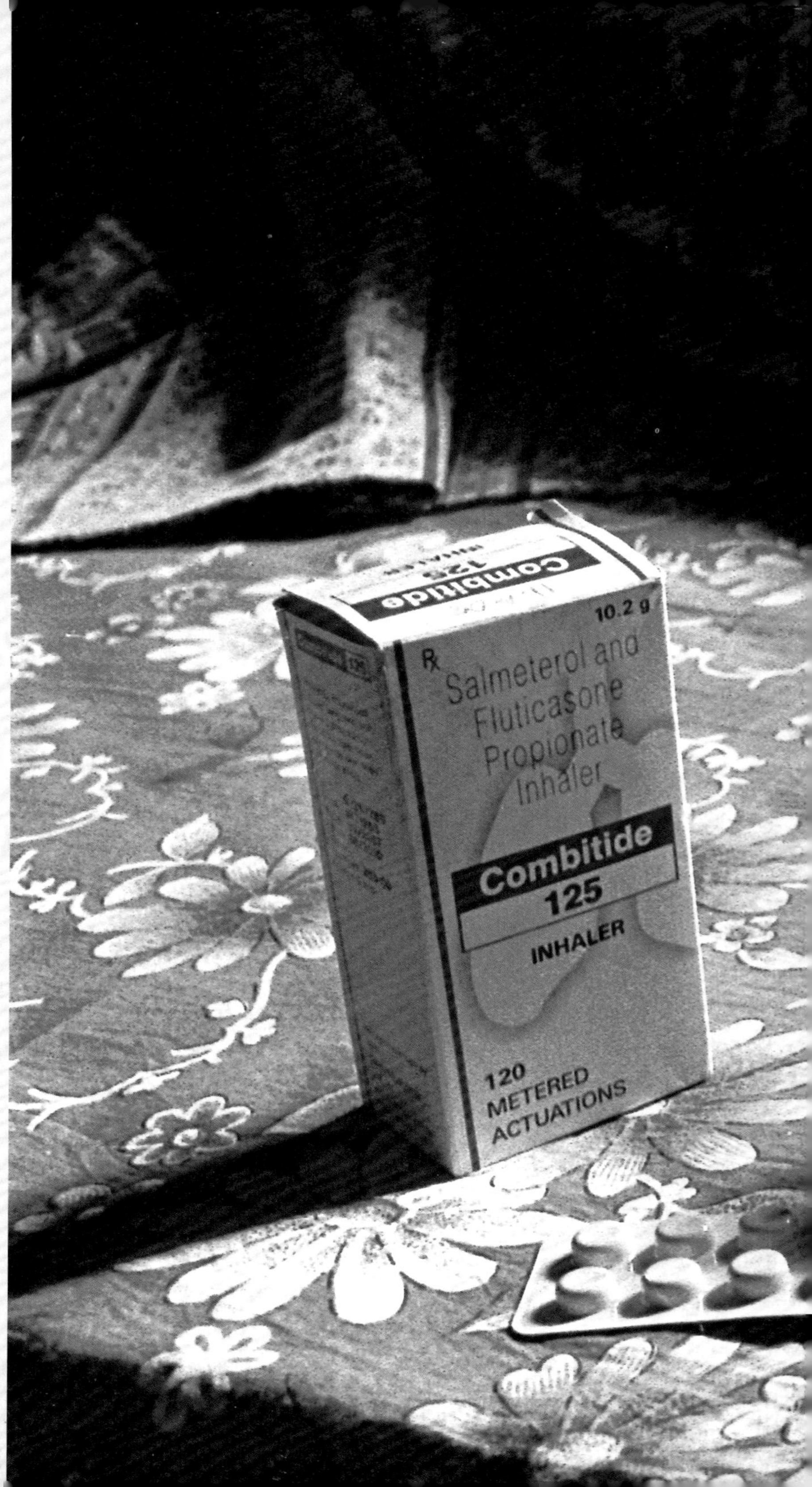

'Put your hand in mind and take a photo of our hands'–Manju Chatterjee

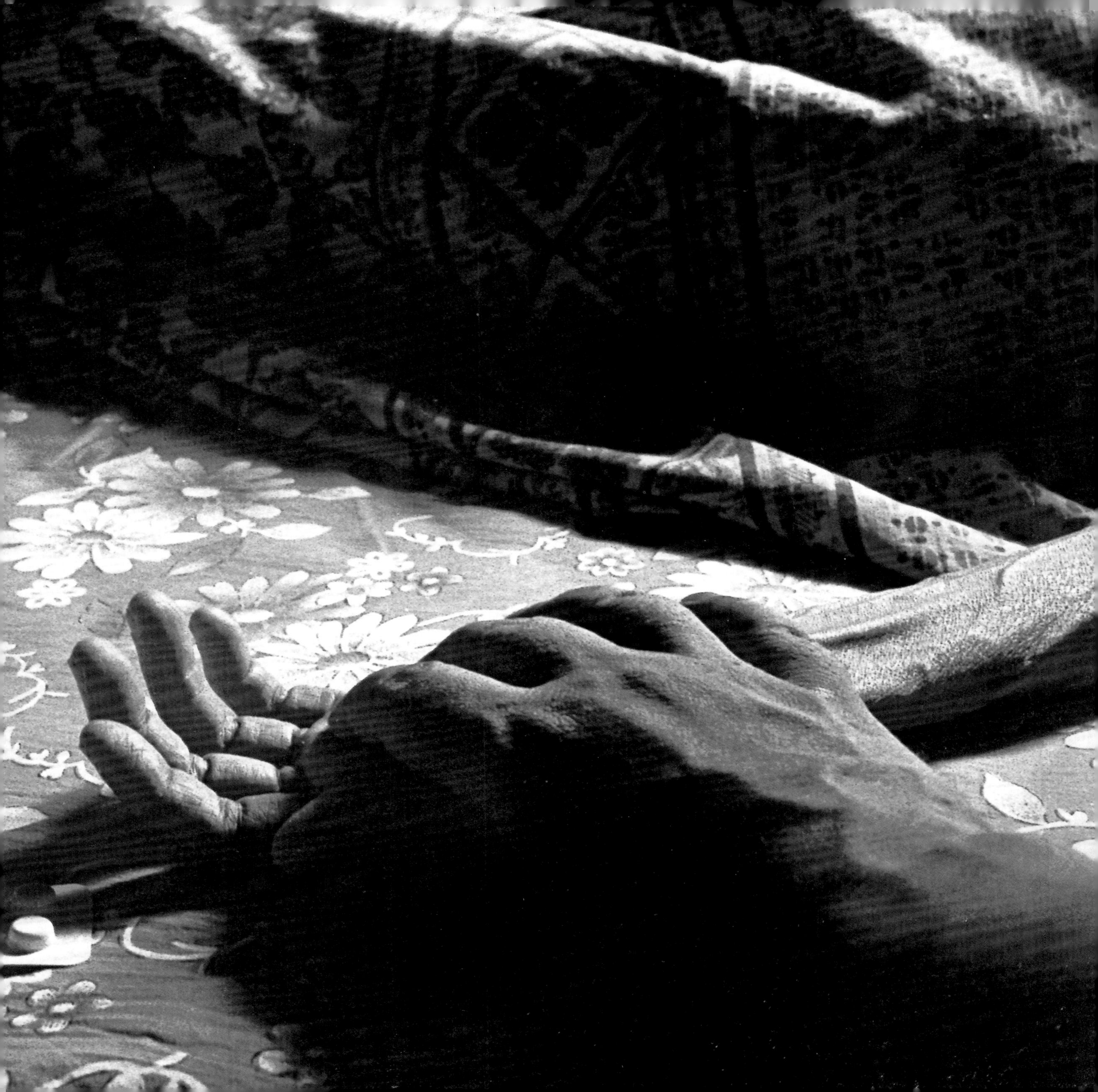

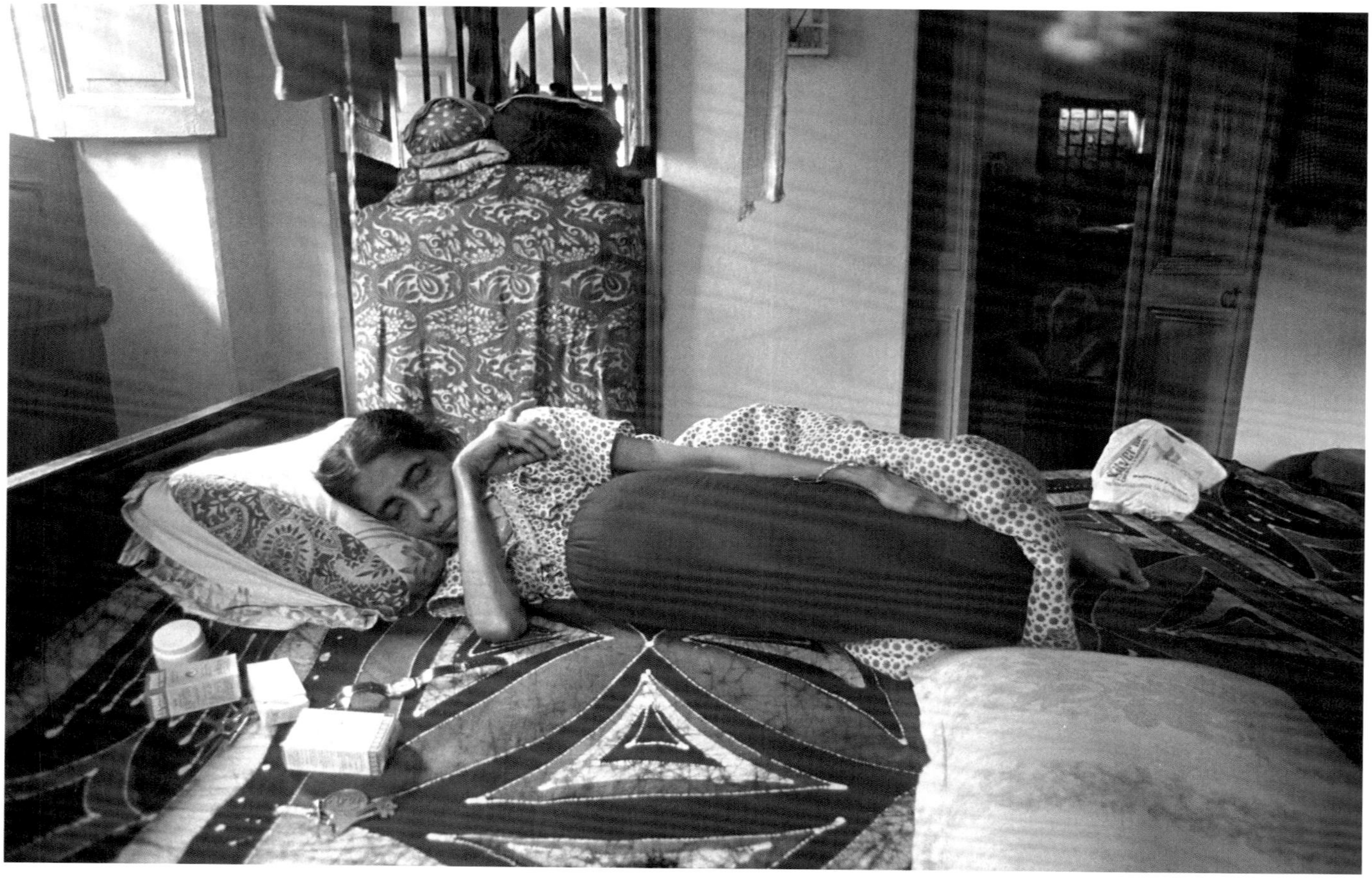

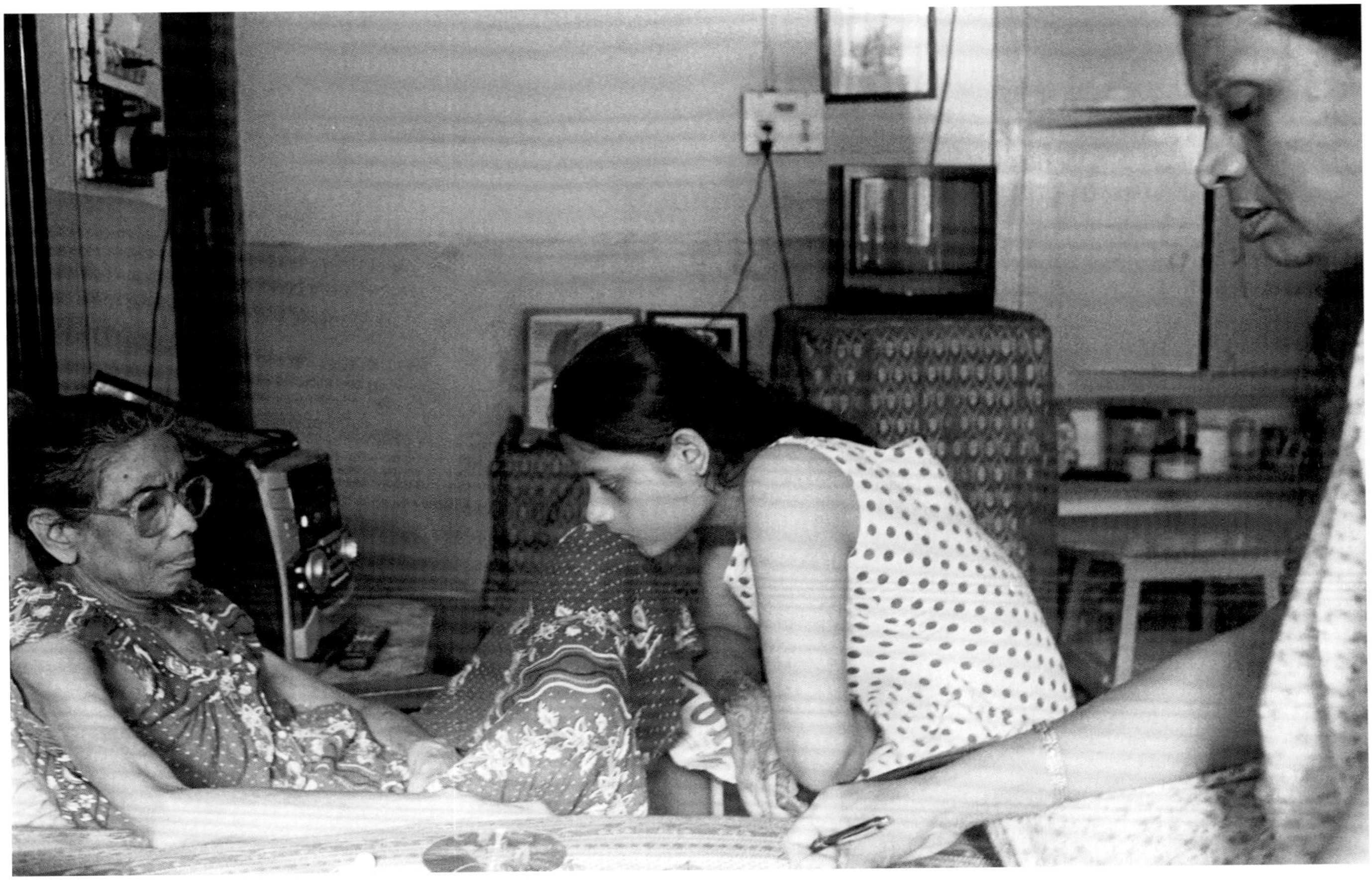

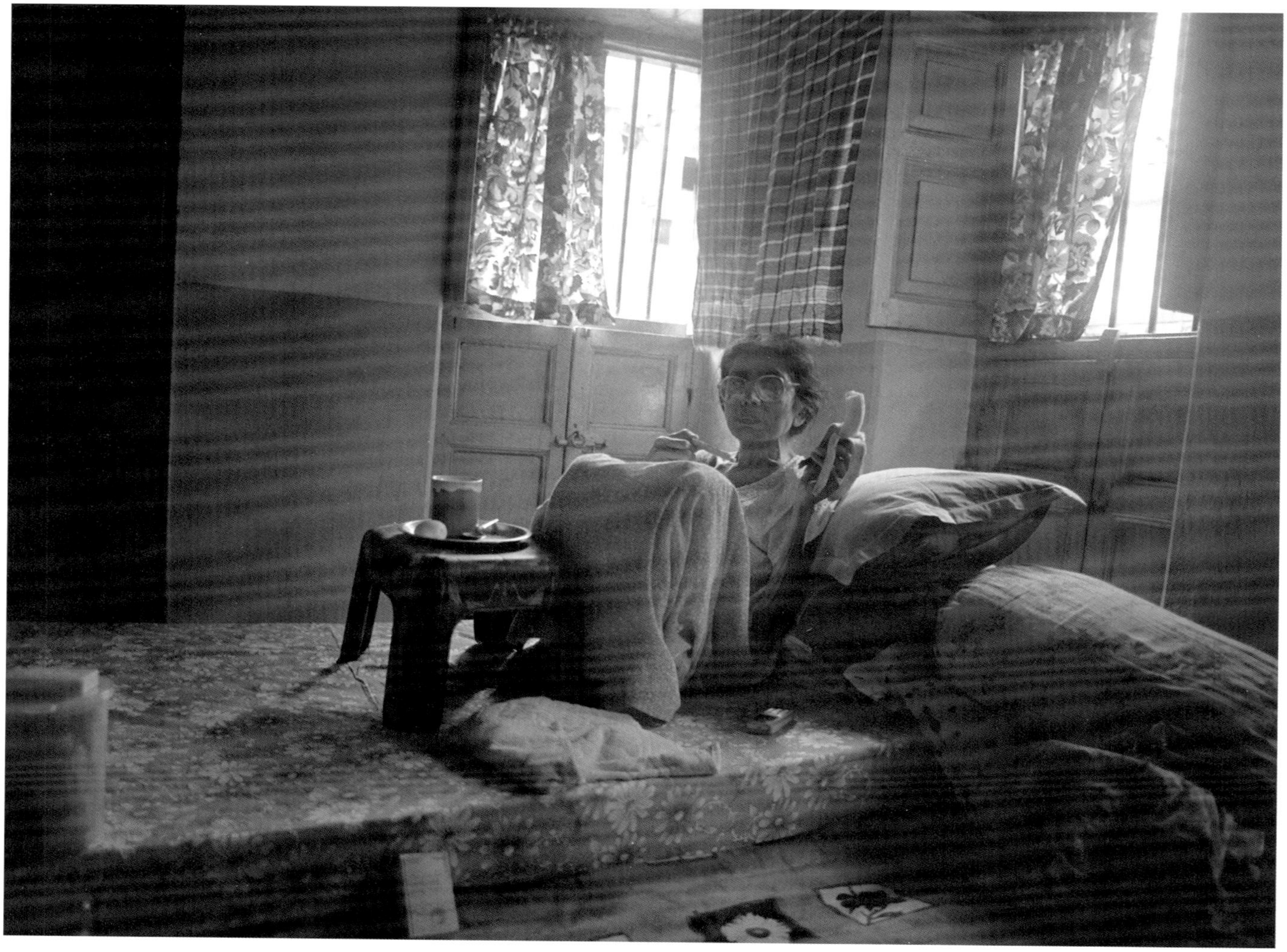

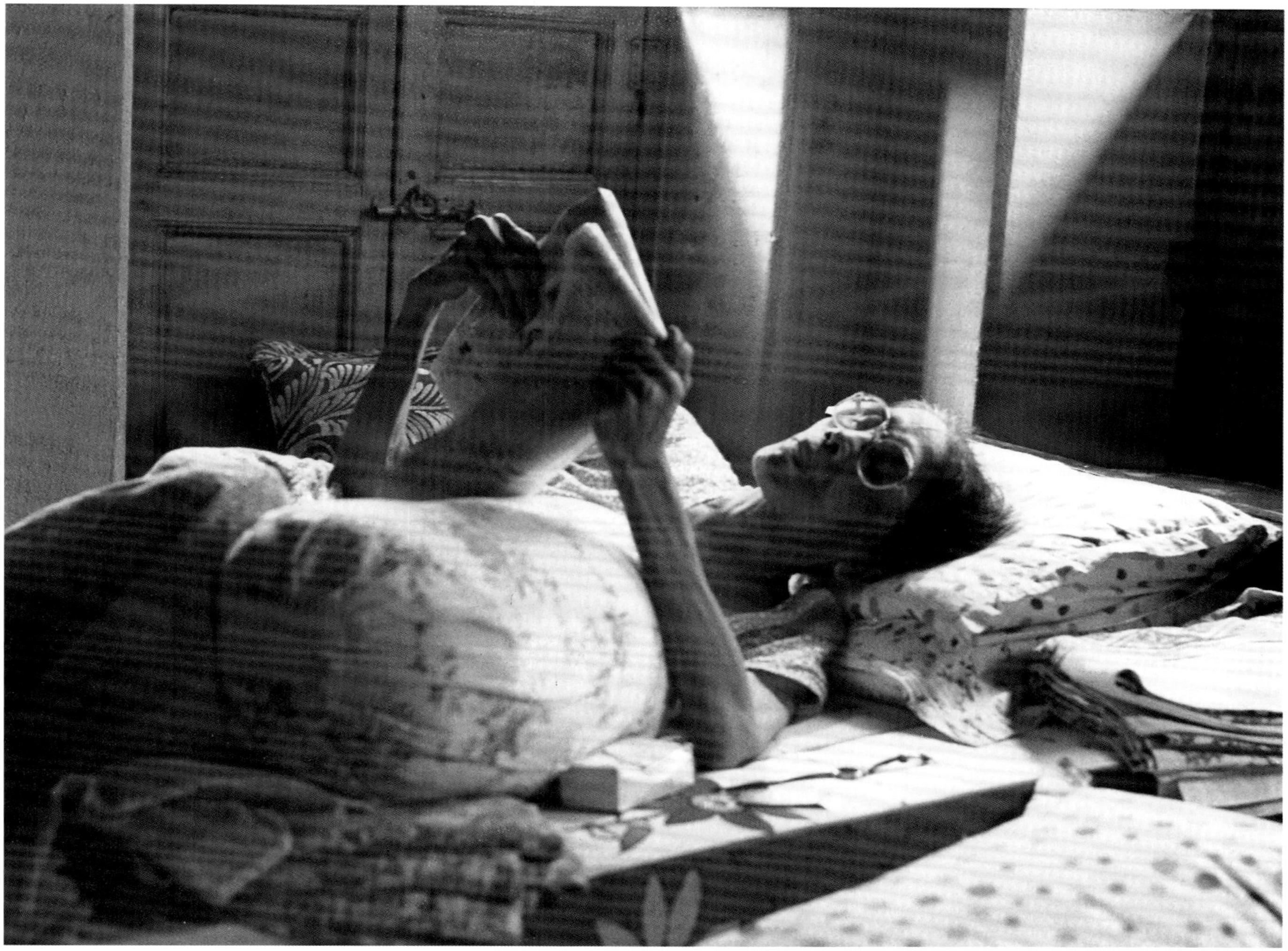

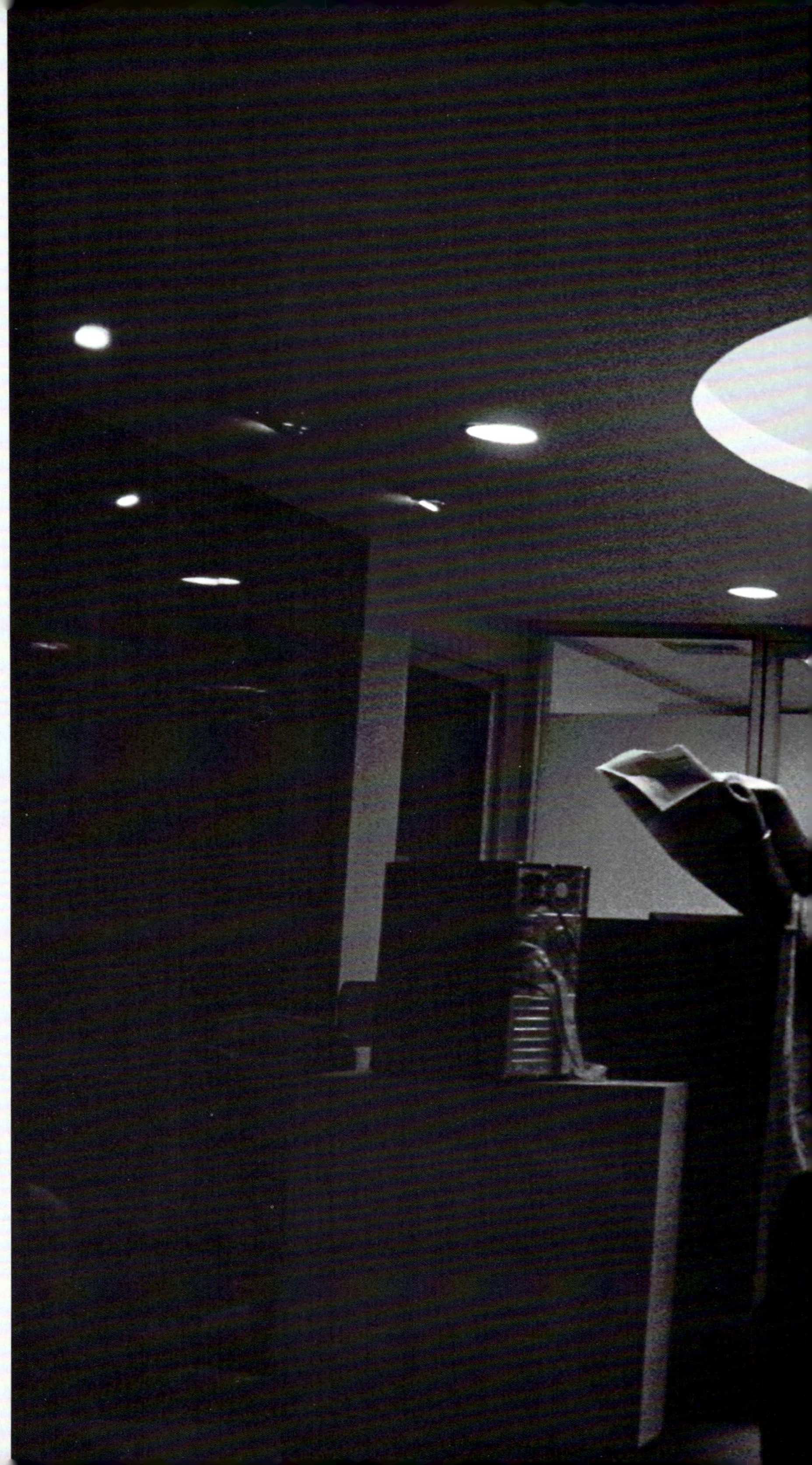

Waiting no longer for the decisive moment

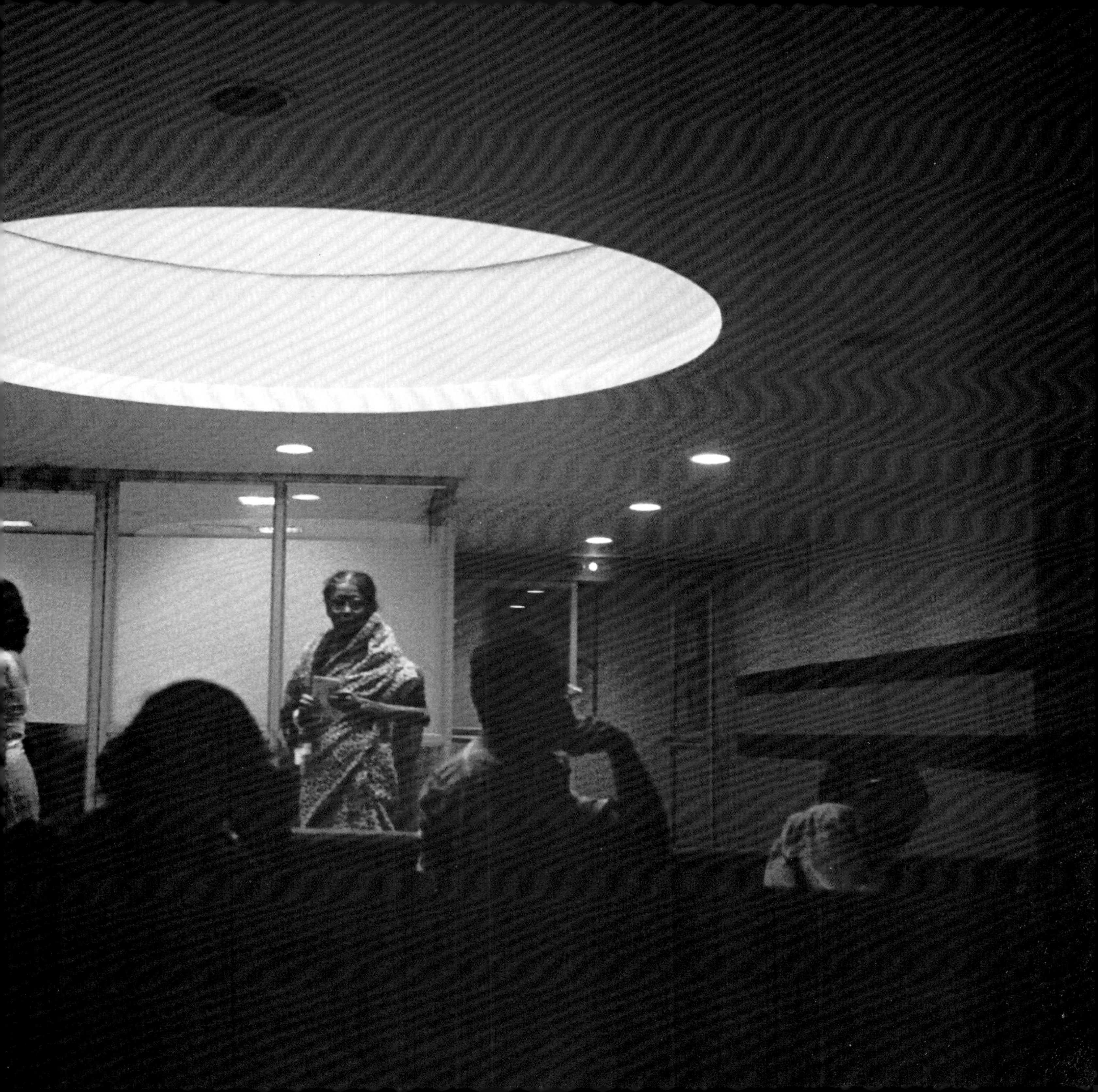

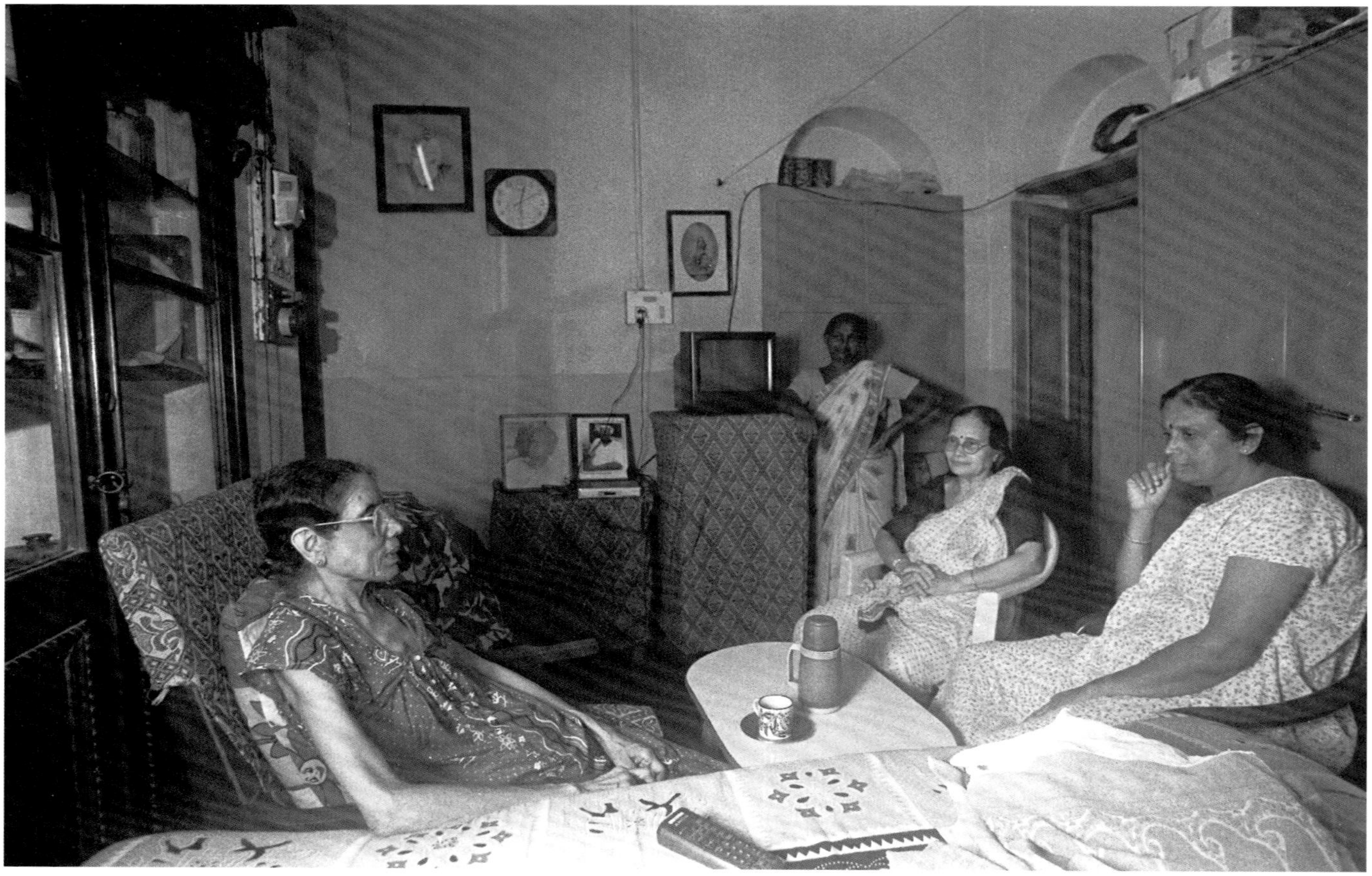

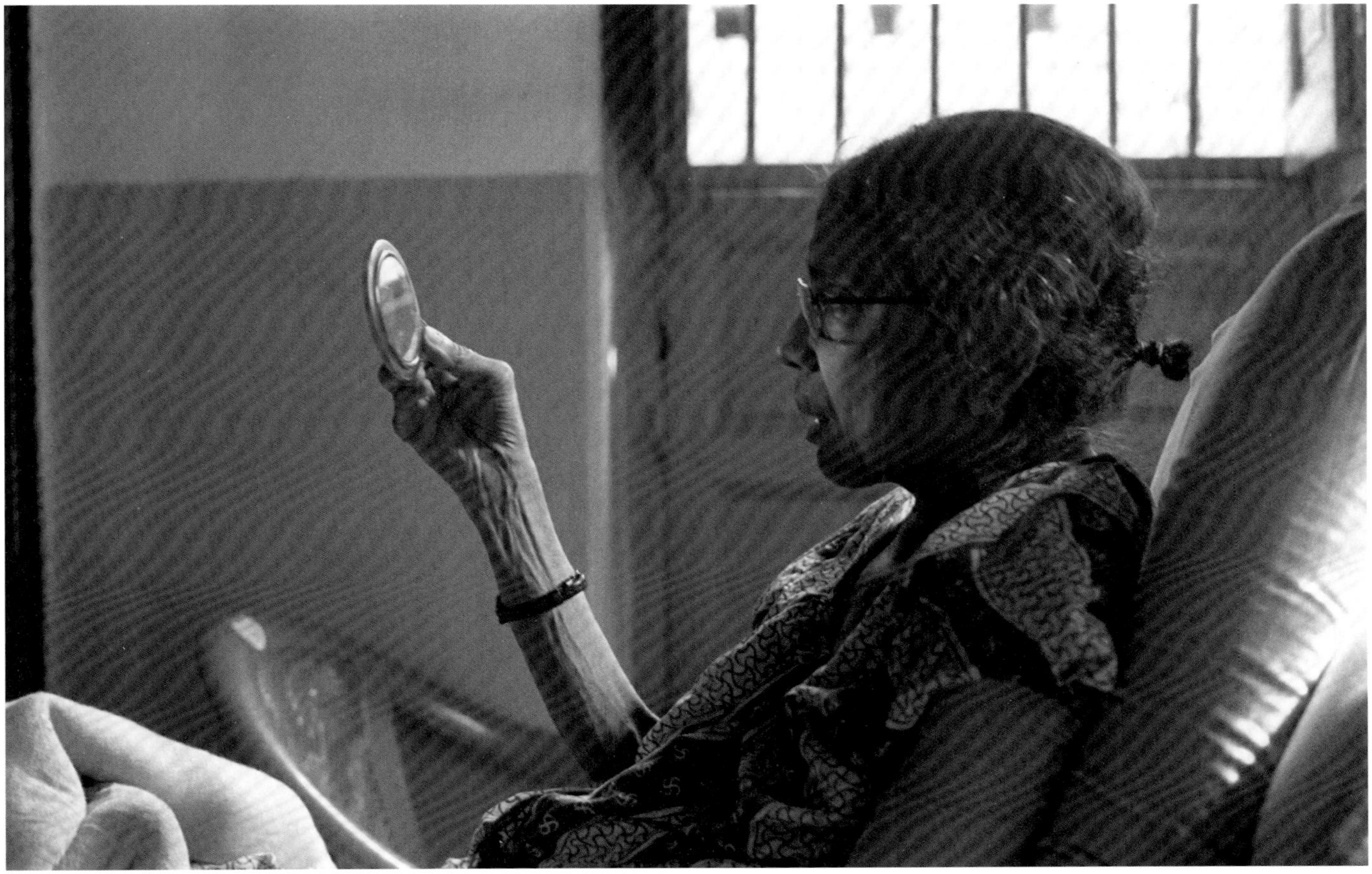

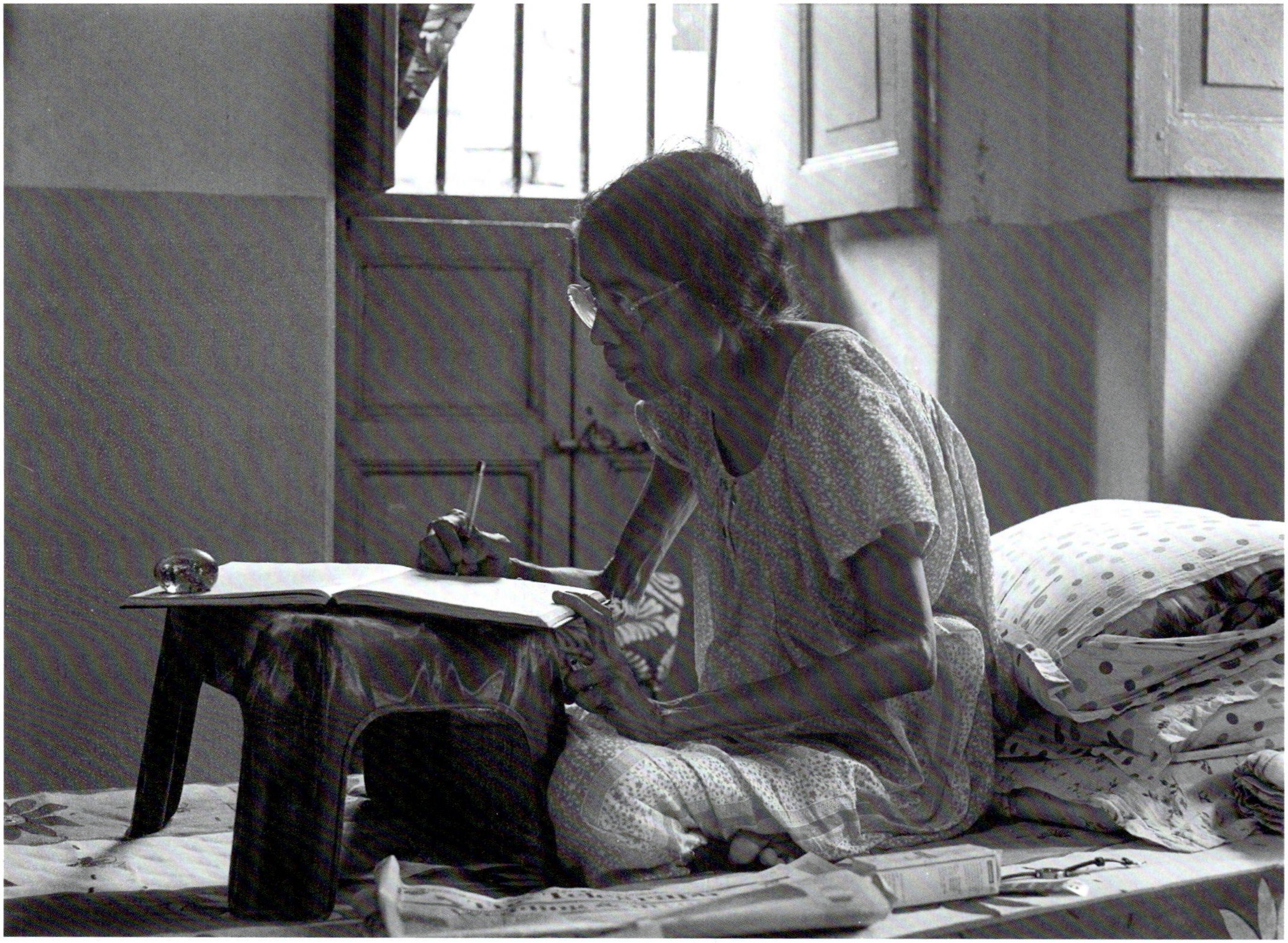

23rd June 2008
This is a new kind of birthday. Now I am a patient of osteoporosis and lung cancer

23 JUNE '08 MONDAY

2008													JUNE
S	M	T	W	T	F	S	S	M	T	W	T	F	S
1	2	3	4	5	6	7	8	9	10	11	12	13	14
15	16	17	18	19	20	21	22	23	24	25	26	27	28
29	30												

জন্মদিন — ৬৭ বছর — এই লেখাটা আগে থেকে লিখেছি,

এ বছর জন্মদিন একেবারে নতুন রকম, এখন আমি শুধু শ্বাসকষ্টের রুগী নই, এখন আমি osteo Porosis ও lung cancer এর patient, ছোটো-কেমো হয়ে গেছে, আবার 6th July N.H. এ ভর্তি হব। এই কথাগুলো শুনে মনে হবে আমি খুব pessimist হয়ে গেছি, আমার মধ্যে pessimism থাকলেও আমি optimist, আমার মনের জোর আমাকে optimist করেছে, optimistic attitude থেকেই আমার পড়াশোনা ও চাকরী করার উদ্যোগ এসেছে, Cancer শুনেও আমার বাঁচার ইচ্ছে চলে যায়নি কুনালের জন্য, আর অনেক বন্ধুর কুনাল আমার রোগের সেবা করছে, ওর মত আন্তরিকতা খুব একটা চোখে পড়েনি — অন্তত আমি তো দেখিনি, আর —। জন্মদিনে আমার খুব ইচ্ছে কুনালের কাজের স্বীকৃতি আমি যেন দেখে যেতে পারি, যদি আর ৪/৫ বছর বাঁচি আমাদের চেষ্টা সফল হবে.

আর — আমার পরে ছবি তোলাও কুনালের ইচ্ছেতেই,

Gas এজেন্সি - 352.50 MC - 176.25 অনি - 21.00

ক্যামেলী - 900.00

ডিম - 8.75

Veg. - 9.50

কলা - 9.00

পাবির - 10.00

1097.25

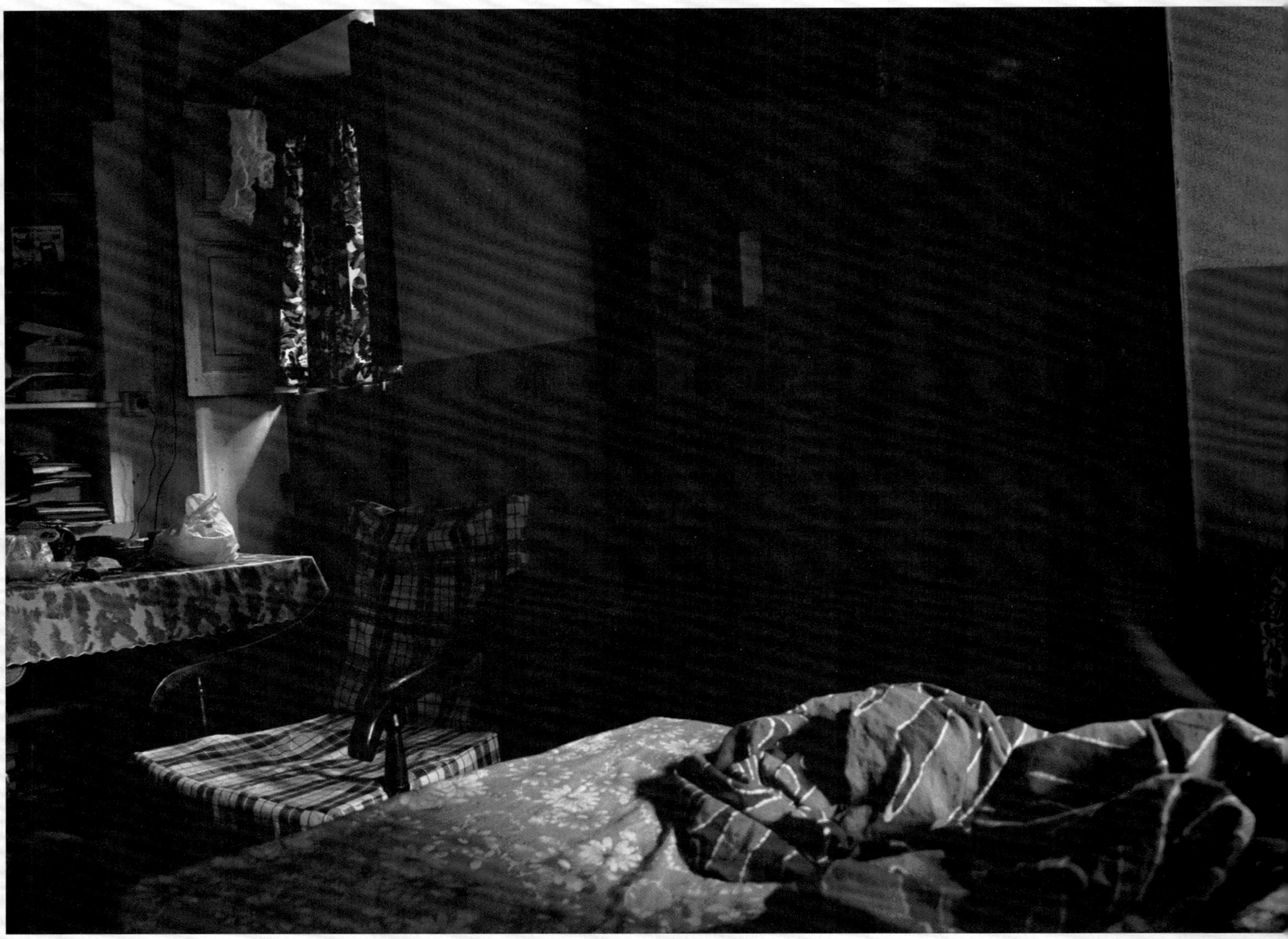

'It was as if I was trying to keep her alive by taking her pictures' - Kushal

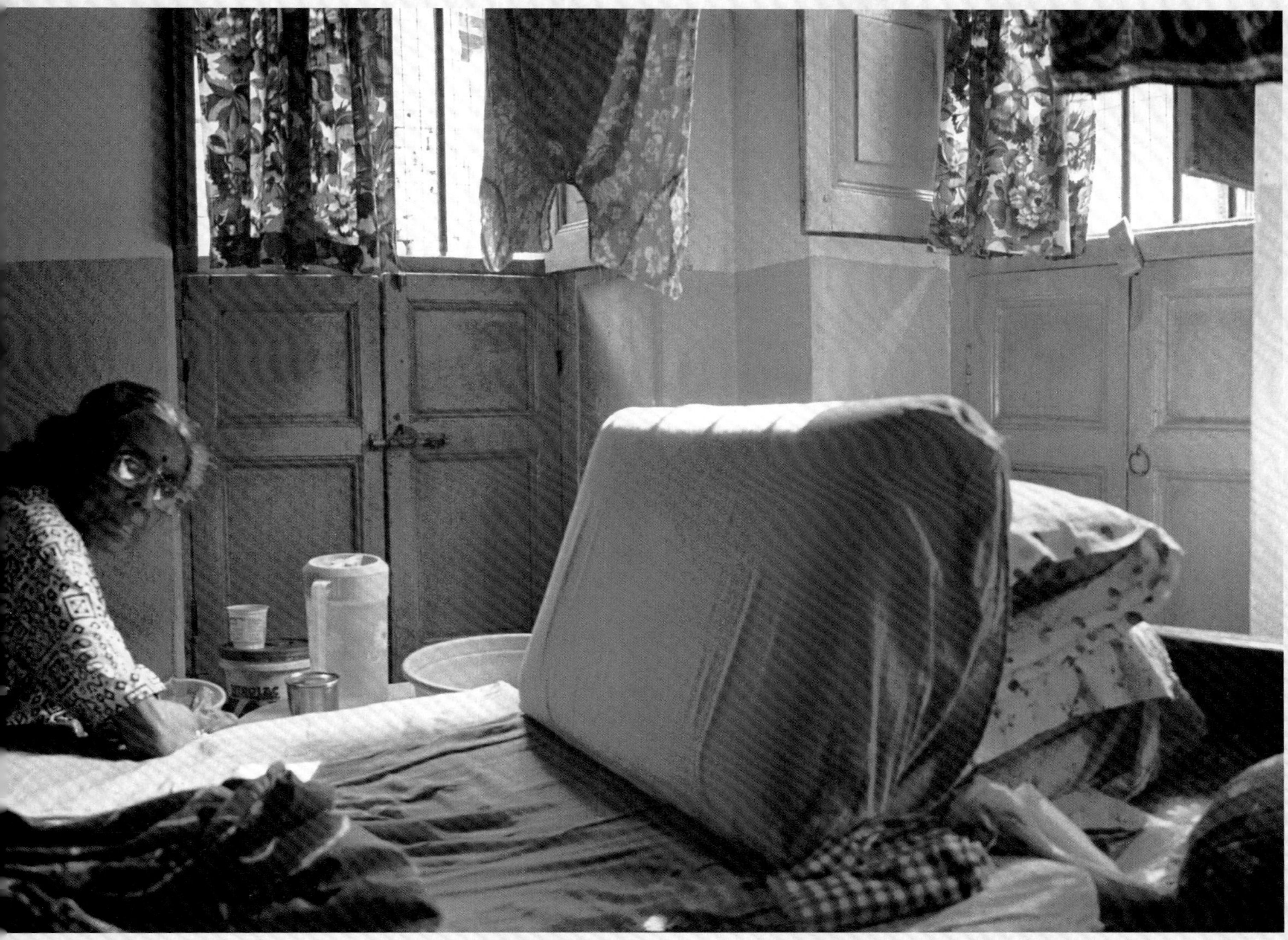

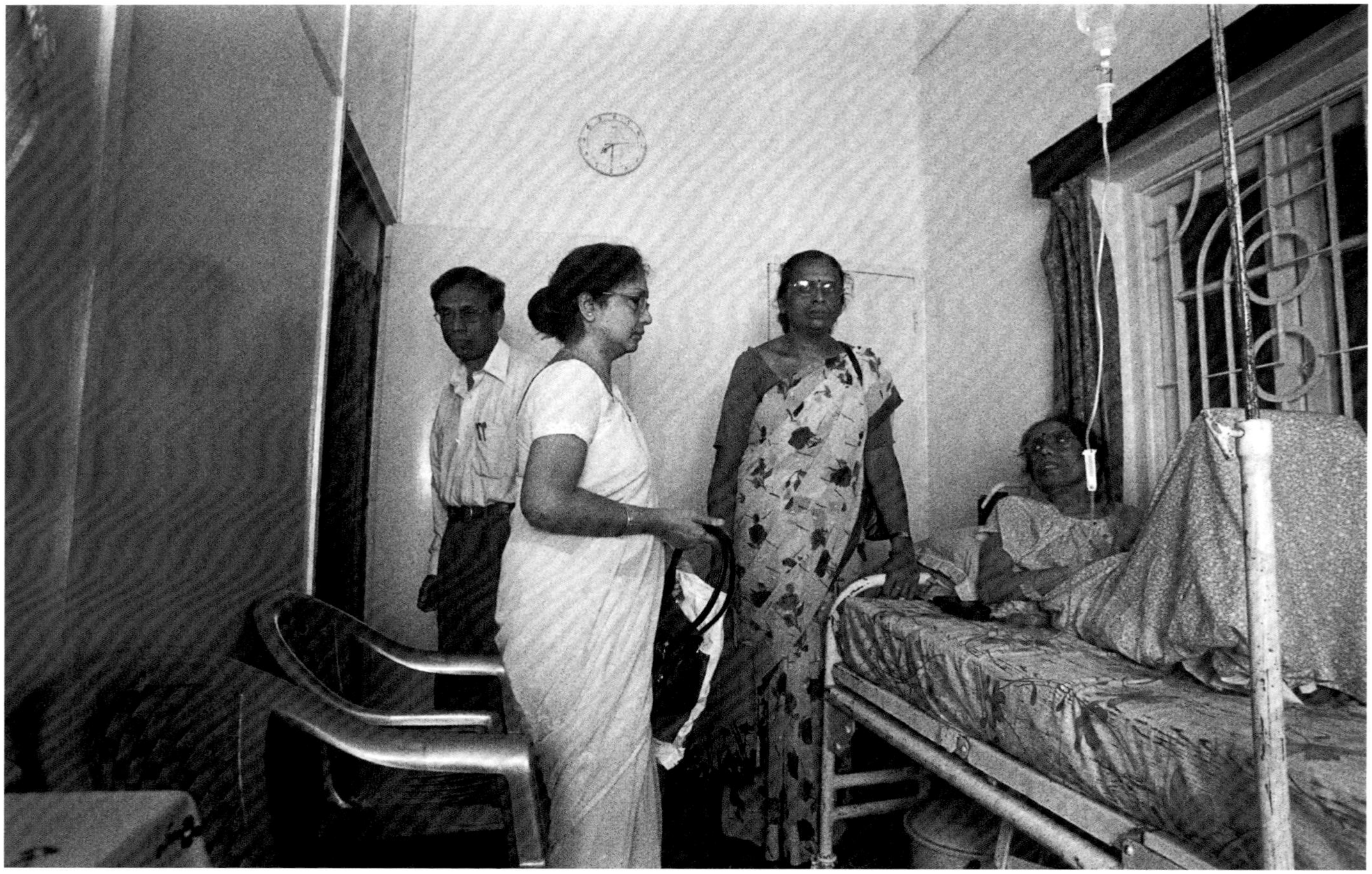

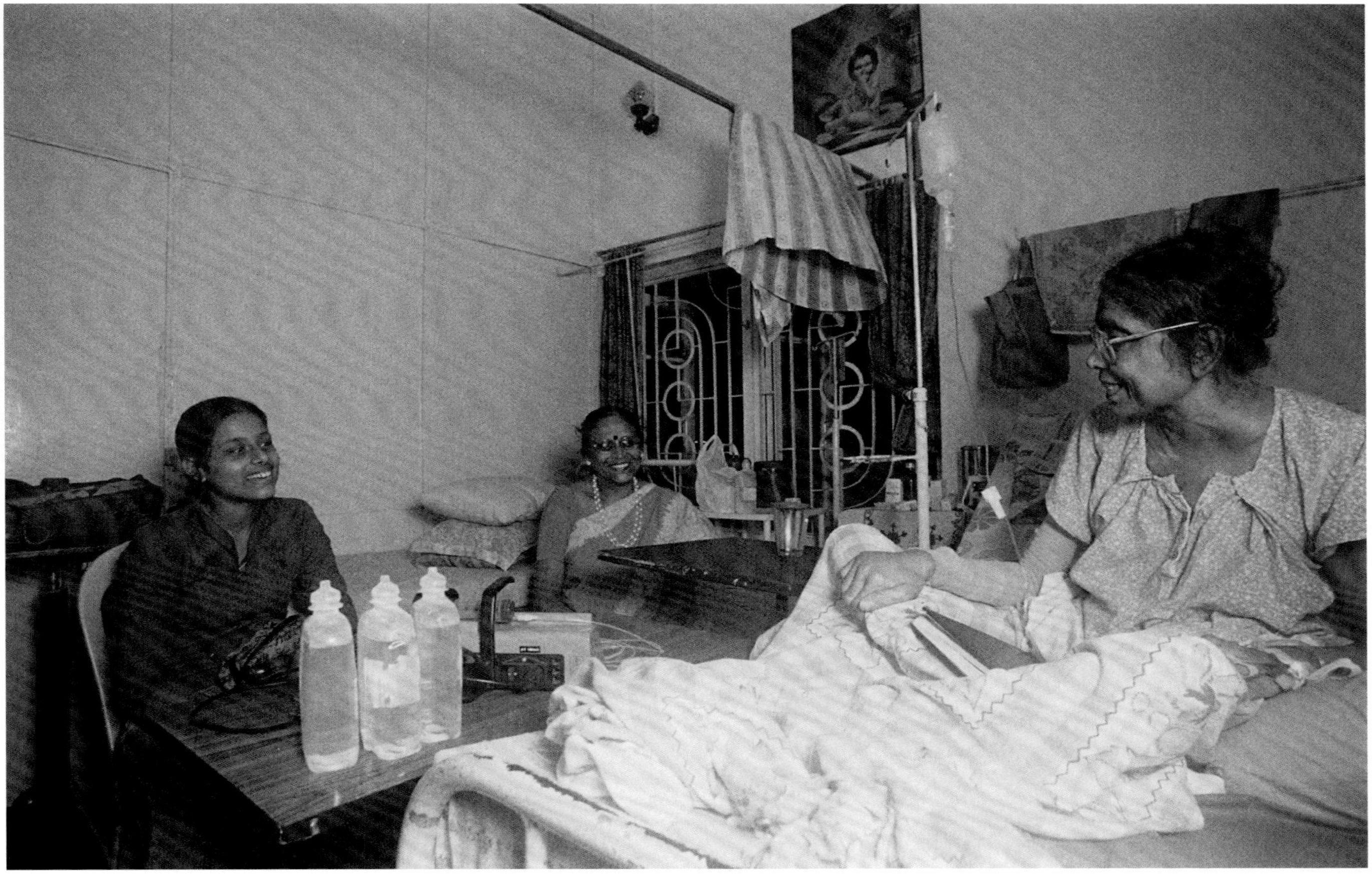

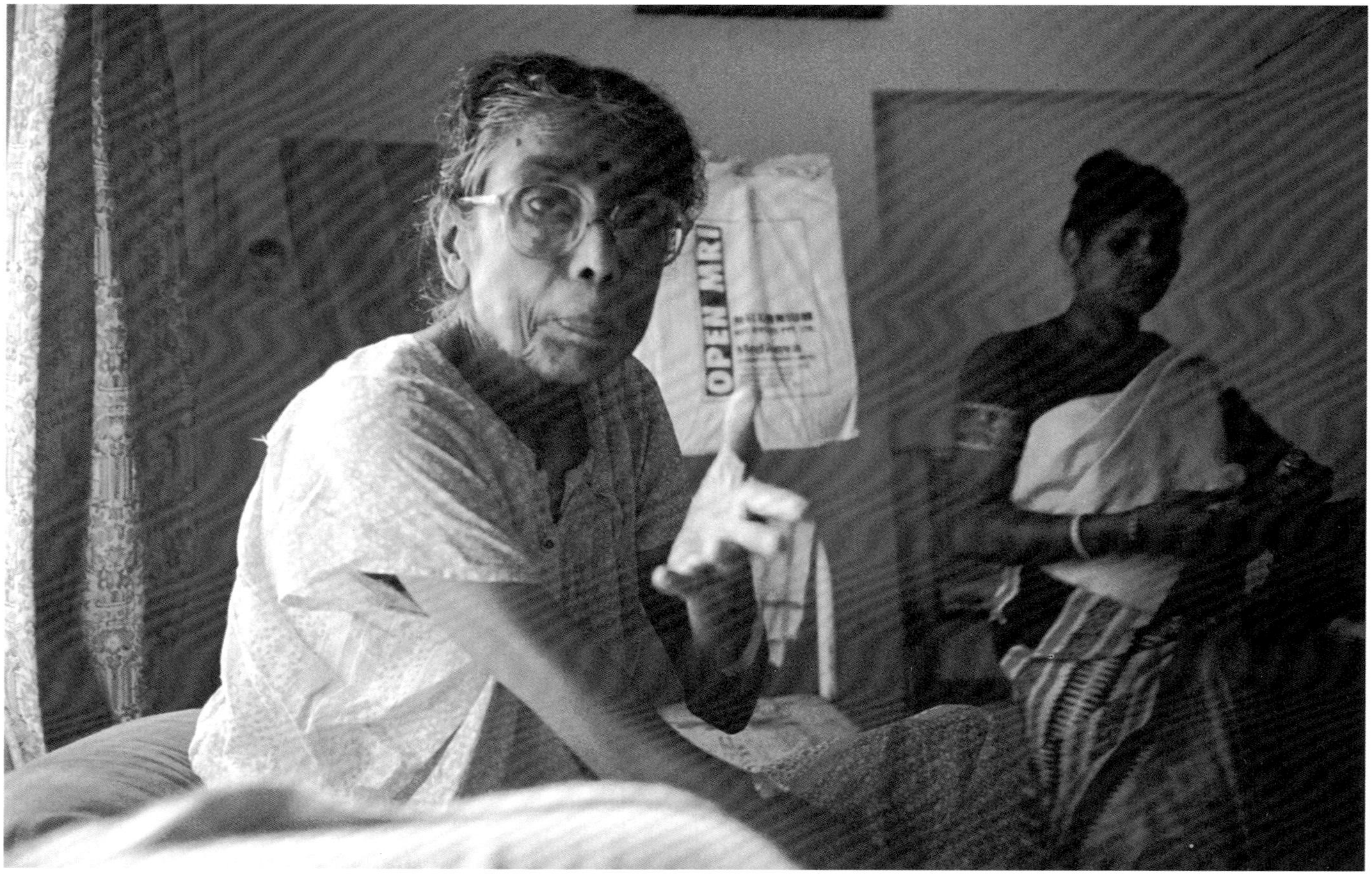
OPEN MRI

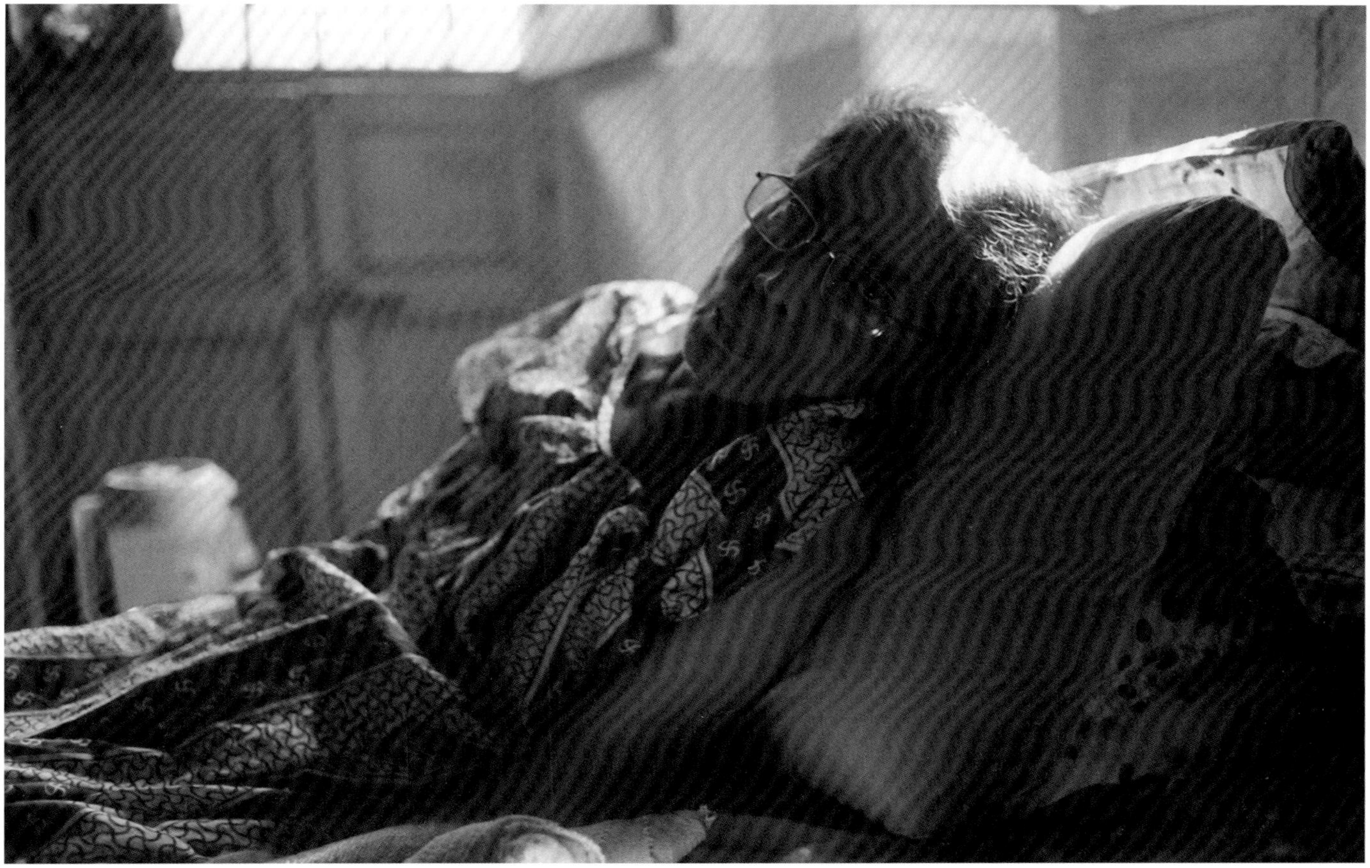

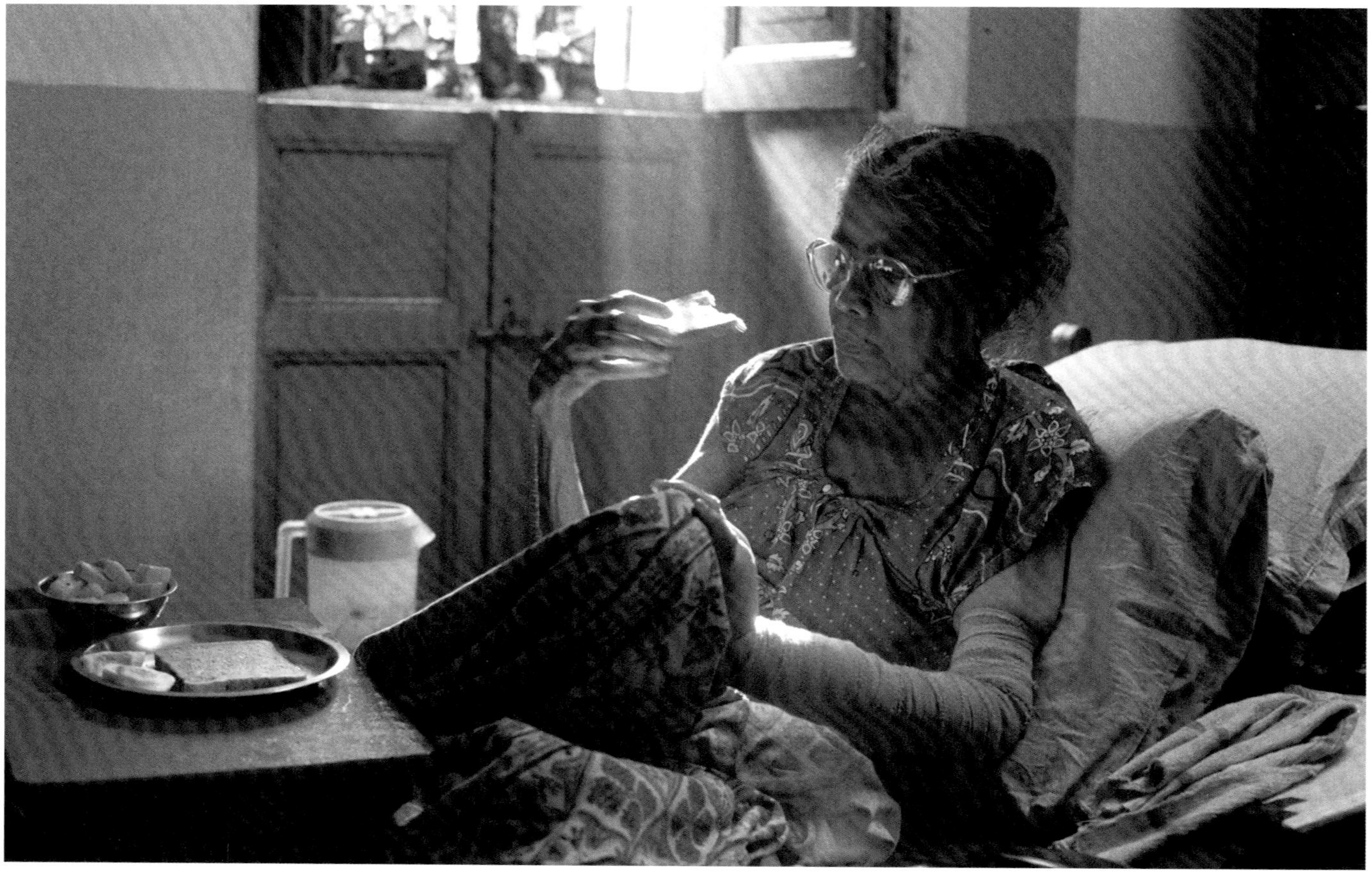

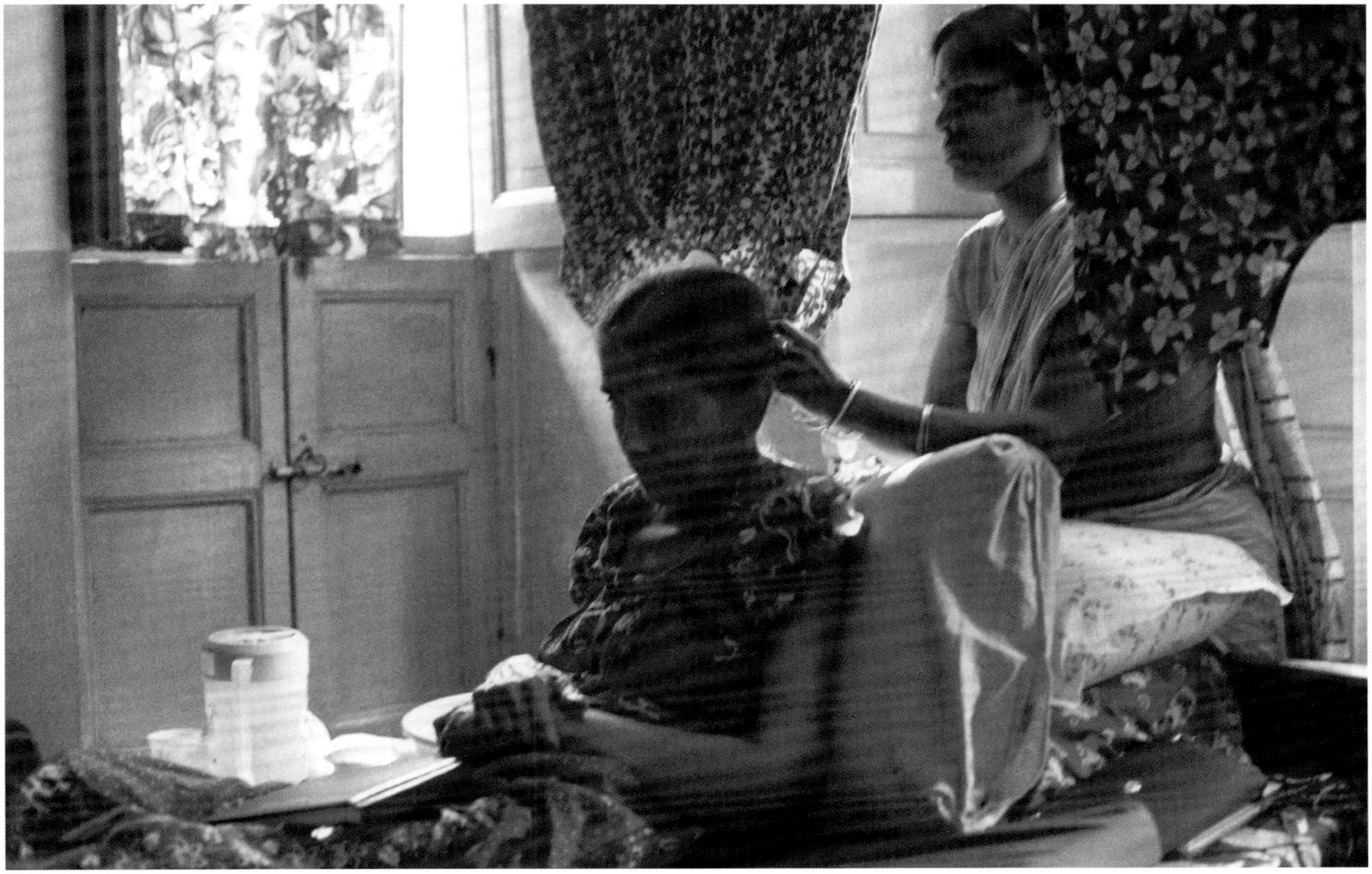

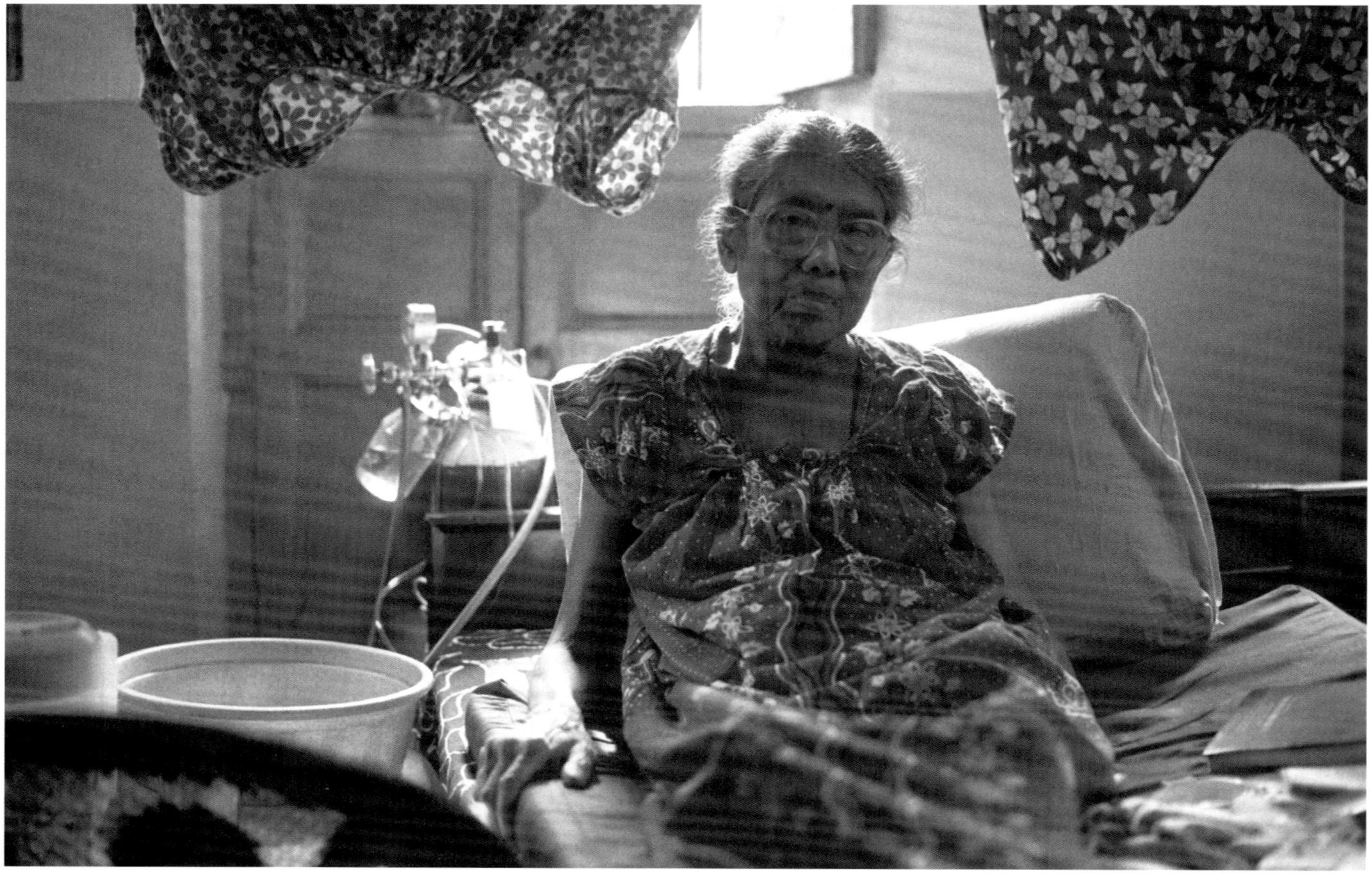

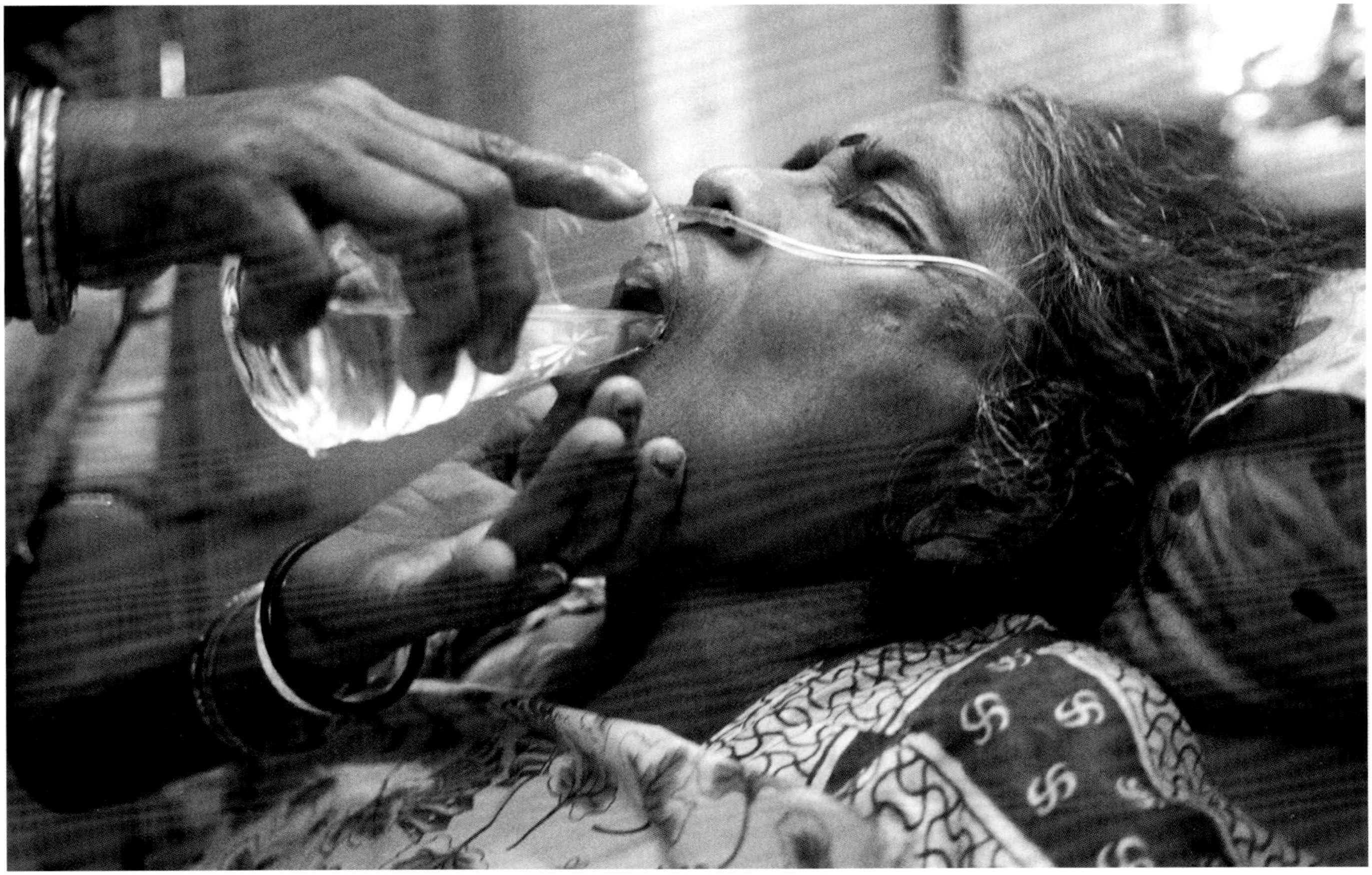

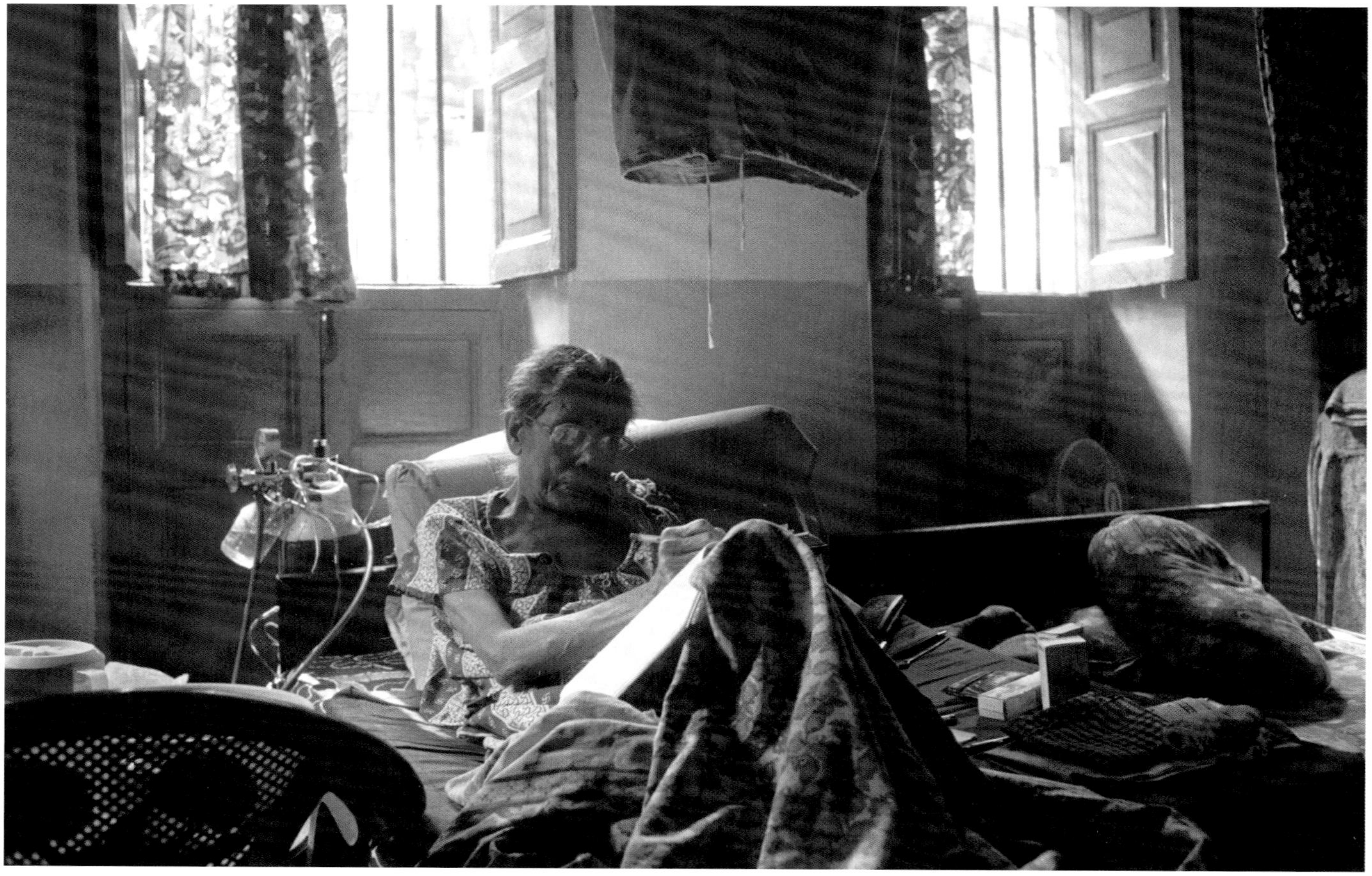

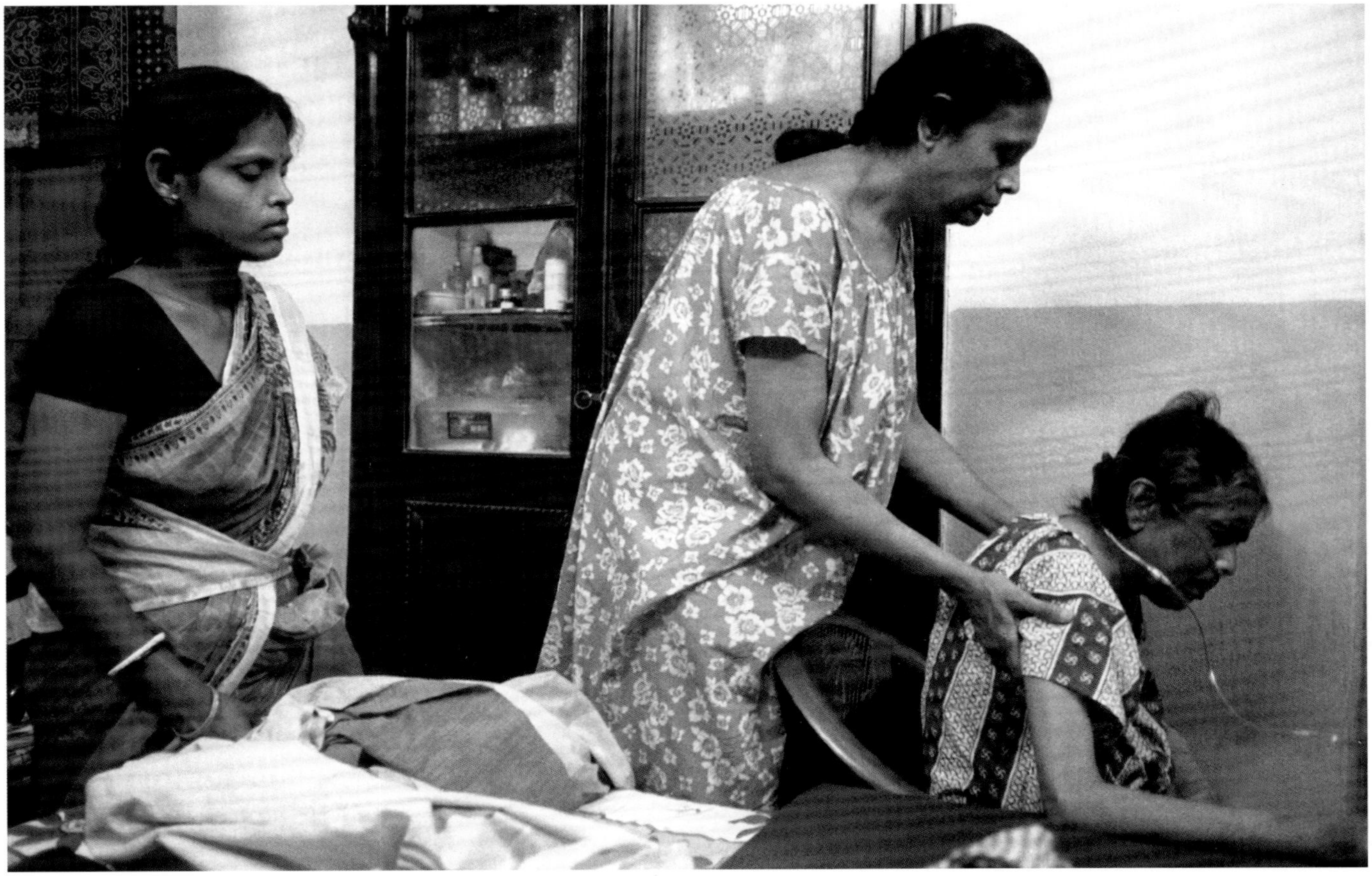

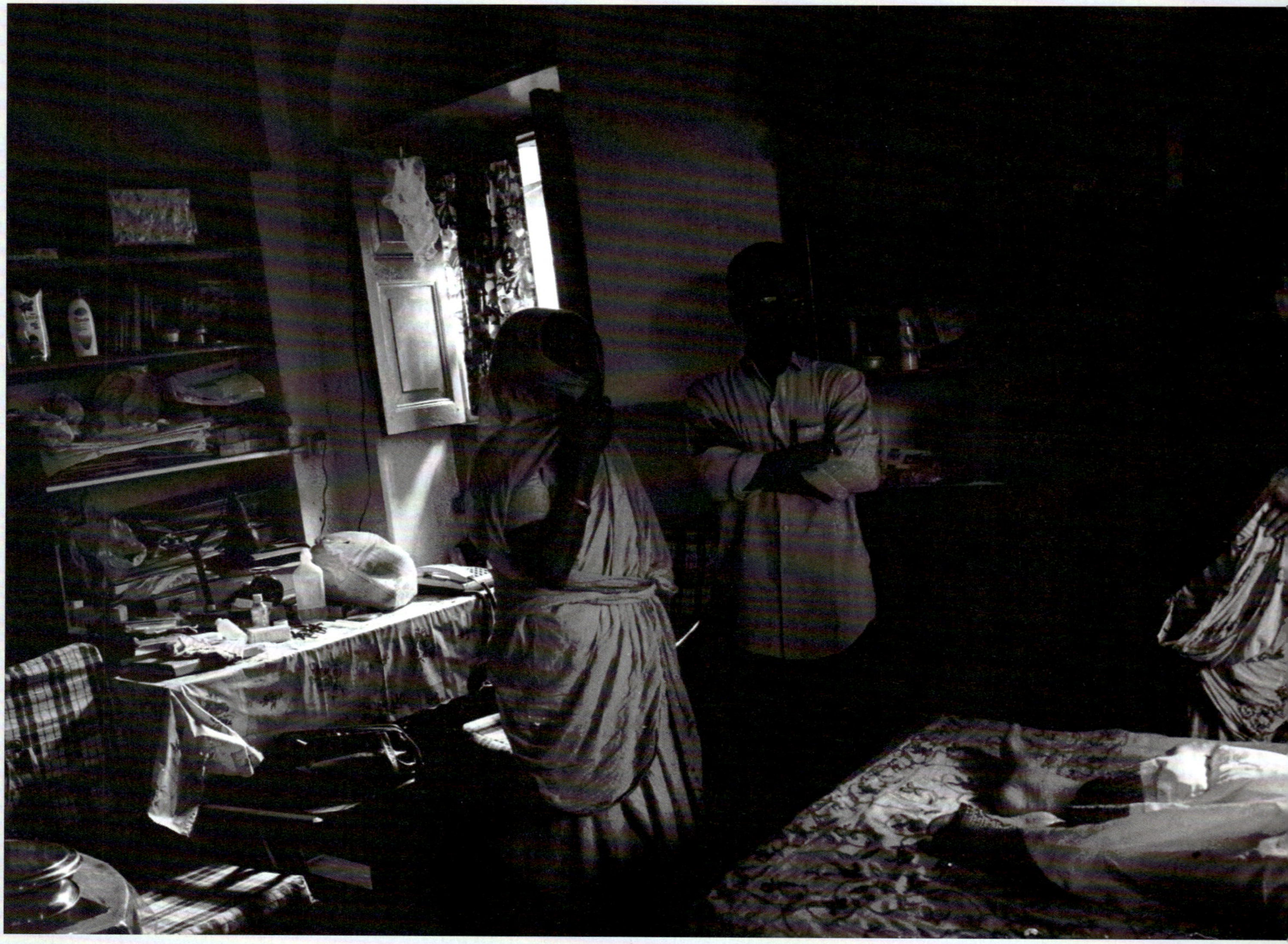

'It broke my heart to take this photo' - Kushal

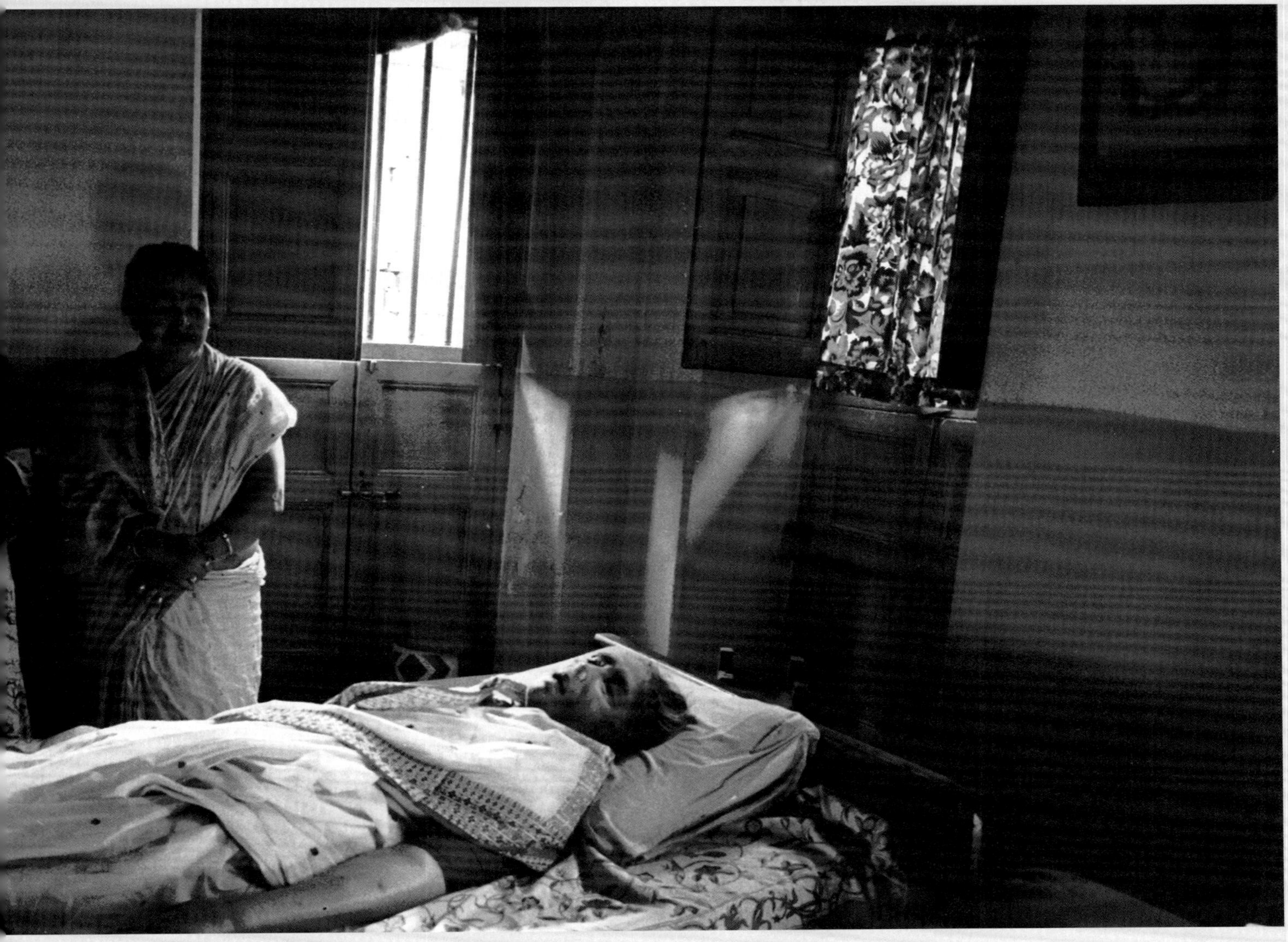

MC (1941-2009)

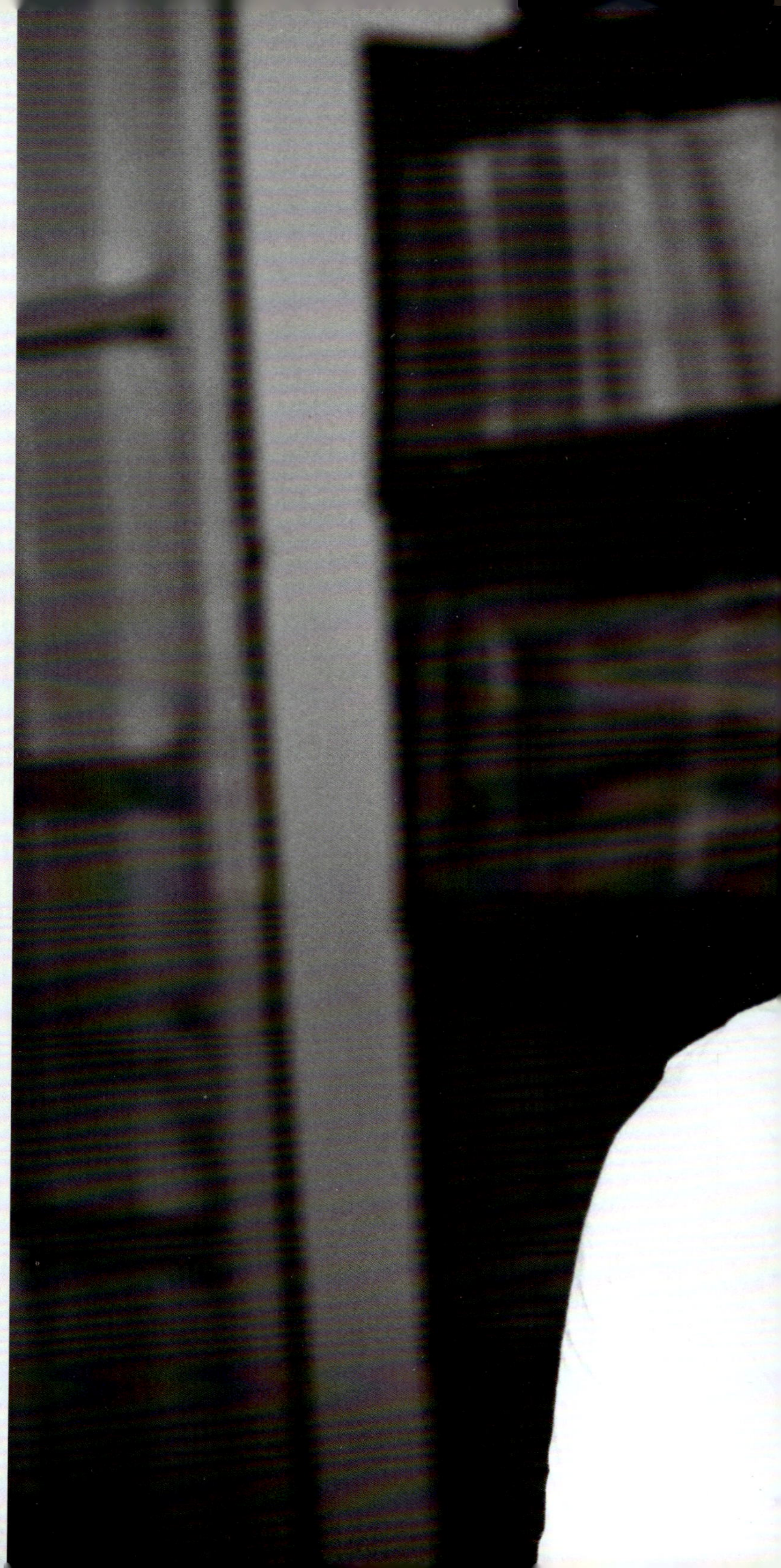

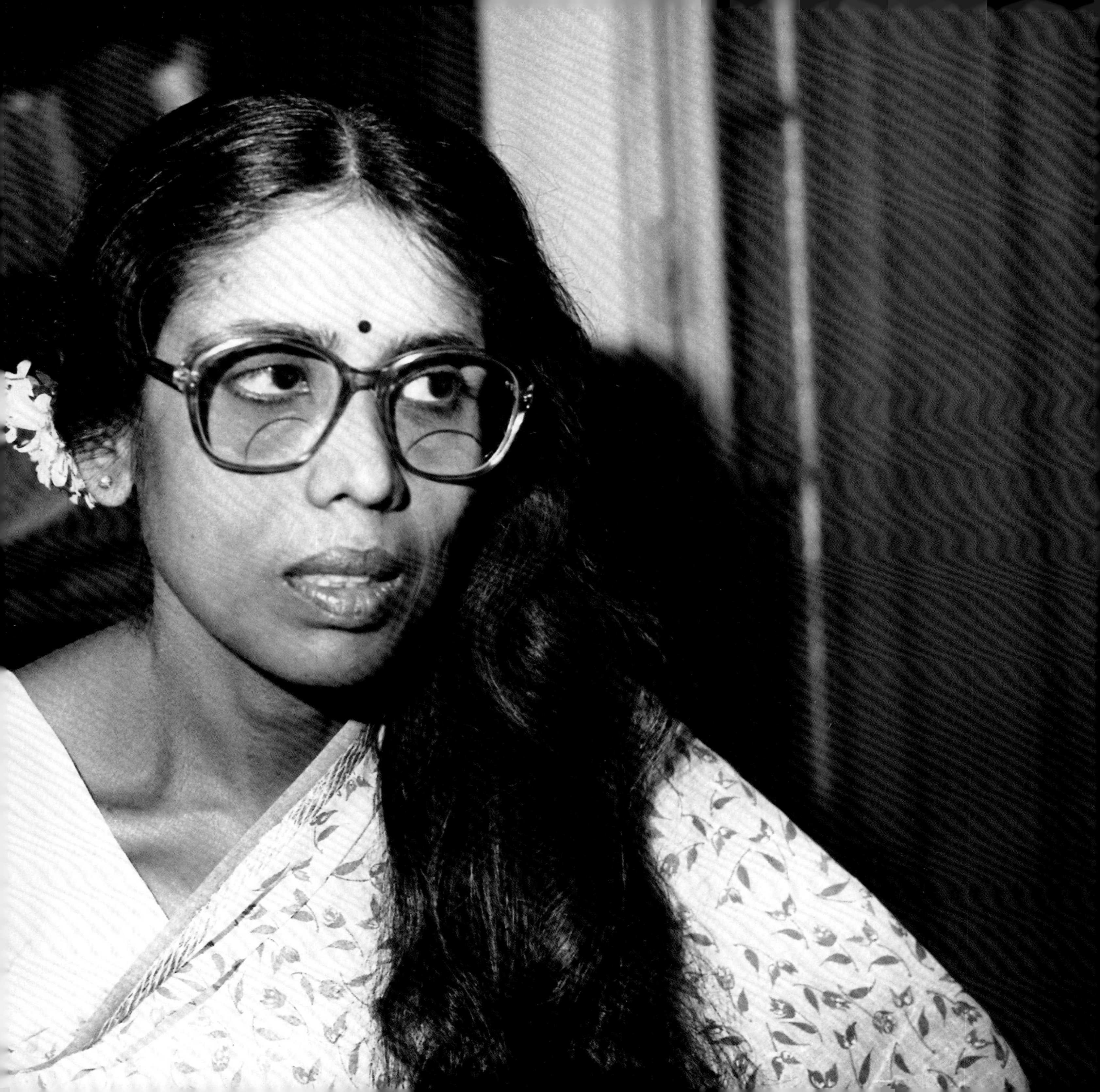

Acknowledgements

Ina Puri; Philippa Brewster; Sunil Gupta; Radhika Singh; Amit Chaudhuri; Dayanita Singh; Suvendu Chatterjee; Shahidul Alam; Eugene Datta; Shankar Sarkar; Ariadne Van de Ven; Vidura Jung Bahadur; Shamik Bag; Christopher Taylor; Bikash Bose; Bivas Bhattacharjee; Bani Chatterjee; Leena Chatterjee; Apurba Chatterjee; Amal Chatterjee; Mithu Chatterjee; Tarun Chatterjee; Padmini Chatterjee; Teesta Chatterjee; Anupam Chattopadhyay; Gopa Chattopadhyay; Sounak Chattopadhyay; Uma Nandi; Dr A. Biswas; Koreman Bibi (Sheila); Rohima Nasrin (Pinky); Jharna Sardar; Kaustav Basu (Bultu); Monika Paul; Savitri Girls' College; Jodhpur Park Nursing Home; Drik India.

Selected Readings

American Photographers of the Depression: Farm Security Administration Photographs, 1935-1942; Introduction by Charles Hagen; Pantheon Photo Library, 1985

Henri Cartier-Bresson: The Early Work, by Peter Galassi; Museum of Modern Art, New York, 1987

Henri Cartier-Bresson; Introduction by Michael Brenson; Pantheon Book, New York/Centra National De La Photographie, Paris, 1985

On Photography, by Susan Sontag; Penguin Books, 1979

W. Eugene Smith; Introduction by William S. Johnson; Thames and Hudson, 1990

Eugene Atget; Introduction by Francoise Reynaud; Thames and Hudson, 1989

Robert Frank; text by Robert Frank; Thames and Hudson, 1991

Bruce Davidson; Text by Bruce Davidson; Thames and Hudson, 1990

Success and Failure of Picasso, by John Berger; Granta, 1991

A Painter of Our Time, by John Berger; Martin Secker & Warburg, London, 1958

'Illustration, Accidents and Ignorance,' by Raghubir Singh; *The Telegraph*, March 23, 1990

'The Vision's the Thing: Lee Friedlander's "Like a One-Eyed Cat",' by Mike Johnston, Camera & Darkroom Photography, Volume 12, No 12, December 1990

Marc Asnin: Uncle Charlie, by Marc Asnin; Contrasto, 2011

Click! Contemporary Photography in India; Introduction by Sunil Gupta; Vadehra Art Gallery, 2008

Where Three Dreams Cross: 150 years of Photography from India, Pakistan and Bangladesh; Whitechapel Gallery, London/Fotomuseum Winterthur, Winterthur/Steidl, 2010

Chobi Tola: Bangali-r Photography Chorcha, by Siddharta Ghosh; Ananda Publishers Limited, 1988

Dayanita Singh, by Donald Albrecht, Aveek Sen, Sunil Khilnani and Adrian Tyler; Fundacion Mapfre, 2010

Dear Theo: The Autobiography of Vincent van Gogh; edited by Irving Stone; Signet 1991

My Life and the Beautiful Game, by Pelé with Robert L. Fish; Warner Books, 1978